JONATHAN EDWARDS:

Basic Writings

JONATHAN EDWARDS:

Basic Writings

Selected, Edited, and with a Foreword by
OLA ELIZABETH WINSLOW

A MERIDIAN BOOK
NEW AMERICAN LIBRARY
TIMES MIRROR
NEW YORK, LONDON AND SCARBOROUGH, ONTARIO

Copyright © 1966 by The New American Library, Inc.

Originally published in a Signet Classic edition by
The New American Library.

MERIDIAN TRADEMARK REG. U.S. PAT. OFF. AND FOREIGN COUNTRIES
REGISTERED TRADEMARK—MARCA REGISTRADA
HECHO EN FORGE VILLAGE, MASS., U.S.A.

SIGNET, SIGNET CLASSICS, MENTOR, PLUME, MERIDIAN
and NAL BOOKS
are published in the United States by
The New American Library, Inc.,
1633 Broadway, New York, New York 10019,
in Canada by The New American Library of Canada Limited,
81 Mack Avenue, Scarborough, Ontario M1L 1M8,
in the United Kingdom by The New English Library Limited,
Barnard's Inn, Holborn, EC1N 2JR, England

First Meridian Printing, October, 1978

2 3 4 5 6 7 8 9 10

PRINTED IN THE UNITED STATES OF AMERICA

CONTENTS

FOREWORD

During the two hundred years since Jonathan Edwards' death, in 1758, his intellectual power and spiritual vision have escaped from the tight theological system in which his generation framed them. As theological systems and arguments have steadily lost their interest and authority for the layman, his thought has no longer been discussed only within traditional boundaries. Historians of ideas have given it a wider hearing and also a wider application. Philosophy, metaphysics, and particularly psychology now claim his ideas as part of their story. Judged in the perspective of two centuries, Jonathan Edwards stands forth today as one of the great original minds of America, a man with few peers in his own day or later. To meet him on almost any one of his thousands of pages is to meet not only a master logician but also a great creative mind, calmly searching out the meanings that have engaged great thinkers since the beginning of time—the meaning of God, the universe, and man in this world and in whatever future there may be. Always the unseen and the immaterial are his subject matter and theme. In the small, distinguished company to which he belongs, he is one of the few men of the far past who still have something to say to men of the present hour.

While he was still a relatively young man he was known beyond his own town borders only as a revival preacher of unusual power. The religious upheaval that began under his preaching in his Northampton parish quickly spread to other towns and prepared the way for the wider triumphs of George Whitefield soon afterward. The Great Awakening, as this wider revival is now called, changed many things in American life. It was a social as well as a religious movement, was in fact a veritable revolution in far more than doctrine and churchly practice. It touched all of colonial America and was both an end and a new beginning. Jonathan Edwards had been its initial spark.

In his early maturity and for years afterward he was the spokesman for one side of the theological controversy that followed this religious upheaval. All but one of his longer treatises belong to this bitter controversy, which divided both colonial pulpit and pew and engaged English as well as American churchmen for more than a generation. His best-known title, *A Careful and Critical Enquiry into the modern prevailing Notions of that Freedom of Will, which is supposed to be essential to Moral Agency. Vertue and Vice, Reward and Punishment, Praise and Blame,* was written as an argument against his theological opponents. It became a Harvard College textbook, and his name carried authority through the lifetimes of those who had studied it.

Little in Edwards' known heritage or training, little in his experience, offer clues to his intellectual power and speculative genius, his originality, his freedom in worlds beyond the local and transient. He was born a third-generation American, with a village minister, Timothy Edwards, as his father; a merchant, Richard Edwards, as grandfather; and a trades-man, William Edwards, who made barrels in the small shop beside his house, as great-grandfather. Behind Esther Stod-dard, his mother, were two ministerial generations, including worthy figures of the New England pulpit in their day. Simple and undistinguished intellectually, all of them, but men of courage and righteousness in the pioneering generations.

Jonathan Edwards grew up in East Windsor, Connecticut, a small frontier village insulated from all except what the village offered. His earliest schoolroom was the "parlour" of the parsonage, with his father as teacher and his ten sisters and a few village boys as his fellow pupils. His father's meetinghouse was the center of his boyhood life, and Sunday was the most important day of the week.

Even as a thirteen-year-old freshman at Yale College he missed the intellectual stimulus of great teachers and a wealth of great books. Yale College, then only two years old, was in the first throes of its stormy beginning. As yet there was no settled location, no building, not even the Yale name. The students were divided into three groups, at Saybrook, Wethersfield, and New Haven. Jonathan Edwards lived with the nine other freshmen in a farmhouse only ten miles from his home in East Windsor. During his undergraduate years came the sensational "battle of the books," when as the precious Jeremiah Dummer gift was being transported to New Haven, it was set upon by certain militant Saybrook citizens, the oxcarts overturned, and the books scattered, with the result that many of the more valuable of them were "conveyed away by unknown Hands, and never could be found again." Undergraduates lived their days in an atmosphere that invited "Tumult and Confusion."

But even as a younger boy Edwards had learned quietude in his own pursuits. He had also found intellectual stimulus close at hand—in the broad fields that stretched away from his boyhood home, in the river that led on to the larger world, and in the Bible and ministerial books on his father's shelf. The few surviving scraps from his boyhood writings, which are probably only a fragment of his day-to-day observations and his wonderings about them, give glimpses of his awakening mind and therefore tell far more than they actually say. Students of Edwards cannot afford to miss them.

When he was eleven he wrote an essay on the flying spiders that "multitudes of times" he had "beheld with wonderment and pleasure." It is worth careful reading not only for its accuracy of observation, which need not be surprising in an alert country boy, but also for the determined persistence of his watching and the experimentation that finally satisfied him that he had found out "the whole mystery" of the spider's way of navigating the air. But this boy did not stop there. He followed the spider and his kind through the whole cycle of their brief life span, and on to their destruction, when "with the greatest ease" they were "swept first and last into the sea" by the winds of early autumn. It must be so, he reasoned, else there would be too many spiders. But they have left their eggs behind. "Admire also the Creator," he concluded in one of the corollaries to this piece, "in so adjusting their Destruction to their multiplication that . . . taking one year with another, there is alwaies Just an equal number of them." At eleven he was placing the spider's story in nature's larger book, where things "are done better than we can imagine beforehand," another wise generalization hardly expected from an eleven-year-old.

There is something more than a boy's curiosity in all this, something more also than a mind that concrete exploration and experimentation could fully satisfy. Similarly with his early reflections on the rainbow. When he had made a little rainbow of his own, asked many questions, and begun to find out the answers, he ended the piece with the sentence, "The next Grand Question is what is it Causes the Colours of the Rainbow?" Already he had learned that to solve one problem in a given field is immediately to confront another in its wake. Already, also, he was moving toward the abstract, which would be his lifetime realm. The short essay on the soul, in spite of its mock seriousness, goes deeper than eyes can see; the one on Being goes deeper still. These brief pieces, never intended for our eyes, reveal a mind breathless with eagerness to know, and more breathless still with the beginnings of discovery. Such a mind would not ask easy questions or be satisfied with easy answers. All of these early efforts were first drafts only, recording his thought as it rushed forth, often in sentences half formed and innocent of punctuation. Fortunately, when he entered Yale, just before his thirteenth birthday, he had already made this start toward independent thinking and was ready for the harder questions college would bring.

The most significant mental experience of his college years, perhaps also of his whole intellectual life, was just ahead. This was the discovery of John Locke's *An Essay Concerning the Human Understanding,* published in 1690, one of the books sent to Yale College in the Dummer gift of 1714. The Dummer books were still stored when he entered the Wethersfield group of freshmen, and how and when he had Locke's book in his own hand is a question that has teased his biographers. No date is recorded, but Samuel Johnson, tutor of the New Haven upperclassmen, had seen a copy in 1715, and by it had become "wholly changed to the New Learning." He and his fellow tutor Daniel Browne had introduced the study of both Newton and Locke to the New Haven students, and it is fair to suppose that this innovation had been duly reported to Wethersfield. Besides, Jonathan Edwards and his classmates were briefly with the New

Haven group in 1716, where he might have seen the book for himself. During his own senior year at New Haven he would have had library privileges and could have borrowed it.

When he recalled this experience in maturity, he put it strongly. He had been "beyond Expression entertained and pleased" with the book and had read it "with more satisfaction and pleasure than the most greedy miser in gathering handfuls of gold from some newly discovered treasure." Had he merely passed on Locke's gold as he found it, there would be nothing more to say. Instead he used what he had found to lead him on to further problems, new realms, sometimes in acceptance of Locke's conclusions, sometimes in challenge of them. His independence and originality would have had the approval of the master, whose account of the "historical, plain method" by which the human understanding attains its notions provides individual contours to the ideas our mental "sensations" imprint on the mind. "Various, different and wholly contradictory" as these ideas may be, Locke wrote, it is our individual mental faculties that have made them so. Let us know the capacities of our own minds, for "The Candle that is set up in us shines light enough for our purposes."

Whatever disagreements might follow as Jonathan Edwards was released to his own thinking, Locke's exposition of the origin and history of human ideas, the certainty of knowledge to which they give rise and his arguments against the current belief in innate ideas, and the extent, limits, and tests of knowledge available to man thrust this young disciple into a world in which he had just begun to be at home and in which he would continue to live. The greatest lesson Locke had taught him was that the "true nature of things" could be part of his own experience, not through effort and strain, but through his own experience. He need not struggle; he would receive it through a wise passivity. Untutored as he yet was in philosophical thinking, he could grasp Locke's concept of objective reality coming to him in the form of ideas. By putting this key in his hand, John Locke had done for this young scholar the best that a teacher can do for a student who is capable of thought. He had struck the flint of a gifted young mind and lighted the fire within.

The surviving series of notes written down by Jonathan

Edwards, probably in the second year of his graduate study,
record the impact of Locke's ideas and also directions in
which some of these ideas were already beginning to take
in his own thought. One series, labeled "The Mind," runs to
some twenty-five thousand words. It is composed of seventy
brief essays on a wide variety of subjects, among them "Existence," "Personal Identity," "Substance," "Matter," "Thought,"
"Perception," "Judgment," "Logick," "Genus," "Excellency,"
"Conscience." Prefixed to this list is another, fifty-six topics
headed "Subjects to be handled in the *Treatise on the Mind.*"
The second series, "Notes on Natural Science," contains
eighty-eight brief essays—"Atoms," "Planets," "Sound,"
"Gravity," "Clouds," "Wind," "Thunder," etc.—and is similarly prefaced by a list of "Things to be Considered, or
Written Fully About."

The brief essays in these two series are not bundles of
notes gathered from Jonathan Edwards' reading and set down
as fact to be remembered. They are the first fruit of his own
thought on these subjects and suggestions for his own
further independent investigation. For example, under "The
Mind":

16. Concerning Liberty, wherein it consists.
18. How far men may be to blame for their judgments; or
    for Believing, or not believing this or that.
21. Whether Self-Love be the ground of all Love.
25. Concerning Moral Sense; what Moral Sense is Natural.
34. Concerning Beauty.
42. How far Imagination is unavoidable in all Thinking; and
    Why?

Several lifetimes longer than his own might not have been
sufficient to complete these projected treatises, assuming that
one mind would have been capable of handling these various
and far-reaching topics. Therein does youthfulness announce
itself, as also in the excitement with which his mind seems
to be reaching out in all directions at once. Throughout his
mature life as well there would be the recurring ambition to
bring vast areas of knowledge within an orderly system, in
which everything would have a place, part relating to part.
He once dreamed of writing *A Rational Account of the
Christian Religion,* in which all art and all science would find
center and meaning in theology. Another prospective title,

The History of the Work of Redemption, was to be similarly all-embracing. Neither book was ever more than begun. Already in his student days his mind was straining toward all-inclusiveness, in an eagerness not only to know but also to relate part to part and to discover the unity that would help to explain all.

In broad terms, these college notes make clear that at this early stage he had begun to understand philosophic idealism, which later would be the basis for recognition of his originality as a thinker.

But the main area of his lifetime thought would claim still another realm, and another experience of the college years would determine the choice. This experience was what he called his conversion, which, though not specifically dated by him, would seem to have occurred shortly before his eighteenth birthday. From all that one can learn of his earlier life, he would seem always to have been deeply religious, but not in his own thought of himself. His conversion taught him that his boyhood "delight in religion" had not come from a visitation of divine grace at all. In comparison with the "new transports of joy," the "inward sweet sense of these Things" he was now experiencing, the hours of prayer from his booth in the East Windsor woods were a mere outward exercise.

His own story of this new certainty of acceptance, as he wrote it down when he was twice as old, is one of the classics of religious experience among surviving first-person records from St. Augustine to Pascal. It places Jonathan Edwards in the small company of men and women through the centuries who in very different ways testify to moments of illumination for which literal description is not adequate. They resort to imagery: a bright light, a fire within, an elevation of spirit, an exquisite harmony, ecstasy, rapture—always sudden, always brief and intense, and always inexpressible. Jonathan Edwards called it "a calm, sweet Abstraction of Soul from all Concerns of this World; and a kind of Vision, or fix'd Ideas and Imaginations, of being alone in the Mountains, or some solitary Wilderness, far from all Mankind; sweetly conversing with Christ, and wrapt and swallowed up in God. The Sense I had of divine Things would often of a sudden as it were, kindle up a sweet burning in my Heart; an ardour of my Soul, that I know not how to express." Those who cannot follow him can only stand aside and respect.

Jonathan Edwards was a man of strong emotions, and this new experience stirred him to the depths. It taught him that religion is of the emotions; and years later, in the most original work of his maturity, *A Treatise Concerning Religious Affections,* he attempted to establish this conviction as truth. Religious emotion with him was never extreme, as he had witnessed it in the Northampton and Whitefield revivals, but he recognized excess for what it was and made due allowance for it. His wife's religious emotion was less controlled than his own, but he spoke no word against it, allowing her story to be put in print just as she had spoken it. Bodily manifestations, even when they went as far as indecorum, were merely excesses of emotion and understandable as such. Over and over he asserted, "True religion lies much in the emotions. There is great power in them and no reason exists why bodily sensations should not follow as a matter of course."

What John Locke had taught him of *perception* now received a new illustration and emphasis in the light of his conversion. The test of religious truth, as he now saw it, was *an inward sense,* "a sense of the heart," a phrase he would use countless times in the years ahead. Not intellectual belief, not acceptance of "a form of words," but a witness within—individual, certain, authentic. This would continue to be the test of his own religious growth; it would be central in all his revival preaching, and later it would shape the issue in his controversy with his Northampton congregation. Still further hence it would put him in the van with religious teachers of another century.

By his own statement his new religious experience confirmed for him what Calvinism called the "sovereignty of God," a doctrine that had previously offended him but which now appeared "exceeding pleasant, bright, and sweet." To the end of his life he did not deny this new realization, but accepted it as the very bedrock of religious truth and built his whole theological system upon it. Calvinism, as he had heard it preached since childhood, presented no contradiction to the emotional raptures of his new youthful experience, and he continued to interpret what had come to pass in his life in words of familiar pulpit doctrine—conviction, conversion, sanctification, assurances of eternal salvation.

When he left Yale College after his two years of tutorship to become a candidate for the pastorate at Northampton, he was as well trained toward the ministry as a young American of his day could be. He was also totally committed to the pulpit calling and was apparently wholly insulated beyond any urge whatsoever toward the secular interests that were calling other gifted young Harvard and Yale graduates.

"Resolved," he wrote on January 12, 1723, "that no other end but religion, shall have any influence at all on any of my actions, and that no action shall be, in the least circumstance, any otherwise, than that the religious end will carry it."

His entire life, it now appears, can bear the test this resolve imposes.

Twenty-three years of preaching and pastoral care were ahead. His Northampton parish, remote as it was in those days, was second only to Boston in size and importance, and for so young a man to succeed Solomon Stoddard was no small honor. It was also a challenge and an even greater risk.

In New England religious matters before Jonathan Edwards was born, Solomon Stoddard had been a power strong enough to change the custom and tradition of more than a century, and at a time when change might have seemed least probable. In his Northampton parish he had instituted the Halfway Covenant of 1662, by which parents not themselves far enough advanced in grace to be full church members might present their children for baptism on the first Sunday after their birth. At the distance of two centuries, one can hardly overstate the magnitude of this privilege to parents of that far-off day. More radically still, somewhat later Solomon Stoddard allowed these Halfway members, provided they were not of scandalous living, to partake of the Lord's Supper on Communion Sunday, a privilege previously guarded for full members only. Halfway privilege though it was, it was eagerly grasped and henceforth regarded as a precious right. For the pastor himself not only to permit but also to advocate such a change was to open the church door very wide indeed, and if Jonathan Edwards as a young pastor thought he could shut it again and return to the former practice, he could not have been more mistaken. The years would tell, as meanwhile "Mr. Stoddard's Way" became quietly accepted all over New England.

During the early years of his pastorate all went well for the young pastor and his beautiful bride, only seventeen years old at the time of her marriage. The house on King Street took a central place in town life, as custom demanded, and Northampton was well pleased. Jonathan Edwards proved to be an acceptable successor to his venerable grandfather. Quietly eloquent, a deep student of the Bible, and with something of a teacher's gift in expounding it, he began with nearly everything in his favor. In addition to pastoral duties, heavy as they were with a membership of nearly six hundred, his life on weekdays was that of a dedicated student. He bought books, borrowed books, imported books, and read avidly. His notebooks, just now beginning to be published, attest his unremitting study, as he sorted, arranged, and commented on the materials of his reading for later use. Little or any of this study had to do with the sermons he was preaching, but nearly all of it concerned religion. First and last, he was a man of this one abiding interest. He investigated many outlying fields, but not for their own detail. Literally hundreds of jottings announce this singlemindedness: "Astronomy, yes; but what has it for the philosopher asking the meaning of existence? Electricity, yes; but remember 'To enquire after some Philosophical Treatise of the Nature of Electricity the best that is extant.' "

During these years he published little, but he had large plans for the future. His first publication was a sermon, preached by invitation at the Boston Public Lecture, July 8, 1731. His audience was largely ministerial, Harvard-trained, and sharply skeptical of a Yale graduate from the doubtful years of Rector Cutler's tutorship. The invitation to preach this sermon implied, as Edwards of course knew, that he was being tested for orthodoxy and also for his fitness as a successor to his grandfather, the unofficial pope of the Connecticut valley. The subject of the sermon was safely orthodox: "God Glorified in the Work of Redemption by the Greatness of Man's Dependence upon him." That the young preacher pleased his audience is apparent in the immediate order that the sermon be published and the laudatory preface signed by Thomas Prince and William Cooper. "May the College in the neighbouring colony . . . be a faithful mother

of many such sons as the author," and may the Stoddard
spirit "long live and shine in his grandson," they wrote in his
praise. Jonathan Edwards had passed a stern test.

After three more years of sermons preached, children
catechized, more books read by dim candlelight, he found
himself suddenly the center of interest far from Northampton. For under his Sunday preaching and his weekly meeting
with small groups, particularly of young people, had come
the greatest revival of religion the parish had ever known.
It surprised even those who had prayed for it. News quickly
spread to neighboring towns, thence to Boston. Clergymen
from all over Massachusetts and Connecticut came to see for
themselves and to carry back personal reports. Meanwhile
converts continued to multiply. Briefly Northampton was a
changed town. The meetinghouse could hardly hold those
who flocked to hear and to see the marvel of it. One Sunday
morning the pastor received into membership one hundred
new applicants. Such an "outpouring of divine grace" seemed
hardly to be solid town history. For several more months
nothing checked the revival progress as excitement continued
to mount. Then one Lord's Day morning Joseph Hawley, an
uncle of Jonathan Edwards and one of the chief men of the
town, cut his throat and died instantly. The town was aghast;
the spell was broken and the revival over. Men looked
around them with new eyes and began to see more realisti-
cally what had been happening in their midst.

But these happenings were now no longer one town's story
alone. Requests had been pouring in from all sides for details, and Jonathan Edwards had already begun to answer
them. His letter to Benjamin Colman of Boston, written before the suicide of Joseph Hawley, was immediately published in London and was followed by more requests for
more details. Jonathan Edwards complied with a book-long
account under the title of *A Faithful Narrative of the sur-
prizing Work of God in the Conversion of Many Hunndred
Souls in Northampton and the Neighboring Towns and Vil-
lages.* It appeared in 1737 and identified the author for
life as a revival preacher. In the first flush of his own success
he had been caught by the more unusual manifestations of
some conversions, and by recounting them while excitement
ran high, he helped to establish some of them as part of a
conversion pattern. Later he would not have done this.

On Christmas Day, 1737, he dedicated the new meeting-house, its widened dimensions an evidence of the great "ingathering." But even before this impressive day the totals were less than he had first reported. There had been many backsliders who, once the excitement was past, had returned to their godless ways. He recognized now that he had been overcredulous, not alert to "False Appearances, corrupt Mixtures," even counterfeits. His own report had included some that he had believed to be genuine. With the story in print, they would be repeated.

The coming of George Whitefield in 1740 and the almost phenomenal success of his preaching soon dwarfed the marvels of the Northampton revival in the popular view. Whitefield's preaching in the fields and the marketplace, his human-interest stories, and his breast-beatings and other innovations of pulpit manner had no parallel in the sedate New England meetinghouse. Innovations such as these invited extravagance in his listeners. Outcries and repentant groans soon punctuated every sermon. The traditional Sunday sermon would never have the same chance again. Whitefield was turning the pulpit into a stage and giving New England its first taste of theater under the flag of salvation. A new era had begun. Discreet men, both ministers and laymen, offered kindly criticism, but it was powerless before the compulsion of his presence and the magic of his voice. While he was in the town, hysteria often prevailed. The next morning he was gone and the local minister had to deal with the aftermath.

Jonathan Edwards was not blind to Whitefield's youthful unwisdom or to the evils he left behind him in every parish, but he was silent as to public criticism. He believed the revival was the work of God Himself and he also wanted to share in making it effective. His sermon at Enfield, Connecticut, in July, 1741, preached at the very height of the excitement, was one of the most spectacular chapters in the story. Its immediate publication, together with reports of the behavior of the congregation who heard it, added terror to Jonathan Edwards' previous reputation as a revival preacher. The reputation he still bears in the twentieth century, in the thought of those who know no more than his name, was made in that one hour in the Enfield meetinghouse.

His subject, eternal torment for sinners, had been preached in every pulpit in America since the beginning, but in an atmosphere of calm it had not been prelude to chaos. Jonathan Edwards preached on it at various times; in fact, he had already preached this same sermon twice in his own pulpit without unusual effect. Characteristically, as he stood before his people on Sunday morning, he chose a positive theme: the glory of salvation, the peace that Christ gives, the reality of spiritual light, comfort in the thought of heaven, the gentleness of Jesus, the duties of Christians. Characteristically also, he spoke quietly, using no gestures, holding the tiny sermon booklet in his left hand and occasionally speaking extemporaneously, by way of illustration or enlargement, as he read what he had written. He preached religion as he had himself experienced it, as an invitation to a better life now and safety for eternity. But this July morning he chose to inspire fear, fear of an eternity without salvation, of an angry God, who would take vengeance on those who had lived without Him, of the uncertainty of human life that might end any minute, of fire and brimstone prepared for the unsaved.

The fact that he was a guest speaker on this occasion, unknown to the congregation except by reputation, gave him a favorable chance. The fact also that a prophecy was current that the end of the world was nigh was the best of preparation for his text, "Their foot shall slide in due time." He had a genius for selecting texts and this time the choice was oracular: Nothing holds you back from slipping into hell but God's hand, and God is very angry. He may loose his hold at any moment. Some of you will remember this discourse in hell.

That was enough. Every "unsaved" man in the house knew he would be that man.

Two centuries and more later, it is still a grim sermon on the printed page, and delivered to a packed auditory under the strain of 1741, it was almost unbearable. What made it so was not only the earnestness of absolute belief for the speaker, as he painted the wrath of God, the pains of fire everlasting, the unending hopelessness of doom, but the fact that the congregation also believed it, ancestrally, as it were. The "unsaved" among them had always intended to accept the terms of eternal safety, but as yet they had postponed the day. What Jonathan Edwards was doing as he turned page after page in the little booklet was to make this July Sunday,

1741, seem their last chance. Accept the terms today or be eternally lost, he seemed to say.

Overwhelmed by this sense of immediacy of doom, no wonder strong men clung to the pillars of the meetinghouse and cried aloud for mercy. It was a scene that could not be reenacted in a later generation to whom these preachments would not spell unqualified certainty. Had the preacher confronted his congregation with a new doctrine, such terror could not have been induced. It was the familiar certainty that had won. Nehemiah Strong, who had heard Jonathan Edwards preach on the last judgment in his home pulpit, wrote in his diary that "without one thought to the contrary," he had expected the "awful judgment to be unfolded on that day and in that place." He had "waited with the deepest and most solemn solicitude to hear the trumpet sound and the archangel call; to see the graves open, the dead arise, and the Judge descend in the glory of his Father, with all the holy angels; and was deeply disappointed, when the day terminated and left the world in its usual state of tranquillity."

Such an effect makes the Enfield sermon likewise a triumph of pulpit power in terms of its intent. It also clarifies, better than many pages of discussion can do, one's impression as to the panic of the Great Awakening. It is itself this panic in miniature, and as such is a landmark in American religious history.

With George Whitefield temporarily out of the country in late 1741, the New England clergy wrestled with the early sequels to the great clamor. A revival season had been newly defined. Noisy demonstrations now had place in it, and if they did not come in volume, noisier new evangelists such as the Tennents or James Davenport could devise new ways of compelling them. By comparison with such extremes, traditional preaching seemed dull and heavy. It lacked the spice of drama. A preacher's performance would henceforth be measured against a new pattern. More ominous still, there was now a new sense of power in the congregation's hands: If the minister's preaching does not please us, we can dismiss him by our vote. Pastorates for life were now all but ended, and nearly every parish would have at least one dismissal on its record.

Whitefield was by no means entirely to blame for these changes, but he had done much to bring them about, particularly as to decorum in the meetinghouse and respect for the settled clergy. He had openly accused individuals among them as unconverted and had disparaged learning as a qualification for the pulpit. He had encouraged "lay preachers" who had only "salvation" as preparation for haranguing the congregation, as scores of them now tried to do, interrupting the Sunday service often with boisterousness. One of the saddest sequels to his new style of preaching was the spirit of strife between members of the clergy over him and his ways. Ministers took sides for or against him and poured forth pamphlets in a flood, stating their reasons. Was the revival a "Great Work" or was it not? Yes, said his supporters, quickly dubbed the New Lights. No, said his opposers, the Old Lights. Bitterness and abuse were the weapons of both sides.

The part of Jonathan Edwards in this paper warfare was the publication of two treatises, *The Disguishing Marks of the Work of the Spirit of God,* in 1741, and *Some Thoughts Concerning the Present Revival of Religion in New England,* in 1742, together with a series of sermons forming the basis of his later *Concerning Religious Affections*, preached in 1743. He decried extremes and viewed with much concern the increasing emphasis on bodily contortions, shriekings, trances, and ecstatic deliriums, although admitting that divine power might cause such manifestations. The concern of the minister is with men's souls, not their bodies, he insisted. In his view, excess had damaged the "Great Work" but had not discredited it. Look at the work as a whole, he said, not at men's follies alone. But at the time, his words were impotent. One had to be either for or against excess, and he was taking a middle ground. Instead of dealing with sensational examples of indecorum, he was looking at the laws of human nature underneath such behavior, and readers in 1741–42 were not interested in abstractions. They wanted concrete marvels. Today this pamphlet outpouring is neglected and forgotten; students of religious psychology read Edwards.

The return of Whitefield in 1744 turned the battle toward him more personally, and again the pamphlets poured forth from New England printing presses, by no means politely. Even civil authorities recognized the threat to religion and proclaimed days of fasting and prayer in view of the "unhappy Divisions and Contentions which prevail both among Ministers and People." Whitefield's attempts to answer criticism were weak and only made matters worse. Presently the "Testimony of the President, Professors, Tutors and Hebrew Instructor of Harvard College in Cambridge against the Reverend Mr. George Whitefield and his Conduct" took him off the front page and dimmed popular interest in the quarrel he had raised, but he had done great damage to the cause he professed.

As one looks back at the Great Awakening through the longer view of history, it appears that an idea had become freshly current, an idea as old as Christianity, namely, that religion is not belief in a creed, nor is it decent living. It is an inner individual experience, or it is nothing. Jonathan Edwards' contribution to the establishment of this idea as authoritative had been to make a place for it in biblical teaching, in theology, and in human nature. He had made religion as "a sense of the heart" a familiar phrase on men's lips and in print, where men may still meet it, most originally in his *Concerning Religious Affections.* In this book he wrote a pioneer chapter in religious psychology and also, except for his *Personal Narrative,* the most self-revealing volume on his entire shelf. He had first lived what he wrote.

But life in the New England meetinghouse would not soon be peaceful again. In the restless years that followed Whitefield's departure, relations between pastor and people continued to be strained. In Northampton, as in other parishes of the midcentury, there was a "salary dispute," perennial and often ugly in its implications. Not only were requests for increases denied, including requests for more cords of wood, but salary as previously arranged was not always paid on time or in full. Northampton town files show such requests and denials, also a humiliating town demand for a detailed family budget and consequent accusations of "lavish expenditure" at the parsonage.

At the height of these local money troubles came the sensational "bad book" episode, which, reduced to its lowest terms, was no more than the discovery that several boys and girls were passing around a book intended as instruction to midwives, with excitement resulting. As soon as this was reported to the pastor, he read out the names of the accused at the close of the Sunday sermon and announced plans for the usual procedure of investigation. Two months of testimony followed, while the town seethed with resentment, and relations between pulpit and pew suffered damage not to be repaired while Jonathan Edwards stood before them as pastor. Publicity given to private offense had been normal procedure in New England meetinghouses since the beginning. The pastor was doing exactly what his father and grandfather before him had done, but the hour had changed. In the late 1740's congregations were in no mood to be publicly rebuked, with culprits brought before the membership for confession and public forgiveness. Some of the children in this misdemeanor were of the best families in the town, and this fact alone made a great difference. Edwards' untactfulness was also a main cause of the uproar, but tactful or not, this was pastoral interference. This was a private affair for the parents to settle, and none of the minister's business. So the town talk ran. The details are shabby enough, but a principle was at stake, and even the public confessions of the three persons chiefly to blame settled nothing. The records of nearly every parish in New England could show some critical case that offered a parallel involving the limits of pastoral authority in a sensitive time. Too late Jonathan Edwards recognized his mistake, but the damage had been done.

Unfortunately, before even surface peace had been restored, an application for membership in the church gave him the opportunity to raise the issue of admission to the ordinance of the Lord's Supper. This was precisely forty-eight years after Solomon Stoddard had allowed Halfway members, not of scandalous living, to partake. Immediately the battle was on. Jonathan Edwards made a formal statement before the church declaring a state of controversy to exist between him and the membership and requesting the privilege of expressing his view in print. His request was granted. He knew himself beaten before he wrote a word, but "experimental piety" as the only qualification for full privileges was a conviction with him and he could not do otherwise than state his position. He did so under the title *A Humble Inquiry into the Rules of the Word of God Concerning the Qualifications Requisite to a Complete Standing and Full Communion with the Visible Christian Church.*

Only twenty copies of his book were distributed in the town, and these were read by very few. The doctrinal issue no longer mattered. Solomon Stoddard had settled that forty-eight years earlier. Jonathan Edwards had offered to resign if

he and his people could not agree, and the majority desired
nothing less than to be rid of him. They denied him the
dignity of resigning and called a packed church council to
decide. Opposition in the town was led by Joseph Hawley,
son of the man who had committed suicide during the
Northampton revivals. He harbored his private grudge. Ver-
dict of the council against Edwards was a foregone conclusion. Dismissal was announced on June 22, 1750, after
three days of deliberation.

"Jonathan Edwards received ye Shock, unshaken," and ten
days later preached his farewell sermon. A painful session it
would be, but such was part of every dismissal drama. No
one in the town or country around would have missed it,
and when it was over, they would be free, or so they thought.

This sermon offers revealing clues for an understanding of
Jonathan Edwards. He had nothing whatever to say of the
controversy itself, nothing of the animosities that had marred
their twenty-three years of relationship. Instead he chose to
set forth the relation between pastor and people in their many
meetings together and to look forward to their final meeting
on the day of judgment, when God Himself would settle
their dispute forever. In page after page of this long sermon,
he was saying over and over that whatever we have done here
together has eternal consequences. This was one of the foundation convictions of his own life. Never before or after did
he say it with more searching plainness.

A chapter closed for him on that day. He would not have
another parish or another people. He was forty-six years old
and had a "numerous and chargeable family" to support.
Offers of other pastorates came, but he did not accept one of
them. After nearly a year of continuing harassed residence
in Northampton, he chose the Stockbridge mission, left vacant
by the death of John Sergeant. The six years that followed
were, in their bare dimensions, sublimely ironic. A great
original mind, one of the most distinguished minds of his
generation, would be set to strange new tasks. His home
would be a tiny outpost in the Indian country, fringed with
hostility and often ravaged by war. The small settlement of
white residents was controlled by a jealous relative of Edwards, sternly opposed to his coming. Jonathan Edwards
would be the missionary, in charge of a small boarding
school for Indian boys. He would try to learn the Housatonic

language in preparation for teaching them. On Sundays he would preach through an interpreter to a small huddle of Indians who would need frequent counsel against the evils of excessive rum. For long periods he would house and feed soldiers sent to guard the mission against destruction by enemy action. When the boarding school burned, he would rebuild it. He would write long and exceedingly wise letters to the Boston commissioners of Indian affairs. For the six years he called Stockbridge home, he would be in virtual exile from all his former life. He would live in constant peril and suffer serious illness.

But during these same years, his life would find center in the tiny four-by-eight nook he called the "study," and here he would write most of the books that have made him a name among philosophers and theologians the world over. In days crowded with strange new responsibilities and ringed with dangers he would begin to reap a rich harvest.

His best-known title while he lived and for a full century afterward was *The Freedom of the Will,* a book he had intended to write ever since his college days. In his "Notes on the Mind" he had entered four brief essays on the will, and in the list of subjects he expected to handle in his projected *Treatise on the Mind,* he had written (12) "Whether any difference between the Will and Inclination." During the twenty-five years since passed, Calvinism had increasingly needed a champion. If man's will were free, as the Arminians made bold to declare, then God's sovereignty, complete and absolute, is limited, and if so, Calvinism is ruined. From time to time church synods and councils passed resolutions and raised voices, but too timidly. When Jonathan Edwards took his turn, the time had grown short for the threat to be safely met, for the Great Awakening had aroused suspicions in the pew and revival preaching seemed to put man's choice of being "saved" or "lost" in his own hands. What else was this but free will?

Jonathan Edwards was fully aware of the peril to traditional belief and he was also well equipped to fight the great intellectual battle of his generation. After completing his *Reply to Solomon Williams* and *The Humble Inquiry,* his tools were sharp. He used his great powers of mind to demolish the arguments of his Arminian opponents, apparently with pleasure. Had he dealt with the subject in complete freedom from these opposing arguments, he would have written a very different book, possibly a greater one. Instead, as the title announces, he was dealing with "modern prevailing Notions," and those "supposed to be essential to Moral Agency, Vertue and Vice, Reward and Punishment, Praise and Blame." Obviously this phrasing puts limitations on a complete examination.

His arguments are strictly disposed to the ends announced. His book is not a philosophical handling, but primarily a theological argument against opposing theological argument. With this intent he framed definitions with knife-blade distinction and argued his case with a scaffolding of logic that is well nigh impregnable. In the conclusion, he had saved both God's sovereignty and man's dignity. The Arminian opponents had been answered and Calvinism was still safe. All this even though neither he nor his opponents had started with the question "What is the truth?" rather than a theological premise that neither stopped to examine. Both had also argued from authority, that of the Bible.

Jonathan Edwards' argument defies condensation. One may say he had won by a new definition of human liberty, in reality a limitation of it. Man is free; yes, free to act on his own choices, but these choices are dependent on motives outside his control. Argument to this conclusion rushes on with a breathlessness that never seems to tire. More amazing still, it proceeds with a coherence that cannot be broken. Take it or leave it as a whole, as one must. It is a web, each part as strong as every other. To demolish his argument, one must begin with his premise and also recognize the foundation of authority upon which it rests. Therein was he a man of his own century, not of two centuries later.

His last polemic, *The Great Christian Doctrine of Original Sin Defended*, was in press at the time of his death and published several months afterward. Once again he was in battle on an issue of moment to theologians. His target of attack was Dr. John Taylor's *The Scripture Doctrine of Original Sin Proposed to a Free and Candid Examination*, published in 1738. Many pens had been busy for and against Dr. Taylor's denial of man's inheritance of Adam's corruption. Jonathan Edwards' contribution to the debate was a brilliant theory of the unity of the race by which Adam's taint remained an inevitable part of man's inheritance. His exposition of the fall also cleared God from being the author of sin. These two contributions gave new directions to the controversy for some time to come.

Seven years after his death the publication of *Two Dissertations: Concerning the End for which God Created the World* and *The Nature of True Vertue* began the long task of putting his manuscript materials in print. In these two pieces he began to be free of controversy, as his thought stretched to realms beyond current doctrinal battle. He wrote these two pieces with a freshness that bespoke new resources of power for new areas of vision and discovery.

Why did God create the world, this "astonishing fabric of the universe"? Because divinity is not self-contained; it must needs flow outward from itself. The fullness of God satisfies itself by diffusing fullness. The process is eternal. The moment of complete satisfaction will never be reached. The poet in Jonathan Edwards is speaking in this mystical speculation. But, as always, the man of intellect pulls him back to consider *chief* ends and *ultimate* ends and to mark reason's carefully chiseled steps. What results, however, is a vision of God made of more than absolute sovereignty.

In *The Nature of True Vertue* he is closer to the next century than in anything else he wrote during these years of exile in Stockbridge. Virtue, as he saw it, is not of the intellect, or perceiving faculty, but of the emotions, or acting faculty. There is nothing of self in it, nor can be. It is pursued for itself alone. It is itself an end, not a means to an end. Only those can recognize it who possess it. His most poetic definition, perhaps also his most precise one, is that virtue is *beauty,* the beauty of holiness, God's own beauty. Beauty is one of his favorite words and is never carelessly used.

Great riches still lie in the manuscript materials, now in process of scholarly publication. Jonathan Edwards will have a chance to be read by a new generation and in the whole corpus of his work, presented against the background of his own time, as modern scholars attempt to reconstruct it.

To understand his theology and philosophy better in the light of two centuries ago will not be the same as to accept it. The certainties of his day are not our certainties. To attempt to translate his thought into more modern idiom is both unfair and impossible. It is also unnecessary. To read what he wrote, as he wrote it, expressed in doctrines and ideas of his own day, still enables one to sense the range of his vision, the depth of his profundity, the symmetry of his design for human life, the richness of the values he lived by. He was a man of far vision and his goals were ultimate.

At the time of his death, in 1758, it was easy to say that he had wasted his powers in years of long battle over the basis for church membership, to name only one battle. Not at all. History stepped in to change many things in American life. After the Revolution, town and parish were no longer one, with the town constable collecting "rates" and enforcing church attendance. It was no longer necessary to devise a basis of church membership suitable for the whole town. The church body became separate and was free to guard its own doors, as in the earliest days. Later, as the church membership split into sects, each sect framed a statement of faith and purpose as basis for membership. "Heart religion" won in all the evangelical sects, and for any one of them either of the statements Jonathan Edwards had proposed in the Northampton dispute would have been satisfactory. He had dealt with the issue for his own day and lost, but he had dealt with it not in its surface application but abstractly, so that what he said was still acceptable when victory turned to his side in a new generation.

There is much in his pages, truly enough, that has scant meaning for later generations, as would be true for men of thought in any day if one stops with local and transient applications. Fortunately the thought of Jonathan Edwards does not stop at these boundaries. He did not concern himself with orthodoxy and unorthodoxy, but wrote of religion in depth and dimension. St. Augustine wrote as a man of his own time and place; so also did Thomas Aquinas, Richard Baxter, John Bunyan, and all great religionists of times past. To read them as men of their own time and setting gives a shape and contour to their thought that is otherwise missed. Strangely also, as we read we are reminded that the great battles of the mind and spirit are not won for all time. Under different banners, and with changed weapons, the same battles are renewed as the generations pass. Jonathan Edwards was such a warrior, and in battles that are perennial.

OLA ELIZABETH WINSLOW

JONATHAN EDWARDS:

Basic Writings

OF INSECTS

Probably written as early as his eleventh year, and at his father's suggestion sent to an English correspondent whose name is unknown. More arresting even than the accuracy and persistence in observation and experiment are the speculative conclusions to which this boy's discovery of fact led him. What this early essay both revealed and promised have often been remarked by students of Edwards. See C. H. Faust, "Jonathan Edwards as a Scientist," *American Literature* (1930), I, pp. 393–404; E. C. Smyth, *The Andover Review* (1890), XIII, pp. 1–19, for comments on this piece. The text is from *The Works of President Edwards,* edited by S. B. Dwight, Vol. I, pp. 23–28.

May it please your Honour,

In the postscript of your letter to my father, you manifest a willingness to receive any thing else that he has observed worthy of remark, respecting the wonders of nature. What there is an account of in the following lines, is by him thought to be such. He has laid it upon me to write the account, I having had advantage to make more full observations than himself. Forgive me that I do not conceal my name, and communicate this to you through a mediator. I do not state it as an hypothesis, but as a plain fact, which my own eyes have witnessed, and which every one's senses may make him as certain of as of any thing else. Although these things appear to me thus certain, still I submit the whole to your better judgment and deeper insight. And I humbly beg to be pardoned for running the venture, though an utter stranger, of troubling you with so prolix an account of that, which I am altogether uncertain, whether you will esteem worthy of the time and pains of reading. If you think the observations childish, and beside the rules of decorum,—with greatness and goodness overlook it in a child. Pardon me, if I thought it might at least give you occasion to make better observations, such as should be worthy of communicating to the learned world, respecting these wondrous animals, from whose glistening web so much of the wisdom of the Creator shines.

I am, Sir,

Your most obedient, humble servant,

JONATHAN EDWARDS

May it please your Honour,

There are some things that I have happily seen of the wondrous way of the working of the spider. Although every thing belonging to this insect is admirable, there are some phenomena relating to them more particularly wonderful. Every body that is used to the country, knows their marching in the air from one tree to another, sometimes at the distance of five or six rods. Nor can one go out in a dewy morning, at the latter end of August and the beginning of September, but he shall see multitudes of webs, made visible by the dew that hangs on them, reaching from one tree, branch and shrub, to another: which webs are commonly thought to be made in the night, because they appear only in the morning; whereas none of them are made in the night, for these spiders never come out in the night when it is dark, as the dew is then falling. But these webs may be seen well enough in the day time by an observing eye, by their reflection in the sunbeams. Especially late in the afternoon, may these webs, that are between the eye and that part of the horizon that is under the sun, be seen very plainly, being advantageously posited to reflect the rays. And the spiders themselves may be very often seen travelling in the air, from one stage to another amongst the trees, in a very unaccountable manner. But I have often seen that, which is much more astonishing. In very calm and serene days in the forementioned time of year, standing at some distance behind the end of an house or some other opake body, so as just to hide the disk of the sun and keep off his dazzling rays, and looking along close by the side of it, I have seen a vast multitude of little shining webs, and glistening strings, brightly reflecting the sunbeams, and some of them of great length, and of such a height, that one would think they were tacked to the vault of the heavens, and would be burnt like tow in the sun, and make a very beautiful, pleasing, as well as surprising appearance. It is wonderful at what a distance, these webs may plainly be seen. Some that are at a great distance appear (it cannot be less than) several thousand times as big as they ought. I believe they appear under as great an angle, as a body of a foot diameter ought to do at such a distance; so greatly doth brightness increase the apparent bigness of bodies at a distance, as is observed of the fixed stars.

But that which is most astonishing, is, that very often appears at the end of these webs, spiders sailing in the air with

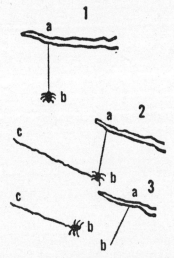

them; which I have often beheld with wonderment and pleasure, and showed to others. And since I have seen these things, I have been very conversant with spiders; resolving if possible, to find out the mysteries of these their astonishing works. And I have been so happy as very frequently to see their manner of working; that when a spider would go from one tree to another, or would fly in the air, he first lets himself down a little way from the twig he stands on by a web, as in Fig. 1; and then, laying hold of it by his fore feet, and bearing himself by that, puts out a web, as in Fig. 2, which is drawn out of his tail with infinite ease, in the gently moving air, to what length the spider pleases; and if the farther end happens to catch by a shrub or the branch of a tree, the spider immediately feels it, and fixes the hither end of it to the web by which he let himself down, and goes over by that web which he put out of his tail as in Fig. 3. And this, my eyes have innumerable times made me sure of.

Now, Sir, it is certain that these webs, when they first proceed from the spider, are so rare a substance, that they are lighter than the air, because they will ascend in it, as they will immediately in a calm air, and never descend except driven by a wind; wherefore 'tis certain. And 'tis as certain, that what swims and ascends in the air is lighter than the air, as that what ascends and swims in water is lighter than water. So that if we should suppose any such time, wherein the air is perfectly calm, this web is so easily drawn out of the spider's tail, that if the end of it be once out, barely the levity of it is sufficient to draw it out to any length; wherefore if it don't happen that the end of this web, *b c,* catches by a tree or some other body, 'till there is so long a web drawn out, that its levity shall be so great as more than to counterbalance the gravity of the spider, or so that the web and the spider, taken together, shall be lighter than such a quantity of air as takes up equal space, then according to the universally acknowledged laws of nature, the web and the spider together will ascend, and not descend, in the air: as when a man is at the bottom of the water, if he has hold of a piece of timber so great, that the wood's tendency upwards is greater than the man's tendency downwards, he together with the wood will ascend to the surface of the water. And therefore, when the spider perceives that the web *b c* is long enough to bear him up by its ascending force, he lets go his hold of the web *a b,* Fig. 3, and ascends in the air with the web *b c.* If there be not web more than enough, just to counterbalance the gravity of the spider, the spider together with the web will hang in equilibrio, neither ascending nor descending, otherwise than as the air moves. But if there is so much web, that its greater levity shall more than equal the greater density of the spider, they will ascend till the air is so thin, that the spider and web together are just of an equal weight with so much air. And in this way, Sir, I have multitudes of times seen spiders mount away into the air, from a stick in my hands, with a vast train of this silver web before them; for, if the spider be disturbed upon the stick by shaking of it, he will presently in this manner leave it. And their way of working may very distinctly be seen, if they are held up in the sun, or against a dark door, or any thing that is black.

Now, Sir, the only remaining difficulty is, how they first put out the end of the web *b c,* Fig. 3, out of their tails. If once the web is out, it is easy to conceive how the levity of it, together with the motion of the air, may draw it out to a great length. But how should they first let out of their tails, the end of so fine and even a string; seeing that the web, while it is in the spider, is a certain cloudy liquor, with which that great bottle tail of theirs is filled; which immediately, upon its being exposed to the air, turns to a dry substance, and exceedingly rarifies and extends itself. Now if it be a liquor, it is hard to conceive how they should let out a fine even thread, without expelling a little drop at the end of it; but none such can be discerned. But there is no need of this; for it is only separating that part of the web *b c,* Fig. 2, from *a b,* and the end of the web is already out. Indeed, Sir, I never could distinctly see them do this: so small a piece of web being imperceptible among the spider's legs. But I cannot doubt but that it is so, because there is a necessity that they should some way or other separate the web *a b,* Fig. 3, from their tails, before they can let out the web *b c.* And then I know they do have ways of dividing their webs by biting them off, or in some other way. Otherwise they could not separate themselves from the web *a b,* Fig. 3.

And this, Sir, is the way of spiders going from one tree to another, at a great distance; and this is the way of their flying in the air. And, although I say I am certain of it, I don't desire that the truth of it should be received upon my word; though I could bring others to testify to it, to whom I have shown it, and who have looked on, with admiration, to see their manner of working. But every one's eyes, that will take the pains to observe, will make them as sure of it. Only those, that would make experiment, must take notice that it is not every sort of spider that is a flying spider, for those spiders that keep in houses are a quite different sort, as also those that keep in the ground, and those that keep in swamps, in hollow trees, and rotten logs; but those spiders, that keep on branches of trees and shrubs, are the flying spiders. They delight most in walnut trees, and are that sort of spiders that make those curious network polygonal webs, that are so frequently to be seen in the latter end of the year. There are more of this sort of spiders by far than of any other.

But yet, Sir, I am assured that the chief end of this faculty, that is given them, is not their recreation, but their destruction; because their destruction is unavoidably the effect of it; and we shall find nothing, that is the continual effect of nature, but what is of the means by which it is brought to pass. But it is impossible, but that the greatest part of the spiders upon the land should, every year, be swept into the ocean. For these spiders never fly, except the weather is fair and the atmosphere dry; but the atmosphere is never clear, neither in this nor any other continent, only when the wind blows from the midland parts, and consequently towards the sea. As here in New-England, the fair weather is only when the wind is westerly, the land being on that side, and the ocean on the easterly. And I never have seen any of these spiders flying, but when they have been hastening directly towards the sea. And the time of their flying being so long, even from about the middle of August every sunshiny day, until about the end of October; (though their chief time, as I observed before, is the latter end of August, and beginning of September;) and they never flying from the sea, but always towards it; must needs get there at last; for its unreasonable to suppose that they have sense enough to stop themselves when they come near the sea; for then they would have hundreds of times as many spiders upon the sea-shore, as any where else.

The same also holds true of other sorts of flying insects; for at these times, that I have viewed the spiders with their webs in the air, there has also appeared vast multitudes of flies, and all flying the same way with the spiders and webs directly to the ocean; and even such as butterflies, millers and moths, which keep in the grass at this time of year, I have seen vastly higher than the tops of the highest trees, all going the same way. These I have seen towards evening, without such a screen to defend my eyes from the sunbeams; which I used to think were seeking a warmer climate.

The reason of their flying at that time of year, I take to be because then the ground and trees, the places of their residence in summer, begin to be chilly and uncomfortable. Therefore when the sun shines pretty warm they leave them, and mount up in the air, and expand their wings to the sun, and flying for nothing but their own ease and comfort, they suffer themselves to go that way, that they find they can go with the greatest ease, and so where the wind pleases; and it being warmth they fly for, they find it cold and laborious flying against the wind. They therefore seem to use their wings, but just so much as to bear them up, and suffer them to go with the wind. So that without doubt almost all aerial insects, and also spiders which live upon trees and are made up of them, are at the end of the year swept away into the sea, and buried in the ocean, and leave nothing behind them but their eggs, for a new stock next year.

OF THE RAINBOW, COLOURS,
THE SOUL, OF BEING

No one of these four essays can be definitely dated, but all would seem to have been written before or during his thirteenth year, the "Rainbow" probably earlier than the others. "Colours" shows some familiarity with Newton's *Opticks,* probably by direct reading. "Of Being" is the most precocious of the four, with its hint of philosophic idealism. The text of these four pieces is edited by E. C. Smyth, "Some Early Writings of Jonathan Edwards, A.D. 1714–1726," *Proceedings of the American Antiquarian Society,* n.s. (1895), X, pp. 237–47. Pages 212–36 include facsimiles from portions of these pieces in Edwards' handwriting. In the transcript, sentence divisions have been indicated and punctuation added. The manuscript spelling has been retained.

OF THE RAINBOW

We shall Endeavour to Give a full Account Of the Rainbow and such an One as we think if Well understood will be satisfactory to Any body If they Are fully satisfied Of Sir Isaac Newtons Different Reflexibility and Refrangibility of the Rays of light and If he be not we Refer him to [what] he has said About it and we are Assured if he be A person Of an ordinary logacity and anything Versed in such matters, by that time he was thoroughly Considered if he[']ll be satisfied and after that let him Peruse what we are about to say. The first Question then shall be What is that Reflection which we Call a Rainbow from I answer from the falling Drops of Rain for we never see any Rainbow except it be so that the sun Can shine full upon the Drops of Rain except the heavens be so Clear on One side as to let the Uninterrupted Rays of the sun Come Directly Upon the Rain that[?] falls on the Other side, thus we say it is a sign of fair Weather when there is a Rainbow in the East, because when there is a Rainbow in the East, it is alwaies already fair in the West for If it be Cloudy there the Rays of the sun will be hindered from Coming thence to the Opposite Drops of Rain. It cannot be the Cloud from whence this Reflection is made, as was once thought, for we almost alwaies see the Ends of Rainbows Come Down Even in amongst the trees below the Hills And to the very Ground where we know there is no part of the Cloud there, but what Descends in Drops of Rain and Can Convince any man by Ocular Demonstration In two Minutes On a fair Day that the Reflection is from Drops by Only taking a little water in my mouth and standing between the sun and something that looks a little Darkish and spirting of it into the Air so as to Disperse all into fine Drops And there will appear as Compleat and plain a Rainbow with all the Colours as ever Was seen in the heavens and there will Appear the same If the sun is near enough to the horizon upon fine Drops of Water Dashd up by a stick from a puddle, the Reason why the Drops must be fine is because they wont be thick enough but here and there a Drop if they Are Large, And I have frequently heard my Countrymen that are Used to sawmills say that they have seen a Rainbow upon the Drops that are Dispersed in the Air by the Violent Concussion of the Waters in the Mill and what Is Equivalent to a Rainbow, If One take a Drop of water upon the end of a Stick and hold it up On the side that is Opposite to the sun and moving it along towards One side or t'other you will Perceive where the Drop is held just at such a Distance from the Point opposite to the sun that the Rays of the sun are much more vividly Reflected by it to your eye, than at any other Place Nearer Or further of[f] and that in the Colours of the Rainbow too, so that If there had been Enough of these Drops there would have appeared a perfect Rainbow. If you have a mind to see more Distinctly you may fill a Globular Glass bottle with water, the Glass of it must be very thin and Clear, and it will serve your turn as well as so big a Drop of Water and by that means you may also Distinctly see that the Reflection is from the Concave and not from the Convex surface.

The Next thing that Wants a solution is what should Cause the Reflection to be Circular, or which is the same thing what should Cause the Reflection to be Just at such a Distance everywhere from the Point that is opposite to the sun, and no reflection at all from the Drops that are within or without that Circle. Why should not all the Drops that are within that Circle Reflect as many rays as those that are in the Circle or where the Circle is to Resolve this we must Consider this One law of Reflection and Refraction; to wit If the Reflecting body be Perfectly Reflective the Angle of

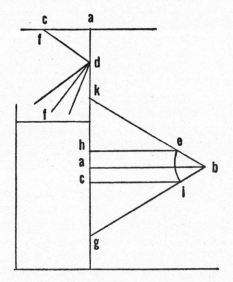

Reflexion will be the same as the Angle but if the body be not perfectly so the Angle will be less than the Angle of incidence by a body Perfectly Reflexive I mean one that is so Solid as Perfectly to Resist the stroke of the incident body and not to Give way to it at all, and by an imperfectly Reflexive a body that Gives way and Does not Obstinately Resist the stroke of the incident Body. So I say that If the body a.b. be Perfectly Reflexive and Does not Give way at all to the stroke of the incident Ray c.d. It will Reflect by an angle that shall be equall to that by which it fell upon the body a.b. from d. to e. but if the body a.b. is not able to Resist the stroke of the Ray c.d. but Gives way to it, it will neither be able to Reflect by so big an angle but will Reflect it may be by the line d.f. or d.g. according as the Reflexive force of a.b. be greater or lesser. And the bare Consideration of this will be enough to Convince any man, for we know that there is need of Greater force by a Great angle than by a little one. If we throw a ball against the floor or Wall it will much easier Rebound side waies than Right back again and [if] we throw it sideways against a body that Gives way by the stroke of (it may be tried at any time) it will not Rebound in so big an angle as if the body were quite hard, so it is the same thing in the body a.b. It might Give way so much as to let the Ray proceed Right on with very little Deviation from its old path and if so the Deviation will be greater and greater in proportion to the Resisting Power of the body, and if so if it Gives way at all it will not Deviate so much as if it Did not at all. Now these Drops of water is one of these imperfectly Reflexive bodies. If they were perfectly Reflexive we should see those Drops that are right opposite to Reflect as many Rays as those that are just so much on one side had the liquor but Resistance enough to Reflect the Rays so Directly back again, but those Rays that fall Perpendicularly or near Perpendicularly upon the Concave surface of the Drop as from a. to b. fig. 2 falling with much Greater force than the Ray, which falls sideways upon it from e. to b. after the Refraction at e which is made in all pellucid Globes. The Concave surface has not force enough to stop it and Reflect it. (What that Reflexive force of the [Concav]e surface is we are not now Disputing) but lets Go through and Pass right on Uninterruptedly [N]ow the Ray h.e.b. and the Rays Which fall about so obliquely Coming with a far light-[er] stroke, the concave surface has force enough to Resist it. and what falls Obliquely being far more easily Reflex[ible] Reflects it along the line b.g. and so in the same manner the Ray c.i.b. will be Reflected to k. so that an eye so much sideways as g. or k. will take the Rays thus Reflected from the Drops and no where Else And it being Only those Rays whose Obliquity is adjusted [to] the Refractive power that are Reflected by it, and they being all Reflected Out again with such a Degree of Obliquity we hence see why the Rays be not Reflected all ways equally, we hence Also see why the Rays are only Reflected out at the sides of the Drop and not Directly back

again by that why the Eye Does not take the Rays from any
Drops but those that are so much sideways of or on one side
of the Point that is Right Opposite to the sun and so why
the Parts that are so Opposite Look Dark, and why the Parts
that are Just so much on one side or just At such A Distance
all Round from the Opposite Point Alone are bright or which
is the same thing why there is such a bright Circle   The
next Grand Question is what is it Causes the Colours of the
Rainbow and this Question indeed is almost answered already for it is very evident. . . .

COLOURS

COLOURS we have already supposed that the Different
Refrangibility of Rays Arises from their Different bulk, we
have also supposed that they Are very Elastic bodies, from
these suppositions the Colours of natural bodies *may be accounted for* that is why some Particles of matter Reflect
such a sort or sorts of Rays and no Other the Different Density of Particles whence Arises a Different attraction and together with their Different firmness will account for all some
bodies have so little of firmness and so Easily Give way
that they Are able to Resist the stroak of no Rays But the
Least and Weakest, and most Reflexible Rays, all the other
Rays that Are bigger and therefore their force not so Easily
Resisted overcome the Resistance of the Particles that stand
in their way such bodies therefore appear blue as the atmosphere or skies, smoke &c.—again tis known that the most
Refrangible Rays are most easily attracted that is are most
easily stay'd or diverted by attraction, for as has been already shown Refraction & Reflection from Concave surfaces
is by attraction because therefore that the most Refrangible
Rays are most Diverted by Refraction and Easiest Reflected
inward from the surface, and most Diverted by Passing by
the edges of bodies it follows that attraction has most influence on the most Refrangible Rays.
'Tis also evident that the Particles of bodies that are the
most Dense have the strongest attraction. the Particles of any

body therefore may be so dense and attract so strongly as to hold fast all the Lesser and more Refrangible Rays so that they shall none of them be Reflected but Only the Greater Rays, on Whom the attraction of these Particles Can have Less influence, hereby the body will become Red

and as for the intermediate Colours the Particles of a body may be so Dense as to hold all the most Refrangible Rays and may yet not be firm Enough to Resist the stroak of the Least Refrangible hereby the body may become Yellow or Green or of any other intermediate Colour

Or a body may be Coloured by the Reflection of a mixture of Rays the body Particles may be able to Reflect three or four sorts of Rays and have too strong an attraction to Reflect those Rays that are Less and too weak a Resistance to Reflect the Bigger Rays, or the Colour of A body may be Compounded of Reflected Rays of very Distant Degrees of Refrangibility and not Reflect any of the intermediate Colours by reason of its being Compounded of very heterogeneous Particles [which] have a very Different Degree of Density and firmness, or the Particles of a body may be firm Enough to Reflect all sorts of Rays yet have so little attraction to hold them that the body will be White, or a body may be Compounded of Particles having so little Resistance as to Reflect no Rays, of so Great Density as to hold all or so full of Pores as to Drink in all, then the body is black

Or the Particles of bodies may have Pores and hollows that may be big enough to Let in the Least Rays not the Rest so that the Pores of Particles may have much to Do in the Causing of Colours

The blue of mountains at a Distance is not made by any Rays Reflected from the mountains but from the Air and vapours that is between us and them. the mountain occasions the blueness by intercepting all Rays that would Come from beyond to Disturb the Colour by their mixture it may therefore seem a Difficulty Why the atmosphere all Round by the horizon Dont appear very blue seeing tis Evident that the atmosphere Reflects Chiefly the blue Rays as Appears In the higher Parts of the atmosphere by the blueness of the skie and near the Earth by the blueness of mountains, and the Redness or Yellowness of the Rising and setting sun, it would therefore seem that the atmosphere should appear most blue where no Rays are Intercepted by mountains because the atmosphere beyond the mountain Reflects blue Rays as well as on this Side, therefore it seems that there would be more blue Rays Come to Our Eyes where none were Intercepted by mountains. And Consequently that the most lively blue would be there. and so it would be, if blue Rays Came to Our Eyes in the same Proportion as they are Reflected but most of those blue Rays that Are Reflected by those Parts of the Atmosphere that Are at a great Distance are intercepted by the intermediate Air before they Come to Our eyes (for the Air by supposition intercepts them Easiest) and only those few Yellow Rays and Less Reflexible Rays that are Reflected by the Air Come to Our eyes whence it Comes to Pass that the Atmosphere near the horizon Dont appear blue but of a Whitish Yellow. And sometimes when it is filled with more Dense exhalations that Can Reflect Less Reflexible Rays still, it appears a little Reddish.

THE SOUL

I am informed y^t you have advan[c]ed a notion y^t the Soul is matereal & keeps wth ye body till ye resur[e]ction as I am a profes't Lover of Novelty you must allow me to be much entertain'd by this discovery wch however old in some parts of ye world is new in this I am informed y^t you have advanced an Notion y^t the Soul is materiall & attends Y^e body till ye resurection as I am a profest Lover of novelty you must immagin I am very much entertained by this discovery (wch however in some parts of ye world is new to us) but suffer my Curiosity a Littel further I w^d know ye manner of ye kingdom before I swear alegance 1st I w^d know whether this materiall Soul keeps wth in ye Coffin and if so whether it might not be convenient to build a repository for it in order to wch I w^d know w^t Shape it is of whether round triangular or fore square or whethe is it a number of Long fine strings reaching from ye head to ye foot and whether it dus not Live a very discontented Life I am afraid when ye Coffin Gives way ye earth will fall in and Crush it but if it should Chuse to Live above Ground and hover about y^e

grave how big is it whether it Covers all ye body or is as-
sined to ye head or breast or how it Covers all ye body wt
it dus when another body is Laid upon yt whether ye 1st
First Gives way and if so where is ye place of retreat but
soppose ye Souls are not so big but yt 10 or a dozen of you
may be about one body whether yy will not Quarril for ye
highest place and as I insist much upon my honnour and
property I wd know wher I must Quit my dear head if a
Superior Soul Comes in ye way but above all I am Con-
searned to know wt they do where a Bureing Place has
bin filled 20 30 or 100 times if they are a top of one another
ye uppermost will be so far of yt it Can take no Care of
ye body I strongly susspect they must march of[f] every
time there Comes anew Set I hope ther is some Good place
provided for them but dupt [d(o)ubt] ye undergoing so
much hard Ship & being deprived of ye body at Last will
make them ill temper'd I Live it wth your phisicall Genus to
determin whether some medesinall applications might not be
proper in such Cases and subscrib your proselite when I can
have solution of these maters.

OF BEING

That there should absolutely be nothing at all is utterly impossible, the Mind Can never Let it stretch its Conceptions
ever so much bring it self to Conceive of a state of Perfect
nothing, it puts the mind into mere Convulsion and Confusion to endeavour to think of such a state, and it Contradicts the very nature of the soul to think that it should be,
and it is the Greatest Contradiction and the Aggregate of all
Contradictions to say that there should not be, tis true we
Cant so Distinctly show the Contradiction by words because
we Cannot talk about it without Speaking horrid Nonsense
and Contradicting our selve at every word, and because nothing is that whereby we Distinctly show other particular Contradictions, but here we are Run up to Our first principle and
have no other to explain the Nothingness or not being of
nothing by, indeed we Can mean nothing else by nothing but

a state of Absolute Contradiction; and if any man thinks he
Can think well Enough how there should be nothing I'll Engage that what he means by nothing is as much something as
any thing that ever He thought of in his Life, and I believe
that if he knew what nothing was it would be intuitively Evident to him that it Could not be. So that we see that it is
necessary some being should Eternally be and tis a more
palpable Contradiction still to say that there must be being
somewhere and not otherwhere for the words absolute nothing, and where, Contradict each other; and besides it Gives
as great a shock to the mind to think of pure nothing being in
any one place, as it Does to think of it in all and it is self
evident that there Can be nothing in one place as well as in
another and so if there Can be in one there Can be in all. So
that we see this necessary eternall being must be infinite and
Omnipresent.

This Infinite And omnipresent being Cannot be solid. Let
us see how Contradictory it is to say that an infinite being is
solid, for Solidity surely is nothing but Resistance to other
solidities.

Space is this Necessary eternal infinite and Omnipresent
being, we find that we can with ease Conceive how all other
beings should not be, we Can remove them out of our Minds
and Place some Other in the Room of them, but Space is the
very thing that we Can never Remove, and Conceive of its
not being, If a man would imagine space any where to be
Divided So as there should be Nothing between the Divided
parts, there Remains Space between notwithstanding and so
the man Contradicts himself, and it is self evident I believe
to every man that space is necessary, eternal, infinite, &
Omnipresent. but I had as Good speak Plain, I have already
said as much as that Space is God, and it is indeed Clear to
me, that all the Space there is not proper to body, all the
space there is without ye Bounds of the Creation, all the
Space there was before the Creation, is God himself, and no
body would in the Least stick at it if it were not because
of the Gross Conception that we have of space.

A state of Absolute nothing is a state of Absolute Contradiction absolute nothing is the Aggregate of all the Absurd [?] contradictions in the World, a state wherein there
is neither body nor spirit, nor space neither empty space nor
full space neither little nor Great, narrow nor broad neither

infinitely Great space, nor finite space, nor a mathematical
point neither Up nor Down neither north nor south (I dont
mean as it is with Respect to the body of the earth or some
other Great body but no Contrary Point, nor Positions nor
Directions) no such thing as either here Or there or that
way or only one way; When we Go About to form an idea of
Perfect nothing we must shut Out all these things we must
shut out of our minds both space that has something in it and
space that has nothing in it we must not allow our selves to
think of the least part of space never so small, nor must we
suffer our thoughts to take sanctuary in a mathematical
point, when we Go to Expell Body out of Our thoughts we
must Cease not to leave empty space in the Room of it and
when we Go to Expell emptiness from Our thoughts we
must not think to squeese it out by any thing Close hard
and solid but we must think of the same that the sleeping
Rocks Dream of and not until then shall we Get a Compleat
idea of nothing. a state of nothing is a state wherein every
Proposition in Euclid is not true, nor any of those self evident
maxims by which they are Demonstrated & all other Eternal
truths are neither true nor false.

when we Go to Enquire whether or no there Can be absolutely nothing we speak nonsense in Enquiring the stating
of the Question is Nonsense because we make a disjunction
where there is none either being or absolute nothing is no
Disjunction no more than whether a t[r]iangle is a t[r]iangle
or not a t[r]iangle there is no other way but only for
there to be existence there is no such thing as absolute
nothing. There is such a thing as nothing with Respect to
this Ink & paper there is such a thing as nothing with
Respect to you & me there is such a thing as nothing with
Respect to this Globe of Earth and with Respect to this
Created universe there is another way besides these things
having existence but there is no such thing as nothing with
Respect to Entity or being absolutely Considered we don't
know what we say if we say we think it Possible in it self
that there should not be Entity.

neither Can be any such thing without consciousness. how is
it possible there should something be from all Eternity and
there be no consciousness of it. it will appear very Plain to

every one that intensely Considers it that Consciousness
and being are the same thing Exactly

and how Doth it Grate upon the mind to think that something should be from all Eternity, and nothing all the while
be Conscious of it let us suppose to illustrate it that the
world had a being from all Eternity, and had many Great
Changes and Wonderful Revolutions, and all the while nothing knew, there was no knowledge in the Universe of any
such thing, how is it possible to bring the mind to imagine
yea it is Really impossible it should be that Any thing
should be and nothing know it then you'll say if it be so it is
because nothing has Any existence any where but in Consciousness no certainly no where else but either in Created
or uncreated Consciousness
supposing there were Another Universe only of bodies Created at a Great Distance from this Created in Excellent
Order and harmonious motions, and a beautiful variety,
and there was no Created intelligence in it nothing but senseless bodies, nothing but God knew anything of it I Demand
in what Respect this world has a being but only in the
Divine Consciousness Certainly in no Respect there would
be figures and magnitudes, and motions and Proportions
but where Else but in the almightie's knowledge how is
it possible there should, then you'll say for the same Reason
in a Room Close Shut Up that no body sees nor hears
nothing in it there is nothing any otherway than in Gods
knowledge I answer Created beings are Conscious of the
Effects of what is in the Room, for Perhaps there is not one
leaf of a tree nor Spire of Grass but what has effects All
over the universe and will have to the End of Eternity but
any otherwise there is nothing in a Room shut up but
only in Gods Consciousness how Can Any thing be there
Any other way this will appear to be truly so to Any one
that thinks of it with the whole united strength of his mind.
Let us suppose for illustration this impossibility that all
the Spirits in the Universe to be for a time to be Deprived
of their Consciousness, and God's Consciousness at the
same time to be intermitted. I say the Universe for that
time would cease to be of it self and not only as we speak
because the almighty Could not attend to Uphold the world
but because God knew nothing of it tis our foolish imagina-

tion that will not suffer us to see we fancy there may be figures and magnitudes Relations and properties without any ones knowing of it, but it is our imagination hurts us we Dont know what figures and Properties are.

Our imagination makes us fancy we see Shapes an[d] Colours and magnitudes tho no body is there to behold it but to help our imagination Let us thus State the Case, Let us suppose the world Deprived of Every Ray of light so that there should not be the least Glimmering of light in the Universe Now all will own that in such Case the Universe would be immediately Really Deprived of all its Colours, one part of the Universe is no More Red or blue, or Green or Yellow or black or white or light or dark or transparent or opake there would be no visible Distinction between the world and the Rest of the incomprehensible Void yea there would be no Difference in these Respect[s] between the world and the infinite void, that is any Part of that void would really be as light and as Dark, as white and as black as Red and Green as blue and as brown as transparent and as opake as Any Part of the universe, or as there would be in such Case no Difference between the world and nothing in these Respects so there would be no Difference between one part of the world and another all in these Respects is alike confounded with and undistinguishable from infinite emptiness At the same time also Let us suppose the Universe to be altogether Deprived of motion, and all part of it be at perfec[t] rest (the same supposition is indeed included in this but we Distinguish them for better Clearness) then the Universe would not Differ from the void in this Respect, there will be no more motion in one than the other then also solidity will cease, all that we mean or Can be meant by solidity is Resistance Resistance to touch, the Resistance of some parts of Space, this is all the knowledge we Get of solidity by our senses and I am sure all that we Can Get any other way, but solidity shall be shown to be nothing Else more fully hereafter. but there Can be no Resistance if there is no motion, one body Can [not] Resist another when there is perfect Rest Amongst them, but you'll say tho there is not actual Resistance yet there is potential existence, that is such and such Parts of space would Resist upon occasion, but this Is all I would have that there is no solidity now not but that God would Cause there to be on occasion and if there is no solidity there is no extension for extension is the extenddedness of the solidity, then all figure, and magnitude and proportion immediately Ceases, put both these suppositions together that is Deprive the world of light and motion and the Case would stand thus with the world, there would [be] neither white nor black neither blew nor brown, bright nor shaded pellucid nor opake, no noise or sound neither heat nor Cold, neither fluid nor Wet nor Drie hard nor soft nor solidity nor Extension, nor figure, nor magnitude nor Proportion nor body nor spirit, what then [is] to become of the Universe Certainly it exists no where but in the Divine mind this will be Abundantly Clearer to one after having Read what I have further to say of solidity &c

So then we see that a world without motion Can Exist no where Else but in the mind either infinite or finite

Corollary. it follows from hence that those beings which have knowledge and Consciousness are the Only Proper and real And substantial beings, inasmuch as the being of other things is Only by these, from hence we may see the Gross mistake of those who think material things the most substantial beings and spirits more like a shadow, whereas spirits Only Are Properly substance.

THE MIND

Written late in his college experience, probably during his second year of graduate study. The impact of John Locke's psychology and of Newton's physics are plainly apparent in these pages, as are also the foundations of Jonathan Edwards' original thought that these studies had stimulated. *The Treatise on the Mind,* for which in part he assembled these notes, was never written, but to the last year of his life he was still dealing with some of the issues raised in these brief essays. For an arrangement of the text more strictly in line with the index to these notes prepared by Jonathan Edwards, and also for critical comment, see Leon Howard, *"The Mind" of Jonathan Edwards: A Reconstructed Text.* The text is from *The Works of President Edwards,* edited by S. B. Dwight, Vol. I, Apendix, pp. 668–70, 673–76.

[12.] BEING. It seems strange sometimes to me, that there should be Being from all Eternity; and I am ready to say, What need was there that any thing should be? I should then ask myself, Whether it seems strange that there should be either Something, or Nothing? If so, it is not strange that there should BE; for that necessity of there being Something, or Nothing, implies it.

[26.] CAUSE is that, after or upon the existence of which, or the existence of it after such a manner, the existence of another thing follows.

[27.] EXISTENCE. If we had only the sense of Seeing, we should not be as ready to conclude the visible world to have been an existence independent of perception, as we do; because the ideas we have by the sense of Feeling, are as much mere ideas, as those we have by the sense of Seeing. But we know, that the things that are objects of this sense, all that the mind views by Seeing, are merely mental Existences; because all these things, with all their modes, do exist in a looking-glass, where all will acknowledge, they exist only mentally.

IT IS now agreed upon by every knowing philosopher, that Colours are not really in the things, no more than Pain is in a needle; but strictly no where else but in the mind. But yet I think that Colour may have an existence out of the mind, with equal reason as any thing in Body has any existence out of the mind, beside the very substance of the body itself, which is nothing but the Divine power, or rather the Constant Exertion of it. For what idea is that, which we call by the name of Body? I find Colour has the chief share in it. 'Tis nothing but Colour, and Figure, which is the termination of this Colour, together with some powers, such as the power of resisting, and motion, &c. that wholly makes up what we call Body. And if that, which we principally mean by the thing itself, cannot be said to be in the thing itself, I think nothing can be. If Colour exists not out of the mind, then nothing belonging to Body, exists out of the mind but Resistance, which is Solidity, and the termination of this Resistance, with its relations, which is Figure, and the communication of this Resistance, from space to space, which is Motion; though the latter are nothing but modes of the former. Therefore, there is nothing out of the mind but Resistance. And not that neither, when nothing is actually resisted. Then, there is nothing but the Power of Resistance. And as Resistance is nothing else but the actual exertion of God's power, so the Power can be nothing else, but the constant Law or Method of that actual exertion. And how is there any Resistance, except it be in some mind, in idea? What is it that is resisted? It is not Colour. And what else is it? It is ridiculous to say, that Resistance is resisted. That, does not tell us at all what is to be resisted. There must be something resisted before there can be Resistance; but to say Resistance is resisted, is ridiculously to suppose Resistance, before there is any thing to be resisted. Let us suppose two globes only existing, and no mind. There is nothing there, *ex confesso,* but Resistance. That is, there is such a Law, that the space within the limits of a globular figure shall resist. Therefore, there is nothing there but a power, or an establishment. And if there be any Resistance really out of the mind, one power and establishment must resist another establishment and law of Resistance, which is exceedingly ridiculous. But yet it cannot be otherwise, if any way out of the mind. But now it is easy to conceive of Resistance, as a mode of an idea. It is easy to conceive of such a power, or constant manner of stopping or resisting a colour. The idea may be resisted, it may move, and stop and rebound; but how a mere power, which is nothing real, can move and stop, is inconceivable, and it is impossible to say a word about it without contradiction. The world is therefore an ideal one; and the Law of creating, and the succession, of these ideas is constant and regular.

[28.] *Coroll.* 1. How impossible is it, that the world should exist from Eternity, without a Mind.

[30.] *Coroll.* 2. SINCE it is so, and that absolute Nothing is such a dreadful contradiction; hence we learn the necessity of the Eternal Existence of an All-comprehending Mind; and that it is the complication of all contradictions to deny such a mind.

[34.] WHEN we say that the World, i.e. the material Universe, exists no where but in the mind, we have got to such a degree of strictness and abstraction, that we must be exceedingly careful, that we do not confound and lose ourselves by misapprehension. That is impossible, that it should be meant, that all the world is contained in the narrow compass of a few inches of space, in little ideas in the place of the brain; for that would be a contradiction; for we are to remember that the human body, and the brain itself, exist only mentally, in the same sense that other things do; and so that, which we call *place,* is an idea too. Therefore things are truly in those places; for what we mean, when we say so, is only, that this mode of our idea of place appertains to such an idea. We would not therefore be understood to deny, that things are where they seem to be. For the principles we lay down, if they are narrowly looked into, do not infer that. Nor will it be found, that they at all make void Natural Philosophy, or the science of the Causes or Reasons of corporeal changes; For to find out the reasons of things, in Natural Philosophy, is only to find out the proportion of God's acting. And the case is the same, as to such proportions, whether we suppose the World, only mental, in our sense, or no.

THOUGH we suppose, that the existence of the whole material Universe is absolutely dependent on Idea, yet we may speak in the old way, and as properly, and truly as ever. God, in the beginning, created such a certain number of Atoms, of such a determinate bulk and figure, which they yet maintain and always will, and gave them such a motion, of such a direction, and of such a degree of velocity; from whence arise all the Natural changes in the Universe, forever, in a continued series. Yet, perhaps all this does not exist any where perfectly, but in the Divine Mind. But then, if it be enquired, What exists in the Divine Mind; and how these things exist there? I answer, There is his determination, his care, and his design, that Ideas shall be united forever, just so, and in such a manner, as is agreeable to such a series. For instance, all the ideas that ever were, or ever shall be to all eternity, in any created mind, are answerable to the existence of such a peculiar Atom in the beginning of the Creation, of such a determinate figure and size, and have such a motion given it: That is, they are all such, as Infinite Wisdom sees would follow, according to the series of nature, from such an Atom, so moved. That is, all ideal changes of creatures are just so, as if just such a particular Atom had actually all along existed even in some finite mind, and never had been out of that mind, and had, in that mind, caused these effects, which are exactly according to nature, that is, according to the nature of other matter, that is actually perceived by the mind. God supposes its existence; that is, he causes all changes to arise, as if all these things had actually existed in such a series, in some created mind, and as if created minds had comprehended all things perfectly. And, although created minds do not; yet, the Divine Mind doth, and he orders all things according to his mind, and his ideas. And these hidden things do not only exist in the Divine idea, but in a sense in created idea; for that exists in created idea, which necessarily supposes it. If a ball of lead were supposed to be let fall from the clouds, and no eye saw it, 'till it got within ten rods of the ground, and then its motion and celerity was perfectly discerned in its exact proportion; if it were not for the imperfection and slowness of our minds, the perfect idea of the rest of the motion would immediately, and of itself arise in the mind, as well as that which is there. So, were our thoughts comprehensive and perfect enough, our view of the present state of the world, would excite in us a perfect idea of all past changes.

And we need not perplex our minds with a thousand questions and doubts that will seem to arise: as, To what purpose is this way of exciting ideas; and, What advantage is there in observing such a series. I answer, It is just all one, as to any benefit or advantage, any end that we can suppose was proposed by the Creator, as if the Material Universe were existent in the same manner as is vulgarly thought. For the corporeal world is to no advantage but to the spiritual; and it is exactly the same advantage this way as the other, for it is all one, as to any thing excited in the mind.

[9.] SPACE. Space, as has been already observed, is a necessary being, if it may be called a being; and yet we have also shown, that all existence is mental, that the existence of all exterior things is ideal. Therefore it is a necessary being, only as it is a necessary idea, so far as it is a simple idea, that is necessarily connected with other simple exterior ideas, and is, as it were, their common substance or subject. It is in the same manner a necessary being, as any thing external is a being.

Coroll. It is hence easy to see in what sense that is true, that has been held by some, That, when there is nothing between any two bodies, they unavoidably must touch.

[13.] THE real and necessary existence of Space, and its Infinity, even beyond the Universe, depend upon a like reasoning as the Extension of Spirits, and to the supposition of the reality of the existence of a Successive Duration, before the Universe: even the impossibility of removing the idea out of the mind. If it be asked, If there be Limits of the Creation, whether or no it be not possible that an Intelligent being shall be removed beyond the limits; and then whether or no there would not be distance between that Intelligent being and the limits of the Universe, in the same manner, and as properly as there is between Intelligent beings and the parts of the Universe, within its limits; I answer, I cannot tell what the Law of Nature, or the Constitution of God, would be in this case.

Coroll. There is, therefore, no difficulty in answering such questions as these. What cause was there why the Universe was placed in such a part of Space? and, Why was the Universe created at such a Time? for, if there be no Space beyond the Universe, it was impossible that it should be created in another place; and if there was no Time before, it was impossible it should be created at another time.

THE idea we have of Space, and what we call by that name, is only *Coloured Space,* and is entirely taken out of the mind, if Colour be taken away. And so all that we call Extension, Motion and Figure, is gone, if Colour is gone. As to any idea of Space, Extension, Distance, or Motion, that a man born blind might form, it would be nothing like what we call by those names. All that he could have would be only certain sensations or feelings, that in themselves would be no more like what we intend by Space, Motion, etc. than the pain we have by the scratch of a pin, or than the ideas of taste and smell. And as to the idea of Motion, that such an one could have, it could be only a diversification of those successions in a certain way, by succession as to time. And then there would be an agreement of these successions of sensations, with some ideas we have by sight, as to number and proportions; but yet the ideas, after all, nothing akin to that idea we now give this name to.—And, as it is very plain, Colour is only in the mind, and nothing like it can be out of all mind. Hence it is manifest, there can be nothing like those things we call by the name of Bodies, out of the mind, unless it be in some other mind or minds.

And, indeed the secret lies here: That, which truly is the Substance of all Bodies, is *the infinitely exact, and precise, and perfectly stable Idea, in God's mind, together with his stable Will, that the same shall gradually be communicated to us, and to other minds, according to certain fixed and exact established Methods, and Laws:* or in somewhat different language, *the infinitely exact and precise Divine Idea, together with an answerable, perfectly exact, precise and stable Will, with respect to correspondent communications to Created Minds, and effects on their minds.*

[61.] *SUBSTANCE.* It is intuitively certain, that, if Solidity be removed from Body, nothing is left but empty space. Now, in all things whatsoever, that, which cannot be removed without removing the whole thing, that thing which is removed is the thing itself, except it be mere circumstance and manner of existence, such as Time and Place; which are in the general necessary, because it implies a contradiction to existence itself, to suppose that it exists at no time and in no place, and therefore in order to remove time and place in the general, we must remove the thing itself: So if we remove Figure and Bulk and Texture, in the general; which may be reduced to that necessary circumstance of Place.

If, therefore, it implies a contradiction to suppose that Body, or any thing appertaining to Body, beside Space, exists, when Solidity is removed; it must be, either because Body is nothing but Solidity and Space, or else, that Solidity is such a mere circumstance and relation of existence, which the thing cannot be without, because whatever exists must exist in some circumstances or other, as at some time or some place. But we know, and every one perceives, it to be a contradiction to suppose, that Body or Matter exists without Solidity, for all the notion we have of Empty Space, is Space without Solidity, and all the notion we have of Full Space, is Space Resisting.

The reason is plain: for if it implies a contradiction to suppose Solidity absent, and the thing existing, it must be because Solidity is that thing, and so it is a contradiction to say the thing is absent from itself; or because it is such a mode, or circumstance, or relation, of the existence, as it is a contradiction to suppose existence at all without it, such as Time and Place, to which both Figure and Texture are reduced. For nothing can be conceived of, so necessarily in an existence, that it is a contradiction to suppose it without it, but the Existence itself, and those general Circumstances or

Relations of existence, which the very supposition of existence itself implies.

Again, Solidity or Impenetrability is as much Action, or the immediate result of Action, as Gravity. Gravity by all will be confessed to be immediately from some active influence. Being a continual tendency in bodies to move, and being that, which will set them in motion though before at perfect rest, it must be the effect of something acting on that body. And it is as clear and evident, that action is as requisite to stop a body, that is already in motion, as in order to set bodies a moving, that are at perfect rest. Now we see continually, that there is a stopping of all motion, at the limits of such and such parts of Space, only this stoppage is modified and diversified according to certain Laws; for we get the idea and apprehension of Solidity, only and entirely, from the observation we make of that ceasing of motion, at the limits of some parts of Space, that already is, and that beginning of motion, that till now was not, according to a certain constant manner.

And why is it not every whit as reasonable, that we should attribute this action or effect, to the influence of some Agent, as that other action or effect which we call Gravity; which is likewise derived from our observation of the beginning and ceasing of motion, according to a certain method? In either case, there is nothing observed, but the beginning, increasing, directing, diminishing and ceasing of motion. And why is it not as reasonable to seek a reason, beside that general one, that it is something; which is no reason at all? I say, Why is it not as reasonable to seek a reason or cause of these actions, as well in one as in the other case? We do not think it sufficient to say, It is the nature of the unknown substance, in the one case; and why should we think it a sufficient explication of the same actions or effects, in the other. By Substance, I suppose it is confessed, we mean only Something; because of Abstract Substance we have no idea, that is more particular than only existence in general. Now why is it not as reasonable, when we see something suspended in the air, set to move with violence towards the Earth, to rest in attributing of it to the nature of the something that is there; as when we see that motion, when it comes to such limits, all on a sudden cease, for this is all that we observe in falling bodies. Their falling is the action we call Gravity: their stopping upon the surface of the Earth, the action whence we gain the idea of Solidity. It was before agreed on all hands, that there is something there, that supports that resistance. It must be granted now, that that Something is a Being, that acts there, as much as that Being, that causes bodies to descend towards the centre. Here is something in these parts of space, that of itself produces effects, without previously being acted upon; for that Being that lays an arrest on bodies in motion, and immediately stops them when they come to such limits and bounds, certainly does as much, as that Being that sets a body in motion, that before was at rest. Now this Being, acting altogether of itself, producing new effects, that are perfectly arbitrary, and that are no way necessary of themselves; must be Intelligent and Voluntary. There is no reason, in the nature of the thing itself, why a body, when set in motion, should stop at such limits, more than at any other. It must therefore be some arbitrary, active and voluntary, Being, that determines it. If there were but one body in the Universe, that always in time past had been at rest, and should now, without any alteration, be set in motion; we might certainly conclude, that some voluntary Being set it in motion, because it can certainly be demonstrated, that it can be for no other reason. So with just the same reason, in the same manner, we may conclude, if the body had hitherto been in motion, and is at a certain point of space now stopped. And would it not be every whit as reasonable to conclude, it must be from such an Agent, as if, in certain portions of space, we observed bodies to be attracted a certain way, and so at once to be set into motion, or accelerated in motion. And it is not at all the less remarkable, because we receive the ideas of light and colours from those spaces; for we know that light and colours are not there, and are made entirely by such a resistance, together with attraction, that is antecedent to these qualities, and would be a necessary effect of a mere resistance of space without other substance.

The whole of what we any way observe, whereby we get the idea of Solidity, or Solid Body, are certain parts of Space, from whence we receive the ideas of light and colours; and certain sensations by the sense of feeling; and we observe that the places, whence we receive these sensations, are not constantly the same, but are successively different, and this light and colours are communicated from one part of space to another. And we observe that these parts of Space, from whence we receive these sensations, resist and stop other bodies, which we observe communicated successively through the parts of Space adjacent; and that those that there were before at rest, or existing constantly in one and the same part of Space, after this exist successively in different parts of Space, and these observations are according to certain stated rules. I appeal to any one that takes notice and asks himself; whether this be not all, that ever he experienced in the world, whereby he got these ideas; and that this is all that we have or can have any idea of, in relation to bodies. All that we observe of Solidity is, that certain parts of Space, from whence we receive the ideas of light and colours, and a few other sensations, do likewise resist any thing coming within them. It therefore follows, that if we suppose there be any thing else, than what we thus observe, it is but only by way of Inference.

I know that it is nothing but the Imagination will oppose me in this: I will therefore endeavour to help the Imagination thus. Suppose that we received none of the sensible qualities of light, colours, etc. from the resisting parts of Space, (we will suppose it possible for resistance to be without them,) and they were, to appearance, clear and pure; and all that we could possibly observe, was only and merely Resistance; we simply observed that Motion was resisted and stopped, here and there, in particular parts of Infinite Space. Should we not then think it less unreasonable to suppose, that such effects should be produced by some Agent, present in those parts of Space, though Invisible. If we, when walking upon the face of the Earth, were stopped at certain limits, and could not possibly enter into such a part of Space, nor make any body enter into it; and we could observe no other difference, no way, nor at any time, between that and other parts of clear space; should we not be ready to say, What is it stops us; What is it hinders all entrance into that place?

THE reason, why it is so exceedingly natural to men, to suppose that there is some Latent *Substance*, or Something that is altogether hid, that upholds the properties of bodies,

is, because all see at first sight, that the properties of bodies
are such as need some Cause, that shall every moment have
influence to their continuance, as well as a Cause of their
first existence. All therefore agree, that there is Something
that is there, and upholds these properties. And it is most
true, there undoubtedly is; but men are wont to content
themselves in saying merely, that it is Something; but that
Something is He, "by whom all things consist."

(Notes on Natural Science)

OF THE PREJUDICES OF THE IMAGINATION

The note "Lemma to the Whole" suggests that "Of the Prejudices of the Imagination" is intended to be preliminary to another demonstration, presumably his argument for idealism. The physical theorems as to swiftness of motion, the smallness of bodies, and the property of a ray of light are designed to "put every man clean out of Conceit with his imagination." For a description of the original manuscript, see E. C. Smyth, "Some Early Writings of Jonathan Edwards, A.D. 1714–1726," *Proceedings of the American Antiquarian Society,* n.s. (1895), X, pp. 212 ff. The text is from *The Works of President Edwards,* edited by S. B. Dwight, Vol. I, Appendix, pp. 703–05.

LEMMA TO THE WHOLE:

Of all prejudices, no one so fights with Natural Philosophy, and prevails more against it, than those of the Imagination. It is these, which make the vulgar so roar out, upon the mention of some very rational philosophical truths. And indeed I have known of some very learned men, that have pretended to a more than ordinary freedom from such prejudices, so overcome by them, that, merely because of them, they have believed things most absurd. And truly I hardly know of any other prejudices, that are more powerful against truth of any kind, than those; and I believe they will not give the hand to any in any case, except to those arising from our ruling self-interest, or the impetuosity of human passions. And there is very good reason for it; for opinions, arising from

62

imagination, take us as soon as we are born, are beat into
us by every act of sensation, and so grow up with us from
our very births, and by that means grow into us so fast,
that it is almost impossible to root them out; being, as it
were, so incorporated with our very minds, that whatsoever
is objected contrary thereunto, is, as if it were dissonant
to the very constitution of them. Hence men come to make
what they can actually perceive by their senses, or by immediate and outside reflection into their own souls, the stand-
ard of possibility and impossibility; so that there must be
no body, forsooth, bigger than they can conceive of, or less
than they can see with their eyes: no motion, either much
swifter, or slower, than they can imagine. As to the greatness, and distances of bodies, the learned world have pretty
well conquered their imagination, with respect to them; neither will any body flatly deny, that it is possible for bodies
to be of any degree of bigness that can be mentioned; yet
imaginations of this kind, among the learned themselves, even
of this learned age, have a very powerful secret influence, to
cause them, either to reject things really true, as erroneous,
or to embrace those that are truly so. Thus some men will
yet say, they cannot conceive, how the Fixed Stars can be so
distant as that the Earth's annual revolution should cause no
parallax among them, and so are almost ready to fall back
into antiquated Ptolemy his system, merely to ease their
imagination.—Thus also, on the other hand, a very learned
man and sagacious astronomer, upon consideration of the
vast magnitude of the visible part of the universe, has, in the
ecstasy of his imagination, been hurried on to pronounce
the universe infinite; which I may say, out of veneration, was
beneath such a man as he. As if it were any more an argument, because what he could see of the universe were so
big, as he was assured it was. And suppose he had discovered
the invisible universe, so vast as it is, to be as a globule of
water to another Universe; the case is the same; as if it would
have been any more of an argument, that that larger Universe was infinite, than if the visible part thereof were no
bigger than a particle of the water of this. I think one is no
nearer to infinite than the other.

To remedy this prejudice, I will, as the best method I
can think of, demonstrate two or three Physical Theorems;
which, I believe, if they are clearly understood, will put

every man clean out of conceit with his imagination: in order whereunto, these two are prerequisite.

PRELIMINARY PROPOSITIONS

Pro. 1. *There is no degree of swiftness of motion whatever, but what is possible.*

That you may not doubt of this, suppose any long piece of matter to move round any point or centre, to which one end shall be fixed, with any given degree of velocity. Now that part of this piece of matter, that is farthest from the centre, to which one end is fixed, must move swiftest. And then suppose this piece of matter to be lengthened out, and that part of it, that moved swiftest before, to move on still with the same degree of velocity. It is evident, that the farther end now moves swifter than the farther end did before, by so much as the piece of matter is longer. And suppose it to be made longer still, the farther end moves still just so much swifter: so that, as the parcel of matter can be protracted to any degree of length whatsoever, so the farther end of it can be moved with any degree of swiftness whatsoever, so that there is no degree of swiftness whatsoever but what is possible.

Prop. 2. *There may be bodies of any infinite degree of smallness.*

Let two perfect spheres, A and B, touch each other in some point of their surfaces at I. It is evident that there can be a globule of matter just so big as to reach from the surface of one sphere to the surface of the other sphere, at any given equal distance in each sphere, from the point of contact I, suppose at *o* and *g*, whether the spheres be greater or smaller. Since therefore the distance *o g*, from the surface of one sphere to that of the other, is less, according as the spheres are greater, and since the touching spheres can be of any degree of magnitude, and since consequently the distance *o g* can be of any degree of smallness, and since the body, that fills up that distance, is small accordingly, it follows that there can be a body of any degree of smallness.

N. B. This I take to be all that is meant by the divisibility of matter, *in infinitum.*

Prop. 3. That it is possible for a body, as small as a ray of light, to strike the surface of a body as big as the earth, or any indefinite magnitude, supposing it to be hard enough

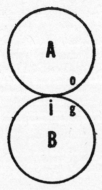

to hold the stroke, so as to impel it along with any indefinite degree of swiftness.

Let the laws of gravity and motion be mentioned; and let it be a postulatum inserted, that these laws hold universally, in all bodies, great or small, at how great distance soever, and however disproportionate.

SARAH PIERREPONT

Sarah Pierrepont was the daughter of the Rev. James Pierrepont of New Haven. According to Sereno B. Dwight, this tribute was written in 1723, when she was only thirteen years old and Jonathan Edwards was twenty. He was taking his M.A. degree in this year. Four years later they were married. The text is from *The Works of President Edwards,* edited by S. B. Dwight, Vol. I, pp. 114–15. Unfortunately the original sheet in Jonathan Edwards' handwriting is lost.

. . . They say there is a young lady in [New Haven] who is beloved of that Great Being, who made and rules the world, and that there are certain seasons in which this Great Being, in some way or other invisible, comes to her and fills her mind with exceeding sweet delight, and that she hardly cares for any thing, except to meditate on him—that she expects after a while to be received up where he is, to be raised up out of the world and caught up into heaven; being assured that he loves her too well to let her remain at a distance from him always. There she is to dwell with him, and to be ravished with his love and delight forever. Therefore, if you present all the world before her, with the richest of its treasures, she disregards it and cares not for it, and is unmindful of any pain or affliction. She has a strange sweetness in her mind, and singular purity in her affections; is most just and conscientious in all her conduct; and you could not persuade her to do any thing wrong or sinful, if you would give her all the world, lest she should offend this Great Being. She is of a wonderful sweetness, calmness and universal benevolence of mind; especially after this Great God has manifested himself to her mind. She will sometimes go about from place to place, singing sweetly; and seems to be always full of joy and pleasure; and no one knows for what. She loves to be alone, walking in the fields and groves, and seems to have some one invisible always conversing with her. . . .

RESOLUTIONS

Compared with other similar lists from other young men in their college years, these resolutions show concern with inner values, chiefly religious, rather than with habits, manners, and various praiseworthy acts such as churchgoing, giving of alms, prayers at stated times, and keeping wide awake in meeting. The resolve not to lose a moment of time is common to many of them. The first thirty-four appear to have been written prior to December 18, 1722. The text is from *The Works of President Edwards,* edited by S. B. Dwight, Vol. I, pp. 68–73.

Being sensible that I am unable to do any thing without God's help, I do humbly entreat him by his grace, to enable me to keep these Resolutions, so far as they are agreeable to his will, for Christ's sake.

REMEMBER TO READ OVER THESE RESOLUTIONS ONCE A WEEK.

1. *Resolved,* That *I will do whatsoever* I think to be most to the glory of God and my own good, profit and pleasure, in the whole of my duration; without any consideration of the time, whether now, or never so many myriads of ages hence. Resolved to do whatever I think to be my *duty,* and most for the good and advantage of mankind in general. Resolved, so to do, whatever *difficulties* I meet with, how many soever, and how great soever.

2. *Resolved,* To be continually endeavouring to find out some *new contrivance,* and invention, to promote the fore-mentioned things.

3. *Resolved,* If ever I shall fall and grow dull, so as to neglect to keep any part of these Resolutions, to repent of all I can remember, when I come to myself again.

4. *Resolved,* Never *to do* any manner of thing, whether in soul or body, less or more, but what tends to the glory of God, nor *be,* nor *suffer* it, if I can possibly avoid it.

5. *Resolved,* Never to lose one moment of time, but to improve it in the most profitable way I possibly can.

6. *Resolved,* To live with all my might, while I do live.

7. *Resolved,* Never to do any thing, which I should be afraid to do, if it were the last hour of my life.

8. *Resolved,* To act, in all respects, both speaking and doing, as if nobody had been so vile as I, and as if I had committed the same sins, or had the same infirmities or failings as others; and that I will let the knowledge of their failings promote nothing but shame in myself, and prove only an occasion of my confessing my own sins and misery to God. *Vid July* 30.

9. *Resolved,* To think much, on all occasions, of my own dying, and of the common circumstances which attend death.

10. *Resolved,* When I feel pain, to think of the pains of Martyrdom, and of Hell.

11. *Resolved,* When I think of any Theorem in divinity to be solved, immediately to do what I can towards solving it, if circumstances do not hinder.

12. *Resolved,* If I take delight in it as a gratification of pride, or vanity, or on any such account, immediately to throw it by.

13. *Resolved,* To be endeavouring to find out fit objects of charity and liberality.

14. *Resolved,* Never to do any thing out of Revenge.

15. *Resolved,* Never to suffer the least motions of anger towards irrational beings.

16. *Resolved,* Never to speak evil of any one, so that it shall tend to his dishonour, more or less, upon no account except for some real good.

17. *Resolved,* That I will live so, as I shall wish I had done when I come to die.

18. *Resolved,* To live so, at all times, as I think is best

in my most devout frames, and when I have the clearest notions of the things of the Gospel, and another world.

19. *Resolved,* Never to do any thing, which I should be afraid to do, if I expected it would not be above an hour, before I should hear the last trump.

20. *Resolved,* To maintain the strictest temperance, in eating and drinking.

21. *Resolved,* Never to do any thing, which, if I should see in another, I should count a just occasion to despise him for, or to think any way the more meanly of him.

22. *Resolved,* To endeavour to obtain for myself as much happiness, in the other world, as I possibly can, with all the power, might, vigour, and vehemence, yea violence, I am capable of, or can bring myself to exert, in any way that can be thought of.

23. *Resolved,* Frequently to take some deliberate action, which seems most unlikely to be done, for the glory of God, and trace it back to the original intention, designs and ends of it; and if I find it not to be for God's glory, to repute it as a breach of the fourth Resolution.

24. *Resolved,* Whenever I do any conspicuously evil action, to trace it back, till I come to the original cause; and then, both carefully endeavour to do so no more, and to fight and pray with all my might against the original of it.

25. *Resolved,* To examine carefully, and constantly, what that one thing in me is, which causes me in the least to doubt of the love of God; and to direct all my forces against it.

26. *Resolved,* To cast away such things, as I find do abate my assurance.

27. *Resolved,* Never wilfully to omit any thing, except the omission be for the glory of God; and frequently to examine my omissions.

28. *Resolved,* To study the Scriptures so steadily, constantly and frequently, as that I may find, and plainly perceive myself to grow in the knowledge of the same.

29. *Resolved,* Never to count that a prayer, nor to let that pass as a prayer, nor that as a petition of a prayer, which is so made, that I cannot hope that God will answer it; nor that as a confession, which I cannot hope God will accept.

30. *Resolved,* To strive, every week, to be brought higher

in Religion, and to a higher exercise of grace, than I was the week before.

31. *Resolved,* Never to say any thing at all against any body, but when it is perfectly agreeable to the highest degree of christian honour, and of love to mankind, agreeable to the lowest humility, and sense of my own faults and failings, and agreeable to the Golden Rule; often, when I have said any thing against any one, to bring it to, and try it strictly by the test of this Resolution.

32. *Resolved,* To be strictly and firmly faithful to my trust, that that, in Prov. xx, 6, *A faithful man, who can find?* may not be partly fulfilled in me.

33. *Resolved,* To do, always, what I can towards making, maintaining and preserving peace, when it can be done without an overbalancing detriment in other respects. *Dec.* 26, 1722.

34. *Resolved,* In narrations, never to speak any thing but the pure and simple verity.

35. *Resolved,* Whenever I so much question whether I have done my duty, as that my quiet and calm is thereby disturbed, to set it down, and also how the question was resolved. *Dec.* 18, 1722.

36. *Resolved,* Never to speak evil of any, except I have some particular good call to it. *Dec.* 19, 1722.

37. *Resolved,* To enquire every night, as I am going to bed, Wherein I have been negligent,—What sin I have committed,—and wherein I have denied myself;—also, at the end of every week, month and year. *Dec.* 22 *and* 26, 1722.

38. *Resolved,* Never to utter any thing that is sportive, or matter of laughter, on a Lord's day. *Sabbath evening, Dec.* 23, 1722.

39. *Resolved,* Never to do any thing, of which I so much question the lawfulness, as that I intend, at the same time, to consider and examine afterwards, whether it be lawful or not; unless I as much question the lawfulness of the omission.

40. *Resolved,* To enquire every night, before I go to bed, whether I have acted in the best way I possibly could, with respect to eating and drinking. *Jan.* 7, 1723.

41. *Resolved,* To ask myself, at the end of every day,

week, month and year, wherein I could possibly, in any respects, have done better.   *Jan.* 11, 1723.

42. *Resolved,* Frequently to renew the dedication of myself to God, which was made at my baptism, which I solemnly renewed, when I was received into the communion of the church, and which I have solemnly re-made this 12th day of January, 1723.

43. *Resolved,* Never, henceforward, till I die, to act as if I were any way my own, but entirely and altogether God's; agreeably to what is to be found in Saturday, Jan. 12th, 1723.

44. *Resolved,* That no other end but religion, shall have any influence at all on any of my actions; and that no action shall be, in the least circumstance, any otherwise than the religious end will carry it.   *Jan.* 12, 1723.

45. *Resolved,* Never to allow any pleasure or grief, joy or sorrow, nor any affection at all, nor any degree of affection, nor any circumstance relating to it, but what helps Religion.   *Jan.* 12 *and* 13, 1723.

46. *Resolved,* Never to allow the least measure of any fretting or uneasiness at my father or mother.   *Resolved,* To suffer no effects of it, so much as in the least alteration of speech, or motion of my eye; and to be especially careful of it with respect to any of our family.

47. *Resolved,* To endeavour, to my utmost, to deny whatever is not most agreeable to a good and universally sweet and benevolent, quiet, peaceable, contented and easy, compassionate and generous, humble and meek, submissive and obliging, diligent and industrious, charitable and even, patient, moderate, forgiving and sincere, temper; and to do, at all times, what such a temper would lead me to; and to examine strictly, at the end of every week, whether I have so done.   *Sabbath Morning, May* 5, 1723.

48. *Resolved,* Constantly, with the utmost niceness and diligence, and the strictest scrutiny, to be looking into the state of my soul, that I may know whether I have truly an interest in Christ or not; that when I come to die, I may not have any negligence respecting this, to repent of. *May* 26, 1723.

49. *Resolved,* That this never shall be, if I can help it.

50. *Resolved,* That I will act so, as I think I shall judge

would have been best, and most prudent, when I come into the future world.   *July* 5, 1723.

51. *Resolved,* That I will act so, in every respect, as I think I shall wish I had done, if I should at last be damned. *July* 8, 1723.

52. I frequently hear persons in old age, say how they would live, if they were to live their lives over again: *Resolved,* That I will live just so as I can think I shall wish I had done, supposing I live to old age.   *July* 8, 1723.

53. *Resolved,* To improve every opportunity, when I am in the best and happiest frame of mind, to cast and venture my soul on the Lord Jesus Christ, to trust and confide in him, and consecrate myself wholly to him; that from this I may have assurance of my safety, knowing that I confide in my Redeemer.   *July* 8, 1723.

54. *Resolved,* Whenever I hear any thing spoken in commendation of any person, if I think it would be praiseworthy in me, that I will endeavour to imitate it.   *July* 8, 1723.

55. *Resolved,* To endeavour, to my utmost, so to act, as I can think I should do, if I had already seen the happiness of Heaven, and Hell torments.   *July* 8, 1723.

56. *Resolved,* Never to give over, nor in the least to slacken, my fight with my corruptions, however unsuccessful I may be.

57. *Resolved,* When I fear misfortunes and adversity, to examine whether I have done my duty, and resolve to do it, and let the event be just as Providence orders it.   I will, as far as I can, be concerned about nothing but my duty, and my sin.   *June* 9, *and July* 13, 1723.

58. *Resolved,* Not only to refrain from an air of dislike, fretfulness, and anger in conversation, but to exhibit an air of love, cheerfulness and benignity.   *May* 27, *and July* 13, 1723.

59. *Resolved,* When I am most conscious of provocations to ill-nature and anger, that I will strive most to feel and act good-naturedly; yea, at such times, to manifest good-nature, though I think that in other respects it would be disadvantageous, and so as would be imprudent at other times. *May* 12, *July* 11, *and July* 13.

60. *Resolved,* Whenever my feelings begin to appear in the least out of order, when I am conscious of the least un-

easiness within, or the least irregularity without, I will then subject myself to the strictest examination. *July* 4, *and* 13, 1723.

61. *Resolved,* That I will not give way to that listlessness which I find unbends and relaxes my mind from being fully and fixedly set on religion, whatever excuse I may have for it—that what my listlessness inclines me to do, is best to be done, &c. *May* 21, *and July* 13, 1723.

62. *Resolved,* Never to do any thing but my duty, and then according to Eph. vi, 6—8, to do it willingly and cheerfully, as unto the Lord, and not to men: knowing that whatever good thing any man doth, the same shall he receive of the Lord. *June* 25, *and July* 13, 1723.

63. On the supposition, that there never was to be but one individual in the world, at any one time, who was properly a complete christian, in all respects of a right stamp, having christianity always shining in its true lustre, and appearing excellent and lovely, from whatever part and under whatever character viewed: *Resolved,* To act just as I would do, if I strove with all my might to be that one, who should live in my time. *Jan.* 14, *and July* 13, 1723.

64. *Resolved,* When I find those *"groanings which cannot be uttered,"* of which the Apostle speaks, and those *"breakings of soul* for the longing it hath," of which the Psalmist speaks, Psalm cxix, 20, That I will promote them to the utmost of my power, and that I will not be weary of earnestly endeavouring to vent my desires, nor of the repetitions of such earnestness. *July* 23, *and August* 10, 1723.

65. *Resolved,* Very much to exercise myself in this, all my life long, viz. With the greatest openness, of which I am capable, to declare my ways to God, and lay open my soul to him, all my sins, temptations, difficulties, sorrows, fears, hopes, desires, and every thing, and every circumstance, according to Dr. Manton's Sermon on the 119th Psalm. *July* 26, *and Aug.* 10, 1723.

66. *Resolved,* That I will endeavour always to keep a benign aspect, and air of acting and speaking in all places and in all companies, except it should so happen that duty requires otherwise.

67. *Resolved,* After afflictions, to enquire, What I am the better for them; What good I have got by them; and, What I might have got by them.

68. *Resolved,* To confess frankly to myself all that which I find in myself, either infirmity or sin; and, if it be what concerns religion, also to confess the whole case to God, and implore needed help.   *July 23, and August* 10, 1723.

69. *Resolved,* Always to do that, which I shall wish I had done when I see others do it.   *Aug.* 11, 1723.

70. Let there be something of benevolence, in all that I speak.   *Aug.* 17, 1723.

DIARY

The diary, like the resolutions, was a fairly common exercise for young men during their college years. This portion of Jonathan Edwards' diary, written during his Yale tutorship, records chiefly self-blame and self-discipline to improve his listlessness in religious exercises. Now that college duties were pressing upon him, there was less time for solitary meditation as he walked alone in the woods and fields, and he was missing the delights that freer days had brought. Introspection would continue for life, but maturity brought adjustment to crowded days, and personal religious growth would soon no longer need the spur of numbered resolutions. The text is from *The Works of President Edwards,* edited by S. B. Dwight, Vol. I, pp. 103–06.

AT YALE COLLEGE

Saturday night, June 6 [1724]. This week has been a very remarkable week with me, with respect to despondencies, fears, perplexities, multitudes of cares, and distraction of mind: it being the week I came hither to New-Haven, in order to entrance upon the office of Tutor of the College. I have now, abundant reason to be convinced, of the troublesomeness and vexation of the world, and that it never will be another kind of world.

Tuesday, July 7. When I am giving the relation of a thing, remember to abstain from altering either in the matter or manner of speaking, so much, as that, if every one, afterwards, should alter as much, it would at last come to be properly false.

Tuesday, Sept. 2. By a sparingness in diet, and eating as much as may be, what is light and easy of digestion, I shall doubtless be able to think more clearly, and shall gain time; 1. By lengthening out my life; 2. Shall need less time for digestion, after meals; 3. Shall be able to study more closely, without injury to my health; 4. Shall need less time for sleep; 5. Shall more seldom be troubled with the head-ache.

Saturday night, Sept. 12. Crosses of the nature of that, which I met with this week, thrust me quite below all comforts in religion. They appear no more than vanity and stubble, especially when I meet with them so unprepared for them. I shall not be fit to encounter them, except I have a far stronger, and more permanent faith, hope and love.

Wednesday, Sept. 30. It has been a prevailing thought with me, to which I have given place in practice, that it is best, sometimes, to eat or drink, when it will do me no good, because the hurt, that it will do me, will not be equal, to the trouble of denying myself. But I have determined, to suffer that thought to prevail no longer. The hurries of commencement, and diversion of the vacancy, has been the occasion of my sinking so exceedingly, as in the three last weeks.

Monday, Oct. 5. I believe it is a good way, when prone to unprofitable thoughts, to deny myself and break off my thoughts, by keeping diligently to my study, that they may not have time to operate to work me to such a listless frame. I am apt to think it a good way, when I am indisposed to reading and study, to read of my own remarks, the fruit of my study in divinity, &c., to set me agoing again.

Friday, Nov. 6. Felt sensibly, somewhat of that trust and affiance, in Christ, and with delight committing of my soul to him, of which our divines used to speak, and about which, I have been somewhat in doubt.

Tuesday, Nov. 10. To mark all that I say in conversation, merely to beget in others, a good opinion of myself, and examine it.

Sabbath, Nov. 15. Determined, when I am indisposed to prayer, always to premeditate what to pray for; and that it is better, that the prayer should be of almost any shortness, than that my mind should be almost continually off from what I say.

Sabbath, Nov. 22. Considering that by-standers always copy some faults, which we do not see, ourselves, or of which, at least, we are not so fully sensible; and that there are many secret workings of corruption, which escape our sight, and of which, others only are sensible: *Resolved,* therefore, that I will, if I can by any convenient means, learn what faults others find in me, or what things they see in me, that appear any way blame-worthy, unlovely, or unbecoming.

Friday, Feb. 12, 1725. The very thing I now want, to give me a clearer and more immediate view of the perfections and glory of God, is as clear a knowledge of the manner of God's exerting himself, with respect to Spirits and Mind, as I have, of his operations concerning Matter and Bodies.

Tuesday, Feb. 16. A virtue, which I need in a higher degree, to give a beauty and lustre to my behaviour, is gentleness. If I had more of an air of gentleness, I should be much mended.

Friday, May 21. If ever I am inclined to turn to the opinion of any other Sect: *Resolved,* Beside the most deliberate consideration, earnest prayer, &c., privately to desire all the help that can possibly be afforded me, from some of the most judicious men in the country, together with the prayers of wise and holy men, however strongly persuaded I may seem to be, that I am in the right.

Saturday, May 22. When I reprove for faults, whereby I am in any way injured, to defer, till the thing is quite over and done with; for that is the way, both to reprove aright, and without the least mixture of spirit, or passion, and to have reproofs effectual, and not suspected.

Friday, May 28. It seems to me, that whether I am now converted or not, I am so settled in the state I am in, that I shall go on in it all my life. But, however settled I may be, yet I will continue to pray to God, not to suffer me to be deceived about it, nor to sleep in an unsafe condition; and ever and anon, will call all into question and try myself, using for helps, some of our old divines, that God may have opportunities to answer my prayers, and the Spirit of God to show me my error, if I am in one.

Saturday night, June 6. I am sometimes in a frame so listless, that there is no other way of profitably improving time, but conversation, visiting, or recreation, or some bodily exercise. However it may be best in the first place, before resorting to either of these, to try the whole circle of my mental employments.

Nov. 16. When confined at Mr. Stiles'. I think it would be of special advantage to me, with respect to my truer interest, as near as I can in my studies, to observe this rule. To let half a day's, or at most, a day's study in other things, be succeeded, by half a day's, or a day's study in Divinity.

One thing wherein I have erred, as I would be complete in all social duties, is, in neglecting to write letters to friends. And I would be forewarned of the danger of neglecting to visit my friends and relations, when we are parted.

When one suppresses thoughts that tend to divert the run of the mind's operations from Religion, whether they are melancholy, or anxious, or passionate, or any others; there is this good effect of it, that it keeps the mind in its freedom. Those thoughts are stopped in the beginning, that would have set the mind agoing in that stream.

There are a great many exercises, that for the present, seem not to help, but rather impede, Religious meditation and affections, the fruit of which is reaped afterwards, and is of far greater worth than what is lost; for thereby the mind is only for the present diverted; but what is attained is, upon occasion, of use for the whole life-time.

Sept. 26, 1726. 'Tis just about three years, that I have been for the most part in a low, sunk estate and condition, miserably senseless to what I used to be, about spiritual things. 'Twas three years ago, the week before commencement; just about the same time this year, I began to be somewhat as I used to be.

Jan. 1728. I think Christ has recommended rising early in the morning, by his rising from the grave very early.

Jan. 22, 1734. I judge that it is best, when I am in a good frame for divine contemplation, or engaged in reading the Scriptures, or any study of divine subjects, that ordinarily, I will not be interrupted by going to dinner, but will forego my dinner, rather than be broke off.

April 4, 1735. When at any time, I have a sense of any divine thing, then to turn it in my thoughts, to a practical improvement. As for instance, when I am in my mind, on some argument for the Truth of Religion, the Reality of a Future State, and the like, then to think with myself, how safely I may venture to sell all, for a future good. So when, at any time, I have a more than ordinary sense of the Glory of the Saints, in another world; to think how well it is worth my while, to deny myself, and to sell all that I have for this Glory, &c.

May, 18. My mind at present is, never to suffer my thoughts and meditations, at all to ruminate.

June 11. To set apart days of meditation on particular subjects; as sometimes, to set apart a day for the consideration of the Greatness of my Sins; at another, to consider the Dreadfulness and Certainty, of the Future Misery of Ungodly men; at another, the Truth and Certainty of Religion; and so, of the Great Future Things promised and threatened in the Scriptures.

PERSONAL NARRATIVE

From the mention of the years 1737 and 1739 one may assume that this account was written when Jonathan Edwards was twice as old as when his conversion took place. Told with the greater restraint of maturity, the poignancy of this remembered experience is no doubt greater than a more youthful telling could have made it. Among the various parallels that come to mind, one might begin with St. Augustine's own story. He also was a man of great power of intellect and will and also of strong emotions. After a long period of turmoil within, when he was often a great riddle to himself, there is the scene in the garden, with Alpheus sitting close by, the voice of the child chanting, "Tolle, lege," and when in obedience Augustine opened the book and read, instantly there was "a peaceful light streaming into my heart, and all the dark shadows of doubt fled away." Jonathan Edwards' narrative has the same simplicity and majesty. The text is from *The Works of President Edwards,* edited by S. B. Dwight, Vol. I, pp. 58–62, 64–67, 98–99, 131–36.

I HAD a variety of concerns and exercises about my soul, from my childhood; but I had two more remarkable seasons of awakening, before I met with that change, by which I was brought to those new dispositions, and that new sense of things, that I have since had. The first time was when I was a boy, some years before I went to college, at a time of remarkable awakening in my father's congregation. I was then very much affected for many months, and concerned about the things of religion, and my soul's salvation; and was abundant in religious duties. I used to pray five times a day in secret, and to spend much time in religious conversation with other boys; and used to meet with them to pray together. I experienced I know not what kind of delight in religion. My mind was much engaged in it, and had much self-righteous pleasure; and it was my delight to abound in religious duties. I, with some of my school-mates, joined together, and built a booth in a swamp, in a very retired spot, for a place of prayer.—And besides, I had particular secret places of my own in the woods, where I used to retire by myself; and was from time to time much affected. My affections seemed to be lively and easily moved, and I seemed to be in my element, when engaged in religious duties. And I am ready to think, many are deceived with such affections, and such a kind of delight as I then had in religion, and mistake it for grace.

But, in process of time, my convictions and affections wore off; and I entirely lost all those affections and delights, and left off secret prayer, at least as to any constant preference of it; and returned like a dog to his vomit, and went on in the ways of sin. Indeed, I was at times very uneasy, especially towards the latter part of my time at college; when it pleased God, to seize me with a pleurisy; in which he brought me nigh to the grave, and shook me over the pit of hell. And yet, it was not long after my recovery, before I fell again into my old ways of sin. But God would not suffer me to go on with any quietness; I had great and violent inward struggles, till, after many conflicts with wicked inclinations, repeated resolutions, and bonds that I laid myself under by a kind of vows to God, I was brought wholly to break off all former wicked ways, and all ways of known outward sin; and to apply myself to seek salvation, and practise many religious duties; but without that kind of affection and delight which I had formerly experienced. My concern now wrought more, by inward struggles, and conflicts, and self-reflections. I made seeking my salvation, the main business of my life. But yet, it seems to me, I sought it after a miserable manner; which has made me sometimes since to question, whether ever it issued in that which was saving; being ready to doubt, whether such miserable seeking ever succeeded. I was indeed brought to seek salvation, in a manner that I never was before; I felt a spirit to part with all things in the world, for an interest in Christ. My concern continued and prevailed, with many exercising thoughts and inward struggles; but yet it never seemed to be proper, to express that concern by the name of terror.

From my childhood up, my mind had been full of objections against the doctrine of God's sovereignty, in choosing whom he would to eternal life, and rejecting whom he pleased; leaving them eternally to perish, and be everlastingly tormented in hell. It used to appear like a horrible doctrine to me. But I remember the time very well, when I seemed to be convinced, and fully satisfied, as to this sovereignty of God, and his justice in thus eternally disposing of men, according to his sovereign pleasure. But never could give an account, how, or by what means, I was thus convinced, not in the least imagining at the time, nor a long time after, that there was any extraordinary influence of God's Spirit in it; but only that now I saw further, and my reason apprehended the justice and reasonableness of it. However, my mind rested in it; and it put an end to all those cavils and objections. And there has been a wonderful alteration in my mind, with respect to the doctrine of God's sovereignty, from that day to this; so that I scarce ever have found so much as the rising of an objection against it, in the most absolute sense, in God shewing mercy to whom he will shew mercy, and hardening whom he will. God's absolute sovereignty and justice, with respect to salvation and damnation, is what my mind seems to rest assured of, as much as of any thing that I see with my eyes; at least it is so at times. But I have often, since that first conviction, had quite another kind of sense of God's sovereignty than I had then. I have often since had not only a conviction, but a *delightful* conviction. The doctrine has very often appeared exceedingly pleasant, bright, and sweet. Absolute sovereignty is what I love to ascribe to God. But my first conviction was not so.

The first instance, that I remember, of that sort of inward, sweet delight in God and divine things, that I have lived much in since, was on reading those words, 1 Tim. i. 17. *Now unto the King eternal, immortal, invisible, the only wise God, be honour and glory for ever and ever, Amen.* As I read the words, there came into my soul, and was as it were diffused through it, a sense of the glory of the Divine Being; a new sense, quite different from any thing I ever experienced before. Never any words of Scripture seemed to me as these words did. I thought with myself, how excellent a Being that was, and how happy I should be, if I might enjoy that God, and be rapt up to him in heaven, and be as it were swallowed up in him for ever! I kept saying, and as it were singing, over these words of scripture to myself; and went to pray to God that I might enjoy him, and prayed in a manner quite different from what I used to do; with a new sort of affection. But it never came into my thought, that there was any thing spiritual, or of a saving nature in this.

From about that time, I began to have a new kind of apprehensions and ideas of Christ, and the work of redemption, and the glorious way of salvation by him. An inward, sweet sense of these things, at times, came into my heart; and my soul was led away in pleasant views and contemplations of them. And my mind was greatly engaged to spend my time in reading and meditating on Christ, on the beauty and excellency of his person, and the lovely way of salvation by free grace in him. I found no books so delightful to me, as those that treated of these subjects. Those words Cant. ii. 1. used to be abundantly with me, *I am the Rose of Sharon, and the Lily of the valleys.* The words seemed to me, sweetly to represent the loveliness and beauty of Jesus Christ. The whole book of Canticles used to be pleasant to me, and I used to be much in reading it, about that time; and found, from time to time, an inward sweetness, that would carry me away, in my contemplations. This I know not how to express otherwise, than by a calm, sweet abstraction of soul from all the concerns of this world; and sometimes a kind of vision, or fixed ideas and imaginations, of being alone in the mountains, or some solitary wilderness, far from all mankind, sweetly conversing with Christ, and wrapt and swallowed up in God. The sense I had of divine things, would often of a sudden kindle up, as it were, a sweet burning in my heart; an ardour of soul, that I know not how to express.

Not long after I first began to experience these things, I gave an account to my father of some things that had passed in my mind. I was pretty much affected by the discourse we had together; and when the discourse was ended, I walked abroad alone, in a solitary place in my father's pasture, for contemplation. And as I was walking there, and looking upon the sky and clouds, there came into my mind so sweet a sense of the glorious *majesty* and *grace* of God, as I know not how to express.—I seemed to see them both in a sweet conjunction; majesty and meekness joined together: it was a sweet, and gentle, and holy majesty; and also a majestic meekness; an awful sweetness; a high, and great, and holy gentleness.

After this my sense of divine things gradually increased, and became more and more lively, and had more of that inward sweetness. The appearance of every thing was altered; there seemed to be, as it were, a calm, sweet, cast, or appearance of divine glory, in almost every thing. God's excellency, his wisdom, his purity and love, seemed to appear in every thing; in the sun, moon and stars; in the clouds and blue sky; in the grass, flowers, trees; in the water and all nature; which used greatly to fix my mind. I often used to sit and view the moon for a long time; and in the day, spent much time in viewing the clouds and sky, to behold the sweet glory of God in these things: in the meantime, singing forth, with a low voice, my contemplations of the Creator and Redeemer. And scarce any thing, among all the works of nature, was so sweet to me as thunder and lightning; formerly nothing had been so terrible to me. Before, I used to be uncommonly terrified with thunder, and to be struck with terror when I saw a thunder-storm rising; but now, on the contrary, it rejoiced me. I felt God, if I may so speak, at the first appearance of a thunder storm; and used to take the opportunity, at such times, to fix myself in order to view the clouds, and see the lightnings play, and hear the majestic and awful voice of God's thunder, which oftentimes was exceedingly entertaining, leading me to sweet contemplations of my great and glorious God. While thus engaged, it always seemed natural for me to sing, or chant forth my meditations; or, to speak my thoughts in soliloquies with a singing voice.

I felt then great satisfaction, as to my good estate; but that did not content me. I had vehement longings of soul after God and Christ, and after more holiness, wherewith my heart seemed to be full, and ready to break; which often brought to my mind the words of the Psalmist, Psal. cxix. 28. *My soul breaketh for the longing it hath.* I often felt a mourning and lamenting in my heart, that I had not turned to God sooner, that I might have had more time to grow in grace. My mind was greatly fixed on divine things; almost perpetually in the contemplation of them. I spent most of my time in thinking of divine things, year after year; often

walking alone in the woods, and solitary places, for meditation, soliloquy, and prayer, and converse with God; and it
was always my manner, at such times, to sing forth my contemplations. I was almost constantly in ejaculatory prayer,
wherever I was. Prayer seemed to be natural to me, as the
breath by which the inward burnings of my heart had vent.
The delights which I now felt in the things of religion, were
of an exceedingly different kind from those before-men-
tioned, that I had when a boy; and what then I had no more
notion of, than one born blind has of pleasant and beautiful
colours. They were of a more inward, pure, soul-animating
and refreshing nature. Those former delights never reached
the heart; and did not arise from any sight of the divine
excellency of the things of God; or any taste of the soul-
satisfying and life-giving good there is in them.

My sense of divine things seemed gradually to increase,
till I went to preach at New-York; which was about a year
and a half after they began; and while I was there, I felt them
very sensibly, in a much higher degree, than I had done
before. My longings after God, and holiness, were much increased. Pure and humble, holy and heavenly, christianity
appeared exceedingly amiable to me. I felt a burning desire to
be, in every thing, a complete christian; and, conformed to
the blessed image of Christ; and that I might live, in all
things, according to the pure, sweet and blessed rules of the
gospel. I had an eager thirsting after progress in these things;
which put me upon pursuing and pressing after them. It was
my continual strife day and night, and constant inquiry,
how I should *be* more holy, and *live* more holily, and more
becoming a child of God, and a disciple of Christ. I now
sought an increase of grace and holiness, and a holy life,
with much more earnestness, than ever I sought grace before
I had it. I used to be continually examining myself, and study-
ing and contriving for likely ways and means, how I should
live holily, with far greater diligence and earnestness, than
ever I pursued any thing in my life; but yet with too great
a dependence on my own strength; which afterwards proved
a great damage to me. My experience had not then taught
me, as it has done since, my extreme feebleness and impotence, every manner of way; and the bottomless depths of
secret corruption and deceit, there was in my heart. How-

ever, I went on with my eager pursuit after more holiness, and conformity to Christ.

The heaven I desired was a heaven of holiness; to be with God, and to spend my eternity in divine love, and holy communion with Christ. My mind was very much taken up with contemplations on heaven, and the enjoyments there; and living there in perfect holiness, humility and love: and it used at that time to appear a great part of the happiness of heaven, that there the saints could express their love to Christ. It appeared to me a great clog and burden, that what I felt within, I could not express as I desired. The inward ardour of my soul, seemed to be hindered and pent up, and could not freely flame out as it would. I used often to think, how in heaven this principle should freely and fully vent and express itself. Heaven appeared exceedingly delightful, as a world of love; and that all happiness consisted in living in pure, humble, heavenly, divine love.

I remember the thoughts I used then to have of holiness; and said sometimes to myself, "I do certainly know that I love holiness, such as the gospel prescribes." It appeared to me, that there was nothing in it but what was ravishingly lovely; the highest beauty and amiableness—a *divine* beauty; far purer than any thing here upon earth; and that every thing else was like mire and defilement, in comparison of it.

Holiness, as I then wrote down some of my contemplations on it, appeared to me to be of a sweet, pleasant, charming, serene, calm nature; which brought an inexpressible purity, brightness, peacefulness and ravishment to the soul. In other words, that it made the soul like a field or garden of God, with all manner of pleasant flowers; enjoying a sweet calm, and the gently vivifying beams of the sun. The soul of a true christian, as I then wrote my meditations, appeared like such a little white flower as we see in the spring of the year; low and humble on the ground, opening its bosom, to receive the pleasant beams of the sun's glory; rejoicing, as it were, in a calm rapture; diffusing around a sweet fragrancy; standing peacefully and lovingly, in the amidst of other flowers round about; all in like manner opening their bosoms, to drink in the light of the sun. There was no part of creature-holiness, that I had so great a sense of its loveliness, as humility, brokenness of heart and poverty of spirit; and there was nothing that I so earnestly longed for.

My heart panted after this—to lie low before God, as in the dust; that I might be nothing, and that God, might be ALL, that I might become as a little child.

While at New York, I sometimes was much affected with reflections on my past life, considering how late it was before I began to be truly religious; and how wickedly I had lived till then: and once so as to weep abundantly, and for a considerable time together.

On *January,* 12, 1723, I made a solemn dedication of myself to God, and wrote it down; giving up myself, and all that I had to God; to be for the future, in no respect, my own; to act as one that had no right to himself, in any respect. And solemnly vowed, to take God for my whole portion and felicity; looking on nothing else, as any part of my happiness, nor acting as if it were; and his law for the constant rule of my obedience: engaging to fight, with all my might, against the world, the flesh, and the devil, to the end of my life. But I have reason to be infinitely humbled, when I consider, how much I have failed, of answering my obligation.

I had, then, abundance of sweet, religious conversation, in the family where I lived, with Mr. John Smith, and his pious mother. My heart was knit in affection, to those, in whom were appearances of true piety; and I could bear the thoughts of no other companions, but such as were holy, and the disciples of the blessed Jesus. I had great longings, for the advancement of Christ's kingdom in the world; and my secret prayer used to be, in great part, taken up in praying for it. If I heard the least hint, of any thing that happened, in any part of the world, that appeared, in some respect or other, to have a favourable aspect, on the interests of Christ's kingdom, my soul eagerly catched at it; and it would much animate and refresh me. I used to be eager to read public news-letters, mainly for that end; to see if I could not find some news, favourable to the interest of religion in the world.

I very frequently used to retire into a solitary place, on the banks of Hudson's River, at some distance from the city, for contemplation on divine things and secret converse with God: and had many sweet hours there. Sometimes Mr. Smith and I walked there together, to converse on the things of God; and our conversation used to turn much on the advancement of Christ's kingdom in the world, and the glorious things that God would accomplish for his church in the latter days. I had then and at other times, the greatest delight in the holy scriptures, of any book whatsoever. Oftentimes in reading it, every word seemed to touch my heart. I felt a harmony between something in my heart, and those sweet and powerful words. I seemed often to see so much light exhibited by every sentence, and such a refreshing food communicated, that I could not get along in reading; often dwelling long on one sentence, to see the wonders contained in it; and yet almost every sentence seemed to be full of wonders.

I came away from New York in the month of *April,* 1723, and had a most bitter parting with Madam Smith and her son. My heart seemed to sink within me, at leaving the family and city, where I had enjoyed so many sweet and pleasant days. I went from New York to Wethersfield, by water; and as I sailed away, I kept sight of the city as long as I could. However, that night after this sorrowful parting, I was greatly comforted in God at Westchester, where we went ashore to lodge: and had a pleasant time of it all the voyage to Saybrook. It was sweet to me to think of meeting dear christians in heaven, where we should never part more. At Saybrook we went ashore to lodge on Saturday, and there kept the Sabbath; where I had a sweet and refreshing season, walking alone in the fields.

After I came home to Windsor, I remained much in a like frame of mind, as when at New York; only sometimes I felt my heart ready to sink, with the thoughts of my friends at New York. My support was in contemplations on the heavenly state; as I find in my Diary of May 1, 1723. It was a comfort to think of that state, where there is fulness of joy; where reigns heavenly, calm, and delightful love, without alloy; where there are continually the dearest expressions of this love; where is the enjoyment of the persons loved, without ever parting; where those persons who appear so lovely in this world, will really be inexpressibly more lovely, and full of love to us. And how sweetly will the mutual lovers join together, to sing the praises of God and the Lamb! How will it fill us with joy to think, that this enjoyment, these sweet exercises, will never cease, but will last to all eternity.

I continued much in the same frame, in the general, as when at New-York, till I went to New-Haven, as Tutor of the College: particularly, once at Bolton, on a journey from Boston, while walking out alone in the fields. After I went to New-Haven, I sunk in religion; my mind being diverted from my eager pursuits after holiness, by some affairs, that greatly perplexed and distracted my thoughts.

In September, 1725, I was taken ill at New-Haven, and while endeavouring to go home to Windsor, was so ill at the North Village, that I could go no farther; where I lay sick, for about a quarter of a year. In this sickness, God was pleased to visit me again, with the sweet influences of his Spirit. My mind was greatly engaged there, on divine and pleasant contemplations, and longings of soul. I observed, that those who watched with me, would often be looking out wishfully for the morning; which brought to my mind those words of the Psalmist, and which my soul with delight made its own language, *My soul waiteth for the Lord, more than they that watch for the morning; I say, more than they that watch for the morning;* and when the light of day came in at the window, it refreshed my soul, from one morning to another. It seemed to be some image of the light of God's glory.

I remember, about that time, I used greatly to long for the conversion of some, that I was concerned with; I could gladly honour them, and with delight be a servant to them, and lie at their feet, if they were but truly holy. But some time after this, I was again greatly diverted with some temporal concerns, that exceedingly took up my thoughts, greatly to the wounding of my soul; and went on, through various exercises, that it would be tedious to relate, which gave me much more experience of my own heart, than I ever had before.

[NOTE] After this entry there is a gap of more than ten years in the personal record. During the time which the entries immediately above report (1725), he was a tutor at Yale College. In 1726 he was invited to become a candidate at the church in Northampton and was ordained Associate Pastor there in 1727. In this same year he was married to Sarah Pierpont and set up his own home in Northampton. The following entries, concluding the *Personal Narrative*, look back on more than ten years of his ministry. The date 1739 appears in the final entry.

Obviously, in comparison with his more leisurely student days, the complications and responsibilities of his tutorship, his marriage, and particularly the care of a large parish, had changed his daily life completely. As he writes this recall as a mature man, no wonder, as he says, these experiences had given him more knowledge of his own heart than he had possessed as a young man. The time for youthful religious raptures had passed. Knowledge of the religious experiences of others, hundreds of them, so different from his own, especially those of converts during the Northampton revivals and the Great Awakening, had enlarged his notions of religion in various ways, new ways. He had been challenged to understand phenomena he would not have understood as a younger man, and to make a place for them in his thought of man and God. In the following entries, recalling his own later religious experiences, we sense the greater maturity of the man speaking, but it is still the same man of the youthful ecstasies.

Since I came to Northampton, I have often had sweet complacency in God, in views of his glorious perfections, and of the excellency of Jesus Christ. God has appeared to me a glorious and lovely Being, chiefly on account of his holiness. The holiness of God has always appeared to me the most lovely of all his attributes. The doctrines of God's absolute sovereignty, and free grace, in shewing mercy to whom he would shew mercy; and man's absolute dependence on the operations of God's Holy Spirit, have very often appeared to me as sweet and glorious doctrines. These doctrines have been much my delight. God's sovereignty has ever appeared to me, a great part of his glory. It has often been my delight to approach God, and adore him as a sovereign God, and ask sovereign mercy of him.

I have loved the doctrines of the gospel; they have been to my soul like green pastures. The gospel has seemed to me the richest treasure; the treasure that I have most desired, and longed that it might dwell richly in me. The way of salvation by Christ, has appeared, in a general way, glorious and excellent, most pleasant and most beautiful. It has often seemed to me, that it would, in a great measure, spoil heaven, to receive it in any other way. That text has often been affecting and delightful to me, Isa. xxxii. 2, *A man shall be an hiding place from the wind, and a covert from the tempest, &c.*

It has often appeared to me delightful, to be united to Christ; to have him for my head, and to be a member of his body; also to have Christ for my teacher and prophet. I very often think with sweetness, and longings, and pantings of soul, of being a little child, taking hold of Christ, to be led by him through the wilderness of this world. That text, Matt. xviii. 3, has often been sweet to me, *Except ye be converted and become as little children, &c.* I love to think of coming to Christ, to receive salvation of him, poor in spirit, and quite empty of self, humbly exalting him alone; cut off entirely from my own root, in order to grow into, and out of Christ: to have God in Christ to be all in all; and to live by faith on the Son of God, a life of humble, unfeigned confidence in him. That Scripture has often been sweet to me, Psal. cxv. 1, *Not unto us, O Lord, not unto us, but unto thy name give glory, for thy mercy, and for thy truth's sake.* And those words of Christ, Luke x. 21, *In that hour Jesus rejoiced in spirit, and said, I thank thee, O Father, Lord of heaven and earth, that thou hast hid these things from the wise and prudent, and hast revealed them unto babes: even so, Father, for so it seemed good in thy sight.* That sovereignty of God, which Christ rejoiced in, seemed to me worthy of such joy; and that rejoicing seemed to show the excellency of Christ, and of what spirit he was.

Sometimes, only mentioning a single word, caused my heart to burn within me; or only seeing the name of Christ, or the name of some attribute of God. And God has appeared glorious to me, on account of the Trinity. It has made me have exalting thoughts of God, that he subsists in three persons; Father, Son, and Holy Ghost. The sweetest joys and delights I have experienced, have not been those that have arisen from a hope of my own good estate; but in a direct view of the glorious things of the gospel. When I enjoy this sweetness, it seems to carry me above the thoughts of my own estate; it seems, at such times, a loss that I cannot bear, to take off my eye from the glorious, pleasant object I behold without me, to turn my eye in upon myself, and my own good estate.

My heart has been much on the advancement of Christ's kingdom in the world. The histories of the past advancement of Christ's kingdom have been sweet to me. When I have read histories of past ages, the pleasantest thing, in all my reading, has been, to read of the kingdom of Christ being promoted. And when I have expected, in my reading, to come to any such thing, I have rejoiced in the prospect, all the way as I read. And my mind has been much entertained and delighted with the scripture promises and prophecies, which relate to the future glorious advancement of Christ's kingdom upon earth.

I have sometimes had a sense of the excellent fulness of Christ, and his meetness and suitableness as a Saviour; whereby he has appeared to me, far above all, the chief of ten thousands. His blood and atonement have appeared sweet, and his righteousness sweet; which was always accompanied with ardency of spirit; and inward strugglings and breathings, and groanings that cannot be uttered, to be emptied of myself, and swallowed up in Christ.

Once, as I rode out into the woods for my health, in 1737, having alighted from my horse in a retired place, as my manner commonly has been, to walk for divine contemplation and prayer, I had a view, that for me was extraordinary, of the glory of the Son of God, as Mediator between God and man, and his wonderful, great, full, pure and sweet grace and love, and meek and gentle condescension. This grace that appeared so calm and sweet, appeared also great above the heavens. The person of Christ appeared ineffably excellent, with an excellency great enough to swallow up all thought and conception—which continued, as near as I can judge, about an hour; which kept me the greater part of the time, in a flood of tears, and weeping aloud. I felt an ardency of soul to be, what I know not otherwise how to express, emptied and annihilated; to lie in the dust, and to be full of Christ alone; to love him with a holy and pure love; to trust in him; to live upon him; to serve and follow him; and to be perfectly sanctified and made pure, with a divine and heavenly purity. I have, several other times, had views very much of the same nature, and which have had the same effects.

I have, many times, had a sense of the glory of the Third Person in the Trinity, in his office of Sanctifier; in his holy operations, communicating divine light and life to the soul. God in the communications of his holy spirit, has appeared as an infinite fountain of divine glory and sweetness; being full and sufficient to fill and satisfy the soul; pouring forth itself in sweet communications; like the sun in its glory, sweetly and pleasantly diffusing light and life. And I have sometimes had an affecting sense of the excellency of the word of God as a word of life; as the light of life; a sweet, excellent, life-giving word; accompanied with a thirsting after that word, that it might dwell richly in my heart.

Often, since I lived in this town, I have had very affecting views of my own sinfulness and vileness; very frequently to such a degree, as to hold me in a kind of loud weeping, sometimes for a considerable time together; so that I have often been forced to shut myself up. I have had a vastly greater sense of my own wickedness, and the badness of my heart, than ever I had before my conversion. It has often appeared to me, that if God should mark iniquity against me, I should appear the very worst of all mankind; of all that have been, since the beginning of the world, to this time: and that I should have by far the lowest place in hell. When others, that have come to talk with me about their soul-concerns, have expressed the sense they have had of their own wickedness, by saying, that it seemed to them, that they were as bad as the devil himself; I thought their expressions seemed exceeding faint and feeble, to represent my wickedness.

My wickedness, as I am in myself, has long appeared to me perfectly ineffable, and swallowing up all thought and imagination; like an infinite deluge, or mountains over my head. I know not how to express better what my sins appear to me to be, than by heaping infinite upon infinite, and multiplying infinite by infinite. Very often, for these many years, these expressions are in my mind, and in my mouth, "Infinite upon infinite—Infinite upon infinite!" When I look into my heart, and take a view of my wickedness, it looks like an abyss, infinitely deeper than hell. And it appears to me, that were it not for free grace, exalted and raised up to the infinite height of all the fulness and glory of the great Jehovah, and the arm of his power and grace stretched forth in all the majesty of his power, and in all the glory of his sovereignty, I should appear sunk down in my sins below hell itself; far beyond the sight of every thing, but the eye of sovereign grace, that can pierce even down to such a depth.

And yet, it seems to me that my conviction of sin is exceedingly small, and faint; it is enough to amaze me, that I have no more sense of my sin. I know certainly, that I have very little sense of my sinfulness. When I have had turns of weeping and crying for my sins, I thought I knew at the time, that my repentance was nothing to my sin.

I have greatly longed of late, for a broken heart, and to lie low before God; and, when I ask for humility, I cannot bear the thoughts of being no more humble than other christians. It seems to me, that though their degrees of humility may be suitable for them, yet it would be a vile self-exaltation in me, not to be the lowest in humility of all mankind. Others speak of their longing to be "humbled to the dust;" that may be a proper expression for them, but I always think of myself, that I ought, and it is an expression that has long been natural for me to use in prayer, "to lie infinitely low before God." And it is affecting to think, how ignorant I was, when a young christian, of the bottomless, infinite depths of wickedness, pride, hypocrisy and deceit, left in my heart.

I have a much greater sense of my universal, exceeding dependance on God's grace and strength, and mere good pleasure, of late, than I used formerly to have; and have experienced more of an abhorrence of my own righteousness. The very thought of any joy arising in me, on any consideration of my own amiableness, performances, or experiences, or any goodness of heart or life, is nauseous and detestable to me. And yet, I am greatly afflicted with a proud and self-righteous spirit, much more sensibly than I used to be formerly. I see that serpent rising and putting forth its head continually, every where, all around me.

Though it seems to me, that in some respects, I was a far better christian, for two or three years after my first conversion, than I am now; and lived in a more constant delight and pleasure; yet of late years, I have had a more full and constant sense of the absolute sovereignty of God, and a delight in that sovereignty; and have had more of a sense of the glory of Christ, as a Mediator revealed in the gospel. On one Saturday night, in particular, I had such a discovery of the excellency of the gospel above all other doctrines, that I could not but say to myself, "This is my chosen light, my chosen doctrine": and of Christ, "This is my chosen Prophet." It appeared sweet, beyond all expression, to follow Christ, and to be taught, and enlightened, and instructed by him; to learn of him, and live to him. Another Saturday night, (*Jan.* 1739) I had such a sense, how sweet and blessed a thing it was to walk in the way of duty; to do that which was right and meet to be done, and agreeable to the holy mind of God; that it caused me to break forth into a kind of loud weeping, which held me some time, so that I was forced to shut myself up, and fasten the doors. I could not but, as it were, cry out, "How happy are they, who do that which is right in the sight of God! They are blessed indeed, *they* are the happy ones!" I had, at the same time, a very affecting sense, how meet and suitable it was that God should govern the world, and order all things according to his own pleasure; and I rejoiced in it, that God reigned, and that his will was done.

A FAITHFUL NARRATIVE OF THE
SURPRISING WORK OF GOD

The various accounts Jonathan Edwards wrote of the Northampton revivals were more widely read in his own day than anything else he ever wrote. His first account was a letter of May 30,
1735, to Benjamin Colman of Boston in reply to a request for
details. Colman published this letter in 1736, and under date of
November 6 of that year Jonathan Edwards complied with a request for still fuller details. This extended account was published
in London in 1737 under the title *A Faithful Narrative . . .*
Three more editions, one translation, and many reprintings followed in the next two years. The present version is from *The
Works of President Edwards,* edited by S. B. Dwight, Vol. IV,
pp. 19–30, with omissions. See also *Some Thoughts concerning
the Present Revival of Religion in New England,* 1742, op. cit.,
IV, 77–280; *The Distinguishing Marks of a Work of the Spirit
of God,* 1741. There are many discussions of Jonathan Edwards
and the Great Awakening. See Perry Miller, *Jonathan Edwards,*
pp. 133–63; Ola Elizabeth Winslow, *Jonathan Edwards, 1703–1758,*
pp. 173–93.

At the latter end of the year 1733, there appeared a very
unusual flexibleness, and yielding to advice, in our young
people. It had been too long their manner to make the evening
after the sabbath, and after our public lecture, to be especially
the times of their mirth, and company-keeping. But a sermon
was now preached on the sabbath before the lecture, to shew
the evil tendency of the practice, and to persuade them to
reform it; and it was urged on heads of families that it
should be a thing agreed upon among them, to govern their
families, and keep their children at home, at these times. It
was also more privately moved, that they should meet to-

gether the next day, in their several neighbourhoods, to know each other's minds; which was accordingly done, and the motion complied with throughout the town. But parents found little or no occasion for the exercise of government in the case. The young people declared themselves convinced by what they had heard from the pulpit, and were willing of themselves to comply with the counsel that had been given: and it was immediately, and, I suppose, almost universally complied with; and there was a thorough reformation of these disorders thenceforward, which has continued ever since.

Presently after this, there began to appear a remarkable religious concern at a little village belonging to the congregation, called Pascommuck, where a few families were settled, at about three miles distance from the main body of the town. At this place a number of persons seemed to be savingly wrought upon. In the April following, anno 1734, there happened a very sudden and awful death of a young man in the bloom of his youth; who being violently seized with the pleurisy, and taken immediately very delirious, died in about two days; which (together with what was preached publicly on that occasion) much affected many young people. This was followed with another death of a young married woman, who had been considerably exercised in mind about the salvation of her soul, before she was ill, and was in great distress, in the beginning of her illness: but seemed to have satisfying evidences of God's saving mercy to her, before her death: so that she died very full of comfort, in a most earnest and moving manner, warning and counselling others. This served to contribute to render solemn the spirits of many young persons; and there began evidently to appear more of a religious concern on people's minds.

In the fall of the year I proposed it to the young people, that they should agree among themselves to spend the evenings after lectures in social religion, and to that end divide themselves into several companies to meet in various parts of the town; which was accordingly done, and those meetings have been since continued, and the example imitated by elder people. This was followed with the death of an elderly person, which was attended with many unusual circumstances, by which many were much moved and affected.

About this time began the great noise, in this part of the country, about Arminianism, which seemed to appear with a very threatening aspect upon the interest of religion here. The friends of vital piety trembled for fear of the issue; but it seemed, contrary to their fear, strongly to be over-ruled for the promoting of religion. Many who looked on themselves as in a Christless condition, seemed to be awakened by it, with fear that God was about to withdraw from the land, and that we should be given up to heterodoxy and corrupt principles; and that then their opportunity for obtaining salvation would be past. Many who were brought a little to doubt about the truth of the doctrines they had hitherto been taught, seemed to have a kind of trembling fear with their doubts, lest they should be led into by-paths, to their eternal undoing; and they seemed; with much concern and engagedness of mind, to enquire what was indeed the way in which they must come to be accepted with God. There were some things said publicly on that occasion, concerning justification by faith alone.

Although great fault was found with meddling with the controversy in the pulpit, by such a person, and at that time —and though it was ridiculed by many elsewhere—yet it proved a word spoken in season here; and was most evidently attended with a very remarkable blessing of heaven to the souls of the people in this town. They received thence a general satisfaction, with respect to the main thing in question, which they had been in trembling doubts and concern about; and their minds were engaged the more earnestly to seek that they might come to be accepted of God, and saved in the way of the gospel, which had been made evident to them to be the true and only way. And then it was, in the latter part of December, that the spirit of God began extraordinarily to set in, and wonderfully to work amongst us; and there were, very suddenly, one after another, five or six persons, who were to all appearance savingly converted, and some of them wrought upon in a very remarkable manner.

Particularly, I was surprised with the relation of a young woman, who had been one of the greatest company-keepers in the whole town. When she came to me, I had never heard that she was become in any wise serious, but by the conversation I then had with her, it appeared to me, that what she gave an account of, was a glorious work of God's infinite power and sovereign grace; and that God had given her a new heart, truly broken and sanctified. I could not then doubt of it, and have seen much in my acquaintance with her since to confirm it.

Though the work was glorious, yet I was filled with concern about the effect it might have upon others. I was ready to conclude, (though too rashly) that some would be hardened by it, in carelessness and looseness of life; and would take occasion from it to open their mouths in reproaches of religion. But the event was the reverse, to a wonderful degree. God made it, I suppose, the greatest occasion of awakening to others, of any thing that ever came to pass in the town. I have had abundant opportunity to know the effect it had, by my private conversation with many. The news of it seemed to be almost like a flash of lightning, upon the hearts of young people, all over the town, and upon many others. Those persons amongst us, who used to be farthest from seriousness, and that I most feared would make an ill improvement of it, seemed greatly to be awakened with it. Many went to talk with her, concerning what she had met with; and what appeared in her seemed to be to the satisfaction of all that did so.

Presently upon this, a great and earnest concern about the great things of religion, and the eternal world, became universal in all parts of the town, and among persons of all degrees, and all ages. The noise amongst the dry bones waxed louder and louder; all other talk but about spiritual and eternal things was soon thrown by; all the conversation, in all companies and upon all occasions, was upon these things only, unless so much as was necessary for people carrying on their ordinary secular business. Other discourse than of the things of religion, would scarcely be tolerated in any company. The minds of people were wonderfully taken off from the world, it was treated amongst us as a thing of very little consequence. They seemed to follow their worldly business, more as a part of their duty, than from any disposition they had to it; the temptation now seemed to lie on that hand, to neglect worldly affairs too much, and to spend too much time in the immediate exercise of religion. This was exceedingly misrepresented by reports that were spread in distant parts of the land, as though the people here had wholly thrown by all worldly business, and betook themselves entirely to reading and praying, and such like religious exercises.

But although people did not ordinarily neglect their worldly business; yet Religion was with all sorts the great concern, and the world was a thing only by the bye. The only thing in their view was to get the kingdom of heaven, and every one appeared pressing into it. The engagedness of their hearts in this great concern could not be hid, it appeared in their very countenances. It then was a dreadful thing amongst us to lie out of Christ, in danger every day of dropping into hell; and what persons minds were intent upon, was to escape for their lives, and to fly from the wrath to come. All would eagerly lay hold of opportunities for their souls; and were wont very often to meet together in private houses, for religious purposes: and such meetings when appointed were greatly thronged.

There was scarcely a single person in the town, old or young, left unconcerned about the great things of the eternal world. Those who were wont to be the vainest, and loosest; and those who had been most disposed to think, and speak slightly of vital and experimental religion, were now generally subject to great awakenings. And the work of conversion was carried on in a most astonishing manner, and increased more and more; souls did as it were come by flocks to Jesus Christ. From day to day, for many months together, might be seen evident instances of sinners brought out of darkness into marvellous light, and delivered out of a horrible pit, and from the miry clay, and set upon a rock with a new song of praise to God in their mouths.

This work of God, as it was carried on, and the number of true saints multiplied, soon made a glorious alteration in the town; so that in the spring and summer following, anno 1735, the town seemed to be full of the presence of God: it never was so full of love, nor of joy, and yet so full of distress, as it was then. There were remarkable tokens of God's presence in almost every house. It was a time of joy in families on account of salvation being brought unto them; parents rejoicing over their children as new born, and husbands over their wives, and wives over their husbands. The goings of God were then seen in his sanctuary, God's day was a delight, and his tabernacles were amiable. Our public assemblies were then beautiful; the congregation was alive in God's service, every one earnestly intent on the public worship, every hearer eager to drink in the words of the minister as they came from his mouth; the assembly in general were, from time to time, in tears while the word was preached; some weeping with sorrow and distress, others with joy and love, others with pity and concern for the souls of their neighbours.

Our public praises were then greatly enlivened; God was then served in our psalmody, in some measure in the beauty of holiness. It has been observable, that there has been scarce any part of divine worship, wherein good men amongst us have had grace so drawn forth, and their hearts so lifted up in the ways of God, as in singing his praises. Our congregation excelled all that ever I knew in the external part of the duty before, the men generally carrying regularly, and well, three parts of music, and the women a part by themselves; but now they were evidently wont to sing with unusual elevation of heart and voice, which made the duty pleasant indeed.

In all companies, on other days, on whatever occasions persons met together, Christ was to be heard of and seen in the midst of them. Our young people when they met, were wont to spend the time in talking of the excellency and dying love of Jesus Christ, the glory of the way of salvation, the wonderful, free, and sovereign grace of God, his glorious work in the conversion of a soul, the truth and certainty of the great things of God's word, the sweetness of the views of his perfections, &c. And even at weddings, which formerly were mere occasions of mirth and jollity, there was now no discourse of any thing but religion, and no appearance of any but spiritual mirth. Those amongst us who had been formerly converted, were greatly enlivened, and renewed with fresh and extraordinary incomes of the spirit of God; though some much more than others, according to the measure of the gift of Christ. Many who before had laboured under difficulties about their own state, had now their doubts removed by more satisfying experience, and more clear discoveries of God's love.

When this work first appeared, and was so extraordinarily carried on amongst us in the winter, others round about us seemed not to know what to make of it. Many scoffed at and ridiculed it; and some compared what we called conversion, to certain distempers. But it was very observable of many, who occasionally came amongst us from abroad with disregardful hearts, that what they saw here cured them of such a temper of mind. Strangers were generally surprised to find things so much beyond what they had heard, and were wont to tell others that the state of the town could not be conceived of by those who had not seen it. The notice that was taken of it by the people who came to town on occasion of the court that sat here in the beginning of March, was very observable. And those who came from the neighbourhood to our public lectures, were for the most part remarkably affected. Many who came to town, on one occasion or other, had their consciences smitten, and awakened; and went home with wounded hearts, and with those impressions that never wore off till they had hopefully a saving issue; and those who before had serious thoughts, had their awakenings and convictions greatly increased. There were many instances of persons who came from abroad on visits, or on business, who had not been long here before, to all appearance, they were savingly wrought upon; and partook of that shower of divine blessing which God rained down here, and went home rejoicing; till at length the same work began evidently to appear and prevail in several other towns in the county.

* * *

This dispensation has also appeared very extraordinary in the numbers of those on whom we have reason to hope it has had a saving effect. We have about six hundred and twenty communicants, which include almost all our adult persons. The church was very large before; but persons never thronged into it, as they did in the late extraordinary time.— Our sacraments are eight weeks asunder, and I received into our communion about a hundred before one sacrament, fourscore of them at one time, whose appearance, when they presented themselves together to make an open explicit profession of christianity, was very affecting to the congregation. I took in near sixty before the next sacrament day: and I had very sufficient evidence of the conversion of their souls, through divine grace, though it is not the custom here, as it is in many other churches in this country, to make a credible relation of their inward experience the ground of admission to the Lord's Supper.

I am far from pretending to be able to determine how many have lately been the subjects of such mercy; but if I may be allowed to declare any thing that appears to me probable in a thing of this nature, I hope that more than 300 souls were savingly brought home to Christ, in this town, in the space of half a year, and about the same number of males as females. By what I have heard Mr. Stoddard say, this was far from what has been usual in years past; for he observed that in his time, many more women were converted than men. Those of our young people who are on other accounts most considerable, are mostly, as I hope, truly pious, and leading persons in the ways of religion. Those who were formerly loose young persons, are generally, to all appearance, become true lovers of God and Christ, and spiritual in their dispositions. I hope that by far the greater part of persons in this town, above sixteen years of age, are such as have the saving knowledge of Jesus Christ. By what I have heard I suppose it is so in some other places; particularly at Sunderland and South Hadley.

This has also appeared to be a very extraordinary dispensation, in that the spirit of God has so much extended not only his awakening, but regenerating influences, both to elderly persons, and also to those who are very young. It has been heretofore rarely heard of, that any were converted past middle age; but now we have the same ground to think, that many such have at this time been savingly changed, as that others have been so in more early years. I suppose there were upwards of fifty persons converted in this town above forty years of age; more than twenty of them above fifty; about ten of them above sixty; and two of them above seventy years of age.

It has heretofore been looked on as a strange thing, when any have seemed to be savingly wrought upon, and remarkably changed in their childhood. But now, I suppose, near thirty were, to appearance, savingly wrought upon, between ten and fourteen years of age; two between nine and ten, and one of about four years of age; and because I suppose this last will be with most difficulty believed, I will hereafter give a particular account of it. The influences of God's Holy Spirit have also been very remarkable on children in some other places; particularly at Sunderland, South Hadley, and the west part of Suffield. There are several families in this town who are all hopefully pious. Yea, there are several numerous families, in which, I think, we have reason to hope that all the children are truly godly, and most of them lately become so. There are very few houses in the whole town, into which salvation has not lately come, in one or more instances. There are several negroes, who from what was seen in them then, and what is discernible in them since, appear to have been truly born again in the late remarkable season.

* * *

This work seemed to be at its greatest height in this town in the former part of the spring, in March and April. At that time, God's work in the conversion of souls was carried on amongst us in so wonderful a manner, that, so far as I can judge, it appears to have been at the rate, at least, of four persons in a day; or near thirty in a week, take one with another, for five or six weeks together. When God in so remarkable a manner took the work into his own hands, there was as much done in a day or two as at ordinary times, with all endeavours that men can use, and with such a blessing as we commonly have, is done in a year.

I am very sensible how apt many would be, if they should see the account I have here given, presently to think with themselves that I am very fond of making a great many converts, and of magnifying the matter; and to think that, for want of judgment, I take every religious pang and enthusiastic conceit for saving conversion. I do not much wonder, if they should be apt to think so; and, for this reason, I have forborne to publish an account of this great work of God, though I have often been solicited. But having now a special call to give an account of it, upon mature consideration I thought it might not be beside my duty to declare this amazing work, as it appeared to me to be indeed divine, and to conceal no part of the glory of it; leaving it with God to take care of the credit of his own work, and running the venture of any censorious thoughts which might be entertained of me to my disadvantage. That distant persons may be under as great advantage as may be, to judge for themselves of this matter, I would be a little more large and particular.

GOD GLORIFIED IN THE WORK OF REDEMPTION

Preached in Boston, July 8, 1731, and immediately published with a commendatory advertisement signed by Thomas Prince and William Cooper, this was Jonathan Edwards' first publication. The invitation to preach on this occasion was obviously to test his orthodoxy, since he had been trained during a portion of his Yale experience under the tutorship of Timothy Cutler, who had shocked New England by going over to the Church of England. Both Edwards and Yale College passed the test. For a discussion of the sermon from this angle, see Perry Miller, *Jonathan Edwards*, pp. 3–34; for the theological importance of this sermon, see Alexander Allen, *Jonathan Edwards*, pp. 56–67. Henceforward (from 1731) the views of Edwards as a theologian received attention. The text is from *The Works of President Edwards*, edited by S. B. Dwight, Vol. VII, pp. 149–62.

1 COR. i. 29–31

That no flesh should glory in his presence. But of him are ye in Christ Jesus, who of God is made unto us wisdom and righteousness, and sanctification, and redemption. That according as it is written, He that glorieth, let him glory in the Lord.

THOSE Christians to whom the apostle directed this epistle, dwelt in a part of the world where human wisdom was in great repute; as the apostle observes in the 22d verse of this chapter, "The Greeks seek after wisdom." Corinth was

not far from Athens, that had been for many ages the most
famous seat of philosophy and learning in the world. The
apostle therefore observes to them how God by the gospel
destroyed, and brought to nought, their wisdom. The learned
Grecians and their great philosophers, by all their wisdom
did not know God, they were not able to find out the truth
in divine things. But, after they had done their utmost to
no effect, it pleased God at length to reveal himself by the
gospel, which they accounted foolishness. He "chose the
foolish things of the world to confound the wise, and the
weak things of the world to confound the things which are
mighty, and the base things of the world, and things that
are despised, yea, and things which are not, to bring to
nought the things that are." And the apostle informs them
in the text why he thus did, *That no flesh should glory in
his presence,* &c. In which words may be observed,

1. What God aims at in the disposition of things in the
affair of redemption, *viz.* that man should not glory in himself, but alone in God; *That no flesh should glory in his
presence,—that according as it is written, He that glorieth,
let him glory in the Lord.*

2. How this end is attained in the work of redemption,
viz. by that absolute and immediate dependence which men
have upon God in that work, for all their good. Inasmuch as,

First, All the good that they have is in and through Christ:
He *is made unto us wisdom, righteousness, sanctification,
and redemption.* All the good of the fallen and redeemed
creature is concerned in these four things, and cannot be
better distributed than into them; but Christ is each of them
to us, and we have none of them any otherwise than in
him. *He is made of God unto us wisdom:* In him are all
the proper good and true excellency of the understanding.
Wisdom was a thing that the Greeks admired; but Christ is
the true light of the world; it is through him alone that true
wisdom is imparted to the mind. It is in and by Christ
that we have *righteousness:* It is by being in him that we
are justified, have our sins pardoned, and are received as
righteous into God's favour. It is by Christ that we have
sanctification: We have in him true excellency of heart,
as well as of understanding; and he is made unto us inherent
as well as imputed righteousness. It is by Christ that we
have *redemption,* or the actual deliverance from all misery,

and the bestowment of all happiness and glory. Thus we have all our good by Christ, who is God.

Secondly, Another instance wherein our dependence on God for all our good appears, is this, That it is God that has given us Christ, that we might have these benefits through him: he *of God is made unto us wisdom, righteousness,* &c.

Thirdly, It is of him that we are in Christ Jesus, and come to have an interest in him, and so do receive those blessings which he is made unto us. It is God that gives us faith whereby we close with Christ.

So that in this verse is shown our dependence on each person in the Trinity for all our good. We are dependent on Christ the Son of God, as he is our wisdom, righteousness, sanctification, and redemption. We are dependent on the Father, who has given us Christ, and made him to be these things to us. We are dependent on the Holy Ghost, for it is *of him that we are in Christ Jesus;* it is the Spirit of God that gives faith in him, whereby we receive him, and close with him.

DOCTRINE

"God is glorified in the work of redemption in this, that there appears in it so absolute and universal a dependence of the redeemed on him."——Here I propose to show, 1st, That there is an absolute and universal dependence of the redeemed on God for all their good. And 2dly, That God hereby is exalted and glorified in the work of redemption.

I. There is an absolute and universal dependence of the redeemed on God. The nature and contrivance of our redemption is such, that the redeemed are in every thing directly, immediately, and entirely dependent on God: They are dependent on him for all, and are dependent on him every way.

The several ways wherein the dependence of one being may be upon another for its good, and wherein the redeemed of Jesus Christ depend on God for all their good, are these, *viz.* That they have all their good of him, and that they have all through him, and that they have all in him: That he is the *cause* and original whence all their good comes, therein it is *of* him; and that he is the *medium* by which it is obtained and conveyed, therein they have it *through* him; and that he is the *good itself* given and conveyed, therein it is *in* him. Now those that are redeemed by Jesus Christ do, in all these respects, very directly and entirely depend on God for their all.

First, The redeemed have all their good *of* God. God is the great *author* of it. He is the *first* cause of it; and not only so, but he is the *only* proper cause. It is of God that we have our Redeemer. It is God that has provided a Saviour for us. Jesus Christ is not only of God in his person, as he is the only begotten Son of God, but he is from God, as we are concerned in him, and in his office of Mediator. He is the gift of God to us: God chose and anointed him, appointed him his work, and sent him into the world. And as it is God that *gives*, so it is God that *accepts* the Saviour. He gives the purchaser, and he affords the thing purchased.

It is of God that Christ becomes ours, that we are brought to him and are united to him. It is of God that we receive faith to close with him, that we may have an interest in him. Eph. ii. 8. "For by grace ye are saved, through faith; and that not of yourselves, it is the gift of God." It is of God that we actually receive all the benefits that Christ has purchased. It is God that pardons and justifies, and delivers from going down to hell; and into his favour the redeemed are received, when they are justified. So it is God that delivers from the dominion of sin, cleanses us from our filthiness, and changes us from our deformity. It is of God that the redeemed receive all their true excellency, wisdom, and holiness: and that two ways, *viz.* as the Holy Ghost by whom these things are immediately wrought is from God, proceeds from him, and is sent by him; and also as the Holy Ghost himself is God, by whose operation and indwelling the knowledge of God and divine things, a holy disposition and all grace, are conferred and upheld. And though means are made use of in conferring grace on men's souls, yet it is of God that we have these means of grace, and it is he that makes them effectual. It is of God that we have the holy scriptures: they are his word. It is of God that we have ordinances, and their efficacy depends on the immediate influence of his Spirit. The ministers of the gospel are

sent of God, and all their sufficiency is of him.—2 Cor.
iv. 7. "We have this treasure in earthen vessels, that the
excellency of the power may be of God, and not of us."
Their success depends entirely and absolutely on the immediate blessing and influence of God.

1. The redeemed have all from the *grace* of God. It was
of mere grace that God gave us his only begotten Son. The
grace is great in proportion to the excellency of what is
given. The gift was infinitely precious, because it was of a
person infinitely worthy, a person of infinite glory; and also
because it was of a person infinitely near and dear to God.
The grace is great in proportion to the benefit we have given
us in him. The benefit is doubly infinite, in that in him we
have deliverance from an infinite, because an eternal misery,
and do also receive eternal joy and glory. The grace in bestowing this gift is great in proportion to our unworthiness
to whom it is given; instead of deserving such a gift, we
merited infinitely ill of God's hands. The grace is great according to the manner of giving, or in proportion to the
humiliation and expense of the method and means by which
a way is made for our having the gift. He gave him to
dwell amongst us; he gave him to us incarnate, or in our
nature; and in the like though sinless infirmities. He gave
him to us in a low and afflicted state; and not only so,
but as slain, that he might be a feast for our souls.

The grace of God in bestowing this gift is most free. It
was what God was under no obligation to bestow. He might
have rejected fallen man, as he did the fallen angels. It
was what we never did any thing to merit; it was given
while we were yet enemies, and before we had so much as
repented. It was from the love of God who saw no excellency
in us to attract it; and it was without expectation of ever
being requited for it.—And it is from mere grace that the
benefits of Christ are applied to such and such particular
persons. Those that are called and sanctified are to attribute
it alone to the good pleasure of God's goodness by which
they are distinguished. He is sovereign, and hath mercy on
whom he will have mercy.

Man hath now a greater dependence on the grace of God
than he had before the fall. He depends on free goodness
of God for much more than he did then. Then he depended on God's goodness for conferring the reward of per-

fect obedience; for God was not obliged to promise and bestow that reward. But now we are dependent on the grace of God for much more; we stand in need of grace, not only to bestow glory upon us, but to deliver us from hell and eternal wrath. Under the first covenant we depended on God's goodness to give us the reward of righteousness; and so we do now: But we stand in need of God's free and sovereign grace to give us that righteousness; to pardon our sin, and release us from the guilt and infinite demerit of it.

And as we are dependent on the goodness of God for more now than under the first covenant, so we are dependent on a much greater, more free and wonderful goodness. We are now more dependent on God's arbitrary and sovereign good pleasure. We were in our first estate dependent on God for holiness. We had our original righteousness from him; but then holiness was not bestowed in such a way of sovereign good pleasure as it is now. Man was created holy, for it became God to create holy all his reasonable creatures. It would have been a disparagement to the holiness of God's nature, if he had made an intelligent creature unholy. But now when fallen man is made holy, it is from mere and arbitrary grace: God may for ever deny holiness to the fallen creature if he pleases, without any disparagement to any of his perfections.

And we are not only indeed more dependent on the grace of God, but our dependence is much more conspicuous, because our own insufficiency and helplessness in ourselves is much more apparent in our fallen and undone state, than it was before we were either sinful or miserable. We are more apparently dependent on God for holiness, because we are first sinful, and utterly polluted, and afterward holy. So the production of the effect is sensible, and its derivation from God more obvious. If man was ever holy and always was so, it would not be so apparent, that he had not holiness necessarily, as an inseparable qualification of human nature. So we are more apparently dependent on free grace for the favour of God, for we are first justly the objects of his displeasure, and afterward are received into favour. We are more apparently dependent on God for happiness, being first miserable, and afterward happy. It is more apparently free and without merit in us, because we are actually without any kind of excellency to merit, if there could be any such thing as merit in creature-excellency. And we are not only without any true excellency, but are full of, and wholly defiled with, that which is infinitely odious. All our good is more apparently from God, because we are first naked and wholly without any good, and afterward enriched with all good.

2. We receive all from the *power* of God. Man's redemption is often spoken of as a work of wonderful power as well as grace. The great power of God appears in bringing a sinner from his low state from the depths of sin and misery, to such an exalted state of holiness and happiness. Eph. i. 19. "And what is the exceeding greatness of his power to us-ward who believe, according to the working of his mighty power."—

We are dependent on God's power through every step of our redemption. We are dependent on the power of God to convert us, and give faith in Jesus Christ, and the new nature. It is a work of creation: "If any man be in Christ, he is a new creature," 2 Cor. v. 17. "We are created in Christ Jesus," Eph. ii. 10. The fallen creature cannot attain to true holiness, but by being created again, Eph. iv. 24. "And that ye put on the new man, which after God is created in righteousness and true holiness." It is a raising from the dead, Colos. ii. 12, 13. "Wherein also ye are risen with him through the faith of the operation of God, who hath raised him from the dead." Yea, it is a more glorious work of power than mere creation, or raising a dead body to life, in that the effect attained is greater and more excellent. That holy and happy being, and spiritual life which is produced in the work of conversion, is a far greater and more glorious effect, than mere being and life. And the state from whence the change is made—a death in sin, a total corruption of nature, and depth of misery—is far more remote from the state attained, than mere death or non-entity.

It is by God's power also that we are preserved in a state of grace. 1 Pet. i. 5. "Who are kept by the power of God through faith unto salvation." As grace is at first from God, so it is continually from him, and is maintained by him, as much as light in the atmosphere is all day long from the sun, as well as at first dawning, or at sun-rising.—Men are dependent on the power of God for every exercise of grace, and for carrying on that work in the heart, for subduing sin and corruption, increasing holy principles, and enabling to bring forth fruit in good works. Man is dependent on divine power in bringing grace to its perfection, in making the soul completely amiable in Christ's glorious likeness, and filling of it with a satisfying joy and blessedness; and for the raising of the body to life, and to such a perfect state, that it shall be suitable for a habitation and organ for a soul so perfected and blessed. These are the most glorious effects of the power of God, that are seen in the series of God's acts with respect to the creatures.

Man was dependent on the power of God in his first estate, but he is more dependent on his power now; he needs God's power to do more things for him, and depends on a more wonderful exercise of his power. It was an effect of the power of God to make man holy at the first; but more remarkably so now, because there is a great deal of opposition and difficulty in the way. It is a more glorious effect of power to make that holy that was so depraved, and under the dominion of sin, than to confer holiness on that which before had nothing of the contrary. It is a more glorious work of power to rescue a soul out of the hands of the devil, and from the powers of darkness, and to bring it into a state of salvation, than to confer holiness where there was no prepossession or opposition. Luke xi. 21, 22. "When a strong man armed keepeth his palace, his goods are in peace; but when a stronger than he shall come upon him, and overcome him, he taketh from him all his armour wherein he trusted, and divideth his spoils." So it is a more glorious work of power to uphold a soul in a state of grace and holiness, and to carry it on till it is brought to glory, when there is so much sin remaining in the heart resisting, and Satan with all his might opposing, than it would have been to have kept man from falling at first, when Satan had nothing in man.—Thus we have shown how the redeemed are dependent on God for all their good, as they have all of him.

Secondly, They are also dependent on God for all, as they have all *through* him. God is the medium of it, as well as the author and fountain of it. All we have, wisdom, the pardon of sin, deliverance from hell, acceptance into God's favour, grace and holiness, true comfort and happiness, eternal life and glory, is from God by a Mediator; and this Mediator is God; which Mediator we have an absolute dependence upon, as he through whom we receive all. So that here is another way wherein we have our dependence on God for all good. God not only gives us the Mediator, and accepts his mediation, and of his power and grace bestows the things purchased by the Mediator; but he the Mediator is God.

Our blessings are what we have by purchase; and the purchase is made of God, the blessings are purchased of him, and God gives the purchaser; and not only so, but God is the purchaser. Yea, God is both the purchaser and the price; for Christ who is God, purchased these blessings for us, by offering up himself as the price of our salvation. He purchased eternal life by the sacrifice of himself. Heb. vii. 27. "He offered up himself." And chap. ix. 26. "He hath appeared to take away sin by the sacrifice of himself." Indeed it was the human nature that was offered; but it was the same person with the divine, and therefore was an infinite price.

As we thus have our good through God, we have a dependence on him in a respect that man in his first estate had not. Man was to have eternal life then through his own righteousness; so that he had partly a dependence upon what was in himself; for we have a dependence upon that through which we have our good, as well as that from which we have it: and though man's righteousness that he then depended on was indeed from God, yet it was his own, it was inherent in himself; so that his dependence was not so *immediately* on God. But now the righteousness that we are dependent on is not in ourselves, but in God. We are saved through the righteousness of Christ: he *is made unto us righteousness;* and therefore is prophesied of, Jer. xxiii. 6, under that name, "the Lord our righteousness." In that the righteousness we are justified by is the righteousness of Christ, it is the righteousness of God. 2 Cor. v. 21. "That we might be made the righteousness of God in him."— Thus in redemption we have not only all things of God, but by and through him, 1 Cor. viii. 6. "But to us there is but one God, the Father, of whom are all things, and we in him; and one Lord Jesus Christ, by whom are all things, and we by him."

Thirdly, The redeemed have all their good *in God.* We not only have it of him, and through him, but it consists in him; he is all our good.—The good of the redeemed is either objective or inherent. By their objective good, I mean that extrinsic object, in the possession and enjoyment of which they are happy. Their inherent good is that excellency or pleasure which is in the soul itself. With respect to both of which the redeemed have all their good in God, or, which is the same thing, God himself is all their good.

1. The redeemed have all their *objective* good in God. God himself is the great good which they are brought to the possession and enjoyment of by redemption. He is the highest good, and the sum of all that good which Christ purchased. God is the inheritance of the saints; he is the portion of their souls. God is their wealth and treasure, their food, their life, their dwelling-place, their ornament and diadem, and their everlasting honour and glory. They have none in heaven but God; he is the great good which the redeemed are received to at death, and which they are to rise to at the end of the world. The Lord God is the light of the heavenly Jerusalem; and is the "river of the water of life" that runs, and "the tree of life that grows, in the midst of the paradise of God." The glorious excellencies and beauty of God will be what will for ever entertain the minds of the saints, and the love of God will be their everlasting feast. The redeemed will indeed enjoy other things; they will enjoy the angels, and will enjoy one another: but that which they shall enjoy in the angels, or each other, or in any thing else whatsoever, that will yield them delight and happiness, will be what shall be seen of God in them.

2. The redeemed have all their *inherent* good in God. Inherent good is two-fold; it is either excellency or pleasure. These the redeemed not only derive from God, as caused by him, but have them in him. They have spiritual excellency and joy by a kind of participation of God. They are made excellent by a communication of God's excellency. God puts his own beauty, *i.e.* his beautiful likeness, upon their souls. They are made partakers of the divine nature, or moral image of God, 2 Pet. i. 4. They are holy by being made partakers of God's holiness, Heb. xii. 10. The saints are beautiful and blessed by a communication of God's holiness and joy, as the moon and planets are bright by the sun's light. The saint hath spiritual joy and pleasure by a kind of effusion of God on the soul. In these things the redeemed have

communion with God; that is, they partake with him and of him.

The saints have both their spiritual excellency and blessedness by the gift of the Holy Ghost, and his dwelling in them. They are not only caused by the Holy Ghost, but are in him as their principle. The Holy Spirit becoming an inhabitant, is a vital principle in the soul. He, acting in, upon, and with the soul, becomes a fountain of true holiness and joy, as a spring is of water, by the exertion and diffusion of itself. John iv. 14. "But whosoever drinketh of the water that I shall give him, shall never thirst; but the water that I shall give him, shall be in him a well of water springing up into everlasting life." Compared with chap. vii. 38, 39. "He that believeth on me, as the scripture hath said, out of his belly shall flow rivers of living water; but this spake he of the Spirit, which they that believe on him should receive." The sum of what Christ has purchased for us, is that spring of water spoken of in the former of those places, and those rivers of living water spoken of in the latter. And the sum of the blessings, which the redeemed shall receive in heaven, is that river of water of life that proceeds from the throne of God and the Lamb, Rev. xxii. 1, which doubtless signifies the same with those rivers of living water, explained John vii. 38, 39, which is elsewhere called the "river of God's pleasures." Herein consists the fulness of good, which the saints receive of Christ. It is by partaking of the Holy Spirit, that they have communion with Christ in his fulness. God hath given the Spirit, not by measure unto him; and they do receive of his fulness, and grace for grace. This is the sum of the saints' inheritance; and therefore that little of the Holy Ghost which believers have in this world, is said to be the earnest of their inheritance, 2 Cor. i. 22. "Who hath also sealed us, and given us the Spirit in our hearts." And chap. v. 5. "Now he that hath wrought us for the self same thing, is God, who also hath given unto us the earnest of the Spirit." And Eph. i. 13, 14. "Ye were sealed with that Holy Spirit of promise, which is the earnest of our inheritance, until the redemption of the purchased possession."

The Holy Spirit and good things are spoken of in scripture as the same; as if the Spirit of God communicated to the soul, comprised all good things. Matt. vii. 11. "How much more shall your heavenly Father give good things to them that ask him?" In Luke it is, chap. xi. 13. "How much more shall your heavenly Father give the Holy Spirit to them that ask him?" This is the sum of the blessings that Christ died to procure, and the subject of gospel-promises. Gal. iii. 13, 14. "He was made a curse for us, that we might receive the promise of the Spirit through faith." The Spirit of God is the great promise of the Father. Luke xxiv. 49. "Behold, I send the promise of my Father upon you." The Spirit of God therefore is called "the Spirit of promise;" Eph. i. 33. This promised thing Christ received, and had given into his hand, as soon as he had finished the work of our redemption, to bestow on all that he had redeemed; Acts ii. 13. "Therefore being by the right hand of God exalted, and having received of the Father the promise of the Holy Ghost, he hath shed forth this, which ye both see and hear." So that all the holiness and happiness of the redeemed is in God. It is in the communications, indwelling, and acting of the Spirit of God. Holiness and happiness are in the fruit, here and hereafter, because God dwells in them, and they in God.

Thus God has given us the Redeemer, and it is by him that our good is purchased. So God is the Redeemer and the price; and he also is the good purchased. So that all that we have is of God, and through him, and in him. Rom. xi. 36. "For of him, and through him, and to him, (or in him,) are all things." The same in the Greek that is here rendered *to him*, is rendered *in him*, 1 Cor. viii. 6.

II. God is glorified in the work of redemption by this means, *viz.* By there being so great and universal a dependence of the redeemed on him.

1. Man hath so much the greater occasion and obligation to notice and acknowledge God's perfections and all-sufficiency. The greater the creature's dependence is on God's perfections, and the greater concern he has with them, so much the greater occasion he has to take notice of them. So much the greater concern any one has with and dependence upon the power and grace of God, so much the greater occasion has he to take notice of that power and grace. So much the greater and more immediate dependence there is on the divine holiness, so much the greater occasion

to take notice of and acknowledge that. So much the greater and more absolute dependence we have on the divine perfections, as belonging to the several persons of the Trinity, so much the greater occasion have we to observe and own the divine glory of each of them. That which we are most concerned with, is surely most in the way of our observation and notice; and this kind of concern with any thing, *viz.* dependence, does especially tend to command and oblige the attention and observation. Those things that we are not much dependent upon, it is easy to neglect; but we can scarce do any other than mind that which we have a great dependence on. By reason of our so great dependence on God, and his perfections and in so many respects, he and his glory are the more directly set in our view, which way soever we turn our eyes.

We have the greater occasion to take notice of God's all-sufficiency, when all our sufficiency is thus every way of him. We have the more occasion to contemplate him as an infinite good, and as the fountain of all good. Such a dependence on God demonstrates his all-sufficiency. So much as the dependence of the creature is on God, so much the greater does the creature's emptiness in himself appear; and so much the greater the creature's emptiness, so much the greater must the fulness of the being be who supplies him. Our having all *of* God, shows the fulness of his power and grace; our having all through him, shows the fulness of his merit and worthiness; and our having all in him, demonstrates his fulness of beauty, love, and happiness. And the redeemed, by reason of the greatness of their dependence on God, have not only so much the greater occasion, but obligation to contemplate and acknowledge the glory and fulness of God. How unreasonable and ungrateful should we be, if we did not acknowledge that sufficiency and glory which we absolutely, immediately and universally depend upon!

2. Hereby is demonstrated how great God's glory is considered comparatively, or as compared with the creature's.— By the creature being thus wholly and universally dependent on God, it appears that the creature is nothing, and that God is all. Hereby it appears that God is infinitely above us; that God's strength, and wisdom, and holiness, are infinitely greater than ours. However great and glorious the creature

apprehends God to be, yet if he be not sensible of the difference between God and him, so as to see that God's glory is great, compared with his own, he will not be disposed to give God the glory due to his name. If the creature in any respects sets himself upon a level with God, or exalts himself to any competition with him, however he may apprehend that great honour and profound respect may belong to God from those that are at a greater distance, he will not be so sensible of its being due from him. So much the more men exalt themselves, so much the less will they surely be disposed to exalt God. It is certainly what God aims at in the disposition of things in redemption, (if we allow the scriptures to be a revelation of God's mind,) that God should appear full, and man in himself empty, that God should appear all, and man nothing. It is God's declared design that others should not "glory in his presence;" which implies that it is his design to advance his own comparative glory. So much the more man "glories in God's presence," so much the less glory is ascribed to God.

3. By its being thus ordered, that the creature should have so absolute and universal a dependence on God, provision is made that God should have our whole souls, and should be the object of our undivided respect. If we had our dependence partly on God, and partly on something else, man's respect would be divided to those different things on which he had dependence. Thus it would be if we depended on God only for a part of our good, and on ourselves, or some other being, for another part: Or, if we had our good only from God, and through another that was not God, and in something else distinct from both, our hearts would be divided between the good itself and him from whom, and him through whom we received it. But now there is no occasion for this, God being not only he from or of whom we have all good, but also through whom, and is that good itself, that we have from him and through him. So that whatsoever there is to attract our respect, the tendency is still directly towards God, all unites in him as the centre.

USE

1. We may here observe the marvellous wisdom of God, in the work of redemption. God hath made man's emptiness and misery, his low, lost and ruined state, into which he sunk by the fall, an occasion of the greater advancement of his own glory, as in other ways, so particularly in this, that there is now much more universal and apparent dependence of man on God. Though God be pleased to lift man out of that dismal abyss of sin and woe into which he has fallen, and exceedingly to exalt him in excellency and honour, and to a high pitch of glory and blessedness, yet the creature hath nothing in any respect to glory of; all the glory evidently belongs to God, all is in a mere, and most absolute, and divine dependence on the Father, Son, and Holy Ghost. And each person of the Trinity is equally glorified in this work: There is an absolute dependence of the creature on every one for all: All is of the Father, all through the Son, and all in the Holy Ghost. Thus God appears in the work of redemption as all in all. It is fit that he who is, and there is none else, should be the Alpha and Omega, the first and the last, the all and the only, in this work.

2. Hence those doctrines and schemes of divinity that are in any respect opposite to such an absolute and universal dependence on God, derogate from his glory, and thwart the design of our redemption. And such are those schemes that put the creature in God's stead, in any of the mentioned respects, that exalt man into the place of either Father, Son, or Holy Ghost, in any thing pertaining to our redemption. However they may allow of a dependence of the redeemed on God, yet they deny a dependence that is so *absolute* and universal. They own an entire dependence on God for *some* things, but not for others; they own that we depend on God for the gift and acceptance of a Redeemer, but deny so absolute a dependence on him for the obtaining of an *interest* in the Redeemer. They own an absolute dependence on the Father for giving his Son, and on the Son for working

out redemption, but not so entire a dependence on the Holy Ghost for *conversion,* and a being in Christ, and so coming to a title to his benefits. They own a dependence on God for *means* of grace, but not absolutely for the benefit and success of those means; a partial dependence on the power of God, for obtaining and exercising holiness, but not a mere dependence on the arbitrary and sovereign grace of God. They own a dependence on the free grace of God for a reception into his favour, so far that it is without any proper merit, but not as it is without being attracted, or moved with any excellency. They own a partial dependence on Christ, as he through whom we have life, as having purchased new terms of life, but still hold that the righteousness through which we have life is inherent in ourselves, as it was under the first covenant. Now whatever scheme is inconsistent with our *entire* dependence on God for all, and of having all of him, through him, and in him, it is repugnant to the design and tenor of the gospel, and robs it of that which God accounts its lustre and glory.

3. Hence we may learn a reason why faith is that by which we come to have an interest in this redemption; for there is included in the nature of faith, a sensible acknowledgment of *absolute dependence* on God in this affair. It is very fit that it should be required of all, in order to their having the benefit of this redemption, that they should be sensible of, and acknowledge their dependence on God for it. It is by this means that God hath contrived to glorify himself in redemption; and it is fit that he should at least have this glory of those that are the subjects of this redemption, and have the benefit of it.—Faith is a sensibleness of what is real in the work of redemption; and the soul that believes doth entirely depend on God for all salvation, in its own sense and act. Faith abases men, and exalts God; it gives all the glory of redemption to him alone. It is necessary in order to saving faith, that man should be emptied of himself, be sensible that he is "wretched, and miserable, and poor, and blind, and naked." Humility is a great ingredient of true faith: He that truly receives redemption, receives it as a little child, Mark x. 15. "Whosoever shall not receive the kingdom of heaven as a little child, he shall not enter therein." It is the delight of a believing soul to abase itself and exalt God alone: that is the language of it, Psalm cxv. 1. "Not unto

us, O Lord, not unto us, but to thy name give glory."

4. Let us be exhorted to exalt God alone, and ascribe to him all the glory of redemption. Let us endeavour to obtain, and increase in, a sensibleness of our great dependence on God, to have our eye on him alone, to mortify a self-dependent, and self-righteous disposition. Man is naturally exceeding prone to exalt himself, and depend on his own power or goodness; as though from himself he must expect happiness. He is prone to have respect to enjoyments alien from God and his Spirit, as those in which happiness is to be found.—But this doctrine should teach us to exalt God *alone;* as by trust and reliance, so by praise. *Let him that glorieth, glory in the Lord.* Hath any man hope that he is converted, and sanctified, and that his mind is endowed with true excellency and spiritual beauty? that his sins are forgiven, and he received into God's favour, and exalted to the honour and blessedness of being his child, and an heir of eternal life? let him give God all the glory; who alone makes him to differ from the worst of men in this world, or the most miserable of the damned in hell. Hath any man much comfort and strong hope of eternal life? let not his hope lift him up, but dispose him the more to abase himself, to reflect on his own exceeding unworthiness of such a favour, and to exalt God alone. Is any man eminent in holiness, and abundant in good works? let him take nothing of the glory of it to himself, but ascribe it to him whose "workmanship we are, created in Christ Jesus unto good works."

A DIVINE AND SUPERNATURAL LIGHT

Preached at Northampton in 1734, a few months before the beginning of the revival, and published at the request of members of the congregation. Both for its choice of subject and for the simple, unadorned treatment, it is fairly representative of Jonathan Edwards' characteristic Sunday preaching. For its theological importance, see Alexander Allen, *Jonathan Edwards,* pp. 68–78; Perry Miller, *Jonathan Edwards,* pp. 44–68. The text is from *The Works of President Edwards,* edited by S. B. Dwight, Vol. VI, pp. 171–88, with omissions.

MATT. XVI. 17.

And Jesus answered and said unto him, Blessed art thou, Simon Bar-jona: for flesh and blood hath not revealed it unto thee, but my Father which is in heaven.

CHRIST addresses these words to Peter upon occasion of his professing his faith in him as the Son of God. Our Lord was inquiring of his disciples, whom men said that he was; not that he needed to be informed, but only to introduce and give occasion to what follows. They answer, that some said he was John the Baptist, and some Elias, and others Jeremias, or one of the prophets. When they had thus given an account whom others said that he was, Christ asks them, whom they said that he was? Simon Peter, whom we find always zealous and forward, was the first to answer: he

123

readily replied to the question, *Thou art Christ the Son of the living God.*

* * *

What had passed in the preceding discourse naturally occasioned Christ to observe this; because the disciples had been telling how others did not know him, but were generally mistaken about him, divided and confounded in their opinions of him: but Peter had declared his assured faith, that he was the *Son of God.* Now it was natural to observe, how it was not *flesh and blood* that had *revealed it to him,* but God; for if this knowledge were dependent on natural causes or means, how came it to pass that they, a company of poor fishermen, illiterate men, and persons of low education, attained to the knowledge of the truth; while the Scribes and Pharisees, men of vastly higher advantages, and greater knowledge and sagacity, in other matters, remained in ignorance? This could be owing only to the gracious distinguishing influence and revelation of the Spirit of God. Hence, what I would make the subject of my present discourse, from these words, is this

DOCTRINE

That there is such a thing as a spiritual and divine light, immediately imparted to the soul by God, of a different nature from any that is obtained by natural means. And on this subject I would,

I. Show what this divine light is.
II. How it is given immediately by God, and not obtained by natural means.
III. Show the truth of the doctrine.
And then conclude with a brief improvement.

I. I would show what this spiritual and divine light is. And in order to it would show,

First, In a few things, what it is not. And here,

1. Those convictions that natural men may have of their sin and misery, is not this spiritual and divine light. Men, in a natural condition, may have convictions of the guilt that lies upon them, and of the anger of God, and their danger of divine vengeance. Such convictions are from the light of truth. That some sinners have a greater conviction of their guilt and misery than others, is because some have more light, or more of an apprehension of truth than others. And this light and conviction may be from the Spirit of God; the Spirit convinces men of sin; but yet nature is much more concerned in it than in the communication of that spiritual and divine light that is spoken of in the doctrine; it is from the Spirit of God only as assisting natural principles, and not as infusing any new principles. Common grace differs from special, in that it influences only by assisting of nature; and not by imparting grace, or bestowing any thing above nature. The light that is obtained, is wholly natural, or of no superior kind to what mere nature attains to, though more of that kind be obtained than would be obtained, if men were left wholly to themselves; or, in other words, common grace only assists the faculties of the soul to do that more fully which they do by nature, as natural conscience or reason will by mere nature make a man sensible of guilt, and will accuse and condemn him when he has done amiss. Conscience is a principle natural to men; and the work that it doth naturally, or of itself, is to give an apprehension of right and wrong, and to suggest to the mind the relation that there is between right and wrong and a retribution. The Spirit of God, in those convictions which unregenerate men sometimes have, assists conscience to do this work in a further degree than it would do if they were left to themselves. He helps it against those things that tend to stupify it, and obstruct its exercise. But in the renewing and sanctifying work of the Holy Ghost, those things are wrought in the soul that are above nature, and of which there is nothing of the like kind in the soul by nature; and they are caused to exist in the soul habitually, and according to such a stated constitution or law, that lays such a foundation for exercises in a continued course, as is called a principle of nature. Not only are remaining principles assisted to do their work more freely and fully, but those principles are restored that were

utterly destroyed by the fall; and the mind thenceforward habitually exerts those acts that the dominion of sin had made it as wholly destitute of as a dead body is of vital acts.

The Spirit of God acts in a very different manner in the one case, from what he doth in the other. He may, indeed, act upon the mind of a natural man, but he acts in the mind of a saint as an indwelling vital principle. He acts upon the mind of an unregenerate person as an extrinsic occasional agent; for, in acting upon them, he doth not unite himself to them: for, notwithstanding all his influences that they may possess, they are still sensual, having not the Spirit. Jude 19. But he unites himself with the mind of a saint, takes him for his temple, actuates and influences him as a new supernatural principle of life and action. There is this difference, that the Spirit of God, in acting in the soul of a godly man, exerts and communicates himself there in his own proper nature. Holiness is the proper nature of the Spirit of God. The Holy Spirit operates in the minds of the godly, by uniting himself to them, and living in them, and exerting his own nature in the exercise of their faculties. The Spirit of God may act upon a creature, and yet not in acting communicate himself. The Spirit of God may act upon inanimate creatures; as, *the Spirit moved upon the face of the waters,* in the beginning of the creation; so the Spirit of God may act upon the minds of men many ways, and communicate himself no more than when he acts upon an inanimate creature. For instance, he may excite thoughts in them, may assist their natural reason and understanding, or may assist other natural principles, and this without any union with the soul, but may act, as it were, upon an external object. But as he acts in his holy influences and spiritual operations, he acts in a way of peculiar communication of himself; so that the subject is thence denominated spiritual.

2. This spiritual and divine light does not consist in any impression made upon the imagination. It is no impression upon the mind, as though one saw any thing with the bodily eyes. It is no imagination or idea of an outward light or glory, or any beauty of form or countenance, or a visible lustre or brightness of any object. The imagination may be strongly impressed with such things; but this is not spiritual light. Indeed when the mind has a lively discovery of spiritual things, and is greatly affected with the power of divine light,

it may, and probably very commonly doth, much affect the imagination; so that impressions of an outward beauty or brightness may *accompany* those spiritual discoveries. But spiritual light is not that impression upon the imagination, but an exceedingly different thing. Natural men may have lively impressions on their imaginations; and we cannot determine but that the devil, who transforms himself into an angel of light, may cause imaginations of an outward beauty, or visible glory, and of sounds and speeches, and other such things; but these are things of a vastly inferior nature to spiritual light.

3. This spiritual light is not the suggesting of any new truths or propositions not contained in the word of God. This suggesting of new truths or doctrines to the mind, independent of any antecedent revelations of those propositions, either in word or writing, is inspiration; such as the prophets and apostles had, and such as some enthusiasts pretend to. But this spiritual light that I am speaking of, is quite a different thing from inspiration. It reveals no new doctrine, it suggests no new proposition to the mind, it teaches no new thing of God, or Christ, or another world, not taught in the Bible, but only gives a due apprehension of those things that are taught in the word of God.

4. It is not every affecting view that men have of religious things that is this spiritual and divine light. Men by mere principles of nature are capable of being affected with things that have a special relation to religion as well as other things. A person by mere nature, for instance, may be liable to be affected with the story of Jesus Christ, and the sufferings he underwent, as well as by any other tragical story. He may be the more affected with it from the interest he conceives mankind to have in it. Yea, he may be affected with it without believing it; as well as a man may be affected with what he reads in a romance, or sees acted in a stage-play. He may be affected with a lively and eloquent description of many pleasant things that attend the state of the blessed in heaven, as well as his imagination be entertained by a romantic description of the pleasantness of fairy land, or the like. And a common belief of the truth of such things, from education or otherwise, may help forward their affection. We read in Scripture of many that were greatly affected with things of a religious nature, who yet are there represented as wholly

graceless, and many of them very ill men. A person therefore may have affecting views of the things of religion, and yet be very destitute of spiritual light. Flesh and blood may be the author of this; one man may give another an affecting view of divine things with but common assistance; but God alone can give a spiritual discovery of them.—But I proceed to show,

Secondly, Positively what this spiritual and divine light is.

And it may be thus described: A true sense of the divine excellency of the things revealed in the word of God, and a conviction of the truth and reality of them thence arising. This spiritual light primarily consists in the former of these, *viz.* A real sense and apprehension of the divine excellency of things revealed in the word of God. A spiritual and saving conviction of the truth and reality of these things, arises from such a sight of their divine excellency and glory; so that this conviction of their truth is an effect and natural consequence of this sight of their divine glory. There is therefore in this spiritual light,

1. A true sense of the divine and superlative excellency of the things of religion; a real sense of the excellency of God and Jesus Christ, and of the work of redemption, and the ways and works of God revealed in the gospel. There is a divine and superlative glory in these things; an excellency that is of a vastly higher kind, and more sublime nature than in other things; a glory greatly distinguishing them from all that is earthly and temporal. He that is spiritually enlightened truly apprehends and sees it, or has a sense of it. He does not merely rationally believe that God is glorious, but he has a sense of the gloriousness of God in his heart. There is not only a rational belief that God is holy, and that holiness is a good thing, but there is a sense of the loveliness of God's holiness. There is not only a speculatively judging that God is gracious, but a sense how amiable God is on account of the beauty of this divine attribute.

There is a twofold knowledge of good of which God has made the mind of man capable. The first, that which is merely notional; as when a person only speculatively judges that any thing is, which, by the agreement of mankind, is called good or excellent, *viz.* that which is most to general advantage, and between which and a reward there is a suitableness,—and the like. And the other is, that which consists in the sense of the heart; as when the heart is sensible of pleasure and delight in the presence of the idea of it. In the former is exercised merely the speculative faculty, or the understanding, in distinction from the will or disposition of the soul. In the latter, the will, or inclination, or heart, are mainly concerned.

Thus there is a difference between having an *opinion*, that God is holy and gracious, and having a *sense* of the loveliness and beauty of that holiness and grace. There is a difference between having a rational judgment that honey is sweet, and having a sense of its sweetness. A man may have the former, that knows not how honey tastes; but a man cannot have the latter unless he has an idea of the taste of honey in his mind. So there is a difference between believing that a person is beautiful, and having a sense of his beauty. The former may be obtained by hearsay, but the latter only by seeing the countenance. When the heart is sensible of the beauty and amiableness of a thing, it necessarily feels pleasure in the apprehension. It is implied in a person's being heartily sensible of the loveliness of a thing, that the idea of it is pleasant to his soul; which is a far different thing from having a rational opinion that it is excellent.

2. There arises from this sense of the divine excellency of things contained in the word of God, a conviction of the truth and reality of them; and that, either indirectly or directly.

First, Indirectly, and that two ways:

1. As the prejudices of the heart, against the truth of divine things, are hereby removed; so that the mind becomes susceptive of the due force of rational arguments for their truth. The mind of man is naturally full of prejudices against divine truth. It is full of enmity against the doctrines of the gospel; which is a disadvantage to those arguments that prove their truth, and causes them to lose their force upon the mind. But when a person has discovered to him the divine excellency of Christian doctrines, this destroys the enmity, removes those prejudices, sanctifies the reason, and causes it to lie open to the force of arguments for their truth.

Hence was the different effect that Christ's miracles had to convince the disciples, from what they had to convince the scribes and Pharisees. Not that they had a stronger reason, or had their reason more improved; but their reason was sanctified, and those blinding prejudices, that the Scribes and Pharisees were under, were removed by the sense they had of the excellency of Christ, and his doctrine.

It not only removes the hindrances of reason, but positively helps reason. It makes even the speculative notions more lively. It engages the attention of the mind, with more fixedness and intenseness to that kind of objects; which causes it to have a clearer view of them, and enables it more clearly to see their mutual relations, and occasions it to take more notice of them. The ideas themselves that other wise are dim and obscure, are by this means impressed with the greater strength, and have a light cast upon them; so that the mind can better judge of them. As he that beholds objects on the face of the earth, when the light of the sun is cast upon them, is under greater advantage to discern them in their true forms and natural relations, than he that sees them in a dim twilight.

The mind, being sensible of the excellency of divine objects, dwells upon them with delight; and the powers of the soul are more awakened and enlivened to employ themselves in the contemplation of them, and exert themselves more fully and much more to the purpose. The beauty of the objects draws on the faculties, and draws forth their exercises; so that reason itself is under far greater advantages for its proper and free exercises, and to attain its proper end, free of darkness and delusion.—But,

Secondly, A true sense of the divine excellency of the things of God's word doth more directly and immediately convince us of their truth; and that because the excellency of these things is so superlative. There is a beauty in them so divine and godlike, that it greatly and evidently distinguishes them from things merely human, or that of which men are the inventors and authors; a glory so high and great, that when clearly seen, commands assent to their divine reality. When there is an actual and lively discovery of this beauty and excellency, it will not allow of any such thought as that it is the fruit of men's invention. This is a kind of intuitive and immediate evidence. They believe the doctrines of God's word to be divine, because they see a divine, and transcendent, and most evidently distinguishing glory in them; such a glory as, if clearly seen, does not leave room to doubt of their being of God, and not of men.

Such a conviction of the truths of religion as this, arising from a sense of their divine excellency, is included in saving faith. And this original of it, is that by which it is most essentially distinguished from that common assent, of which unregenerate men are capable.

II. I proceed now to the *second* thing proposed, *viz.* To shew how this light is immediately given by God, and not obtained by natural means. And here,

1. It is not intended that the natural faculties are not used in it. They are the subject of this light: and in such a manner, that they are not merely passive, but active in it. God, in letting in this light into the soul, deals with man according to his nature, and makes use of his rational faculties. But yet this light is not the less immediately from God for that; the faculties are made use of as the subject, and not as the cause. As the use we make of our eyes in beholding various objects, when the sun arises, is not the cause of the light that discovers those objects to us.

2. It is not intended that outward means have no concern in this affair. It is not in this affair, as in inspiration, where new truths are suggested; for, by this light is given only a due apprehension of the same truths that are revealed in the word of God: and therefore it is not given without the word. The gospel is employed in this affair. This light is the "light of the glorious gospel of Christ." 2 Cor. iv. 4. The gospel is as a glass, by which this light is conveyed to us. 1 Cor. xiii. 12. "Now we see through a glass."——But,

3. When it is said that this light is given immediately by God, and not obtained by natural means, hereby is intended, that it is given by God without making use of any means that operate by their own power or natural force. God makes use of means; but it is not as mediate causes to produce this effect. There are not truly any second causes of it; but it is produced by God immediately. The word of God is no proper cause of this effect; but is made use of only to convey to the mind the subject-matter of this saving instruction: And this indeed it doth convey to us by natural force or influence. It conveys to our minds these doctrines; it is the cause of a notion of them in our heads, but not of the sense of their divine excellency in our hearts. Indeed a person cannot have spiritual light without the word. But that does not argue, that

the word properly causes that light. The mind cannot see the excellency of any doctrine, unless that doctrine be first in the mind; but seeing the excellency of the doctrine may be immediately from the Spirit of God; though the conveying of the doctrine, or proposition, itself, may be by the word. So that the notions which are the subject-matter of this light, are conveyed to the mind by the word of God; but that due sense of the heart, wherein this light formally consists, is immediately by the Spirit of God. as, for instance, the notion that there is a Christ, and that Christ is holy and gracious, is conveyed to the mind by the word of God: But the sense of the excellency of Christ, by reason of that holiness and grace, is, nevertheless, immediately the work of the Holy Spirit.—I come now,

III. To show the truth of the doctrine; that is, to show that there is such a thing as that spiritual light that has been described, thus immediately let into the mind by God. And here I would show, briefly, that this doctrine is both *scriptural* and *rational.*

First, It is scriptural. My text is not only full to the purpose, but it is a doctrine with which the Scripture abounds. . . .

* * *

Secondly, This doctrine is rational.

I will conclude with a very brief improvement of what has been said.

First, This doctrine may lead us to reflect on the goodness of God, that has so ordered it, that a saving evidence of the truth of the gospel is such, as is attainable by persons of mean capacities and advantages, as well as those that are of the greatest parts and learning. If the evidence of the gospel depended only on history, and such reasonings as learned men only are capable of, it would be above the reach of far the greatest part of mankind. But persons with an ordinary degree of knowledge, are capable, without a long and subtile train of reasoning, to see the divine excellency of the things of religion: they are capable of being taught by the Spirit of God, as well as learned men. The evidence that is this way obtained, is vastly better and more satisfying, than all that can be obtained by the arguings of those that are most learned, and greatest masters of reason. And babes are as capable of knowing these things, as the wise and prudent; and they are often hid from these, when they are revealed to those. 1 Cor. i. 26, 27. "For ye see your calling, brethren, how that not many wise men, after the flesh, not many mighty, not many noble, are called. But God hath chosen the foolish things of the world."—

Secondly. This doctrine may well put us upon examining ourselves, whether we have ever had this divine light let into our souls. If there be such a thing, doubtless it is of great importance whether we have thus been taught by the Spirit of God; whether the light of the glorious gospel of Christ, who is the image of God, hath shined unto us, giving us the light of the knowledge of the glory of God in the face of Jesus Christ; whether we have seen the Son, and believed on him, or have that faith of gospel doctrines which arises from a spiritual sight of Christ.

Thirdly. All may hence be exhorted, earnestly to seek this spiritual light. To influence and move to it, the following things may be considered.

1. This is the most excellent and divine wisdom that any creature is capable of. It is more excellent than any human learning; it is far more excellent than all the knowledge of the greatest philosophers or statesmen. Yea, the least glimpse of the glory of God in the face of Christ doth more exalt and ennoble the soul, than all the knowledge of those that have the greatest speculative understanding in divinity without grace. This knowledge has the most noble object that can be, *viz.* the divine glory and excellency of God and Christ. The knowledge of these objects is that wherein consists the most excellent knowledge of the angels, yea, of God himself.

2. This knowledge is that which is above all others sweet and joyful. Men have a great deal of pleasure in human knowledge, in studies of natural things; but this is nothing to that joy which arises from this divine light shining into the soul. This light gives a view of those things that are immensely the most exquisitely beautiful, and capable of delighting the eye of the understanding. This spiritual light is the dawning of the light of glory in the heart. There is nothing so powerful as this to support persons in affliction,

and to give the mind peace and brightness in this stormy and dark world.

3. This light is such as effectually influences the inclination, and changes the nature of the soul. It assimilates our nature to the divine nature, and changes the soul into an image of the same glory that is beheld. 2 Cor. iii. 18. "But we all with open face, beholding as in a glass the glory of the Lord, are changed into the same image, from glory to glory, even as by the Spirit of the Lord." This knowledge will wean from the world, and raise the inclination to heavenly things. It will turn the heart to God as the fountain of good, and to choose him for the only portion. This light, and this only, will bring the soul to a saving close with Christ. It conforms the heart to the gospel, mortifies its enmity and opposition against the scheme of salvation therein revealed; it causes the heart to embrace the joyful tidings, and entirely to adhere to, and acquiesce in, the revelation of Christ as our Saviour; it causes the whole soul to accord and symphonize with it, admitting it with entire credit and respect, cleaving to it with full inclination and affection; and it effectually disposes the soul to give up itself entirely to Christ.

4. This light, and this only, has its fruit in an universal holiness of life. No merely notional or speculative understanding of the doctrines of religion will ever bring to this. But this light, as it reaches the bottom of the heart, and changes the nature, so it will effectually dispose to an universal obedience. It shows God as worthy to be obeyed and served. It draws forth the heart in a sincere love to God, which is the only principle of a true, gracious, and universal obedience: and it convinces of the reality of those glorious rewards that God has promised to them that obey him.

THE CHRISTIAN PILGRIM

Another example of the typical Sunday sermon to which the parish listened. Bunyan's *The Pilgrim's Progress* had been widely read in America and the preacher's use of the image of life as a journey toward heaven would have gained effectiveness for the sermon for those who knew Christian's story. Jonathan Edwards was quite as literal as Bunyan when he painted the joys of heaven for those who were among the blessed. It was a frequent subject with him. The text is from *The Works of President Edwards,* edited by S. B. Dwight, Vol. VII, pp. 135–46.

HEBREWS xi. 13, 14.

And confessed that they were strangers and pilgrims on the earth. For they that say such things declare plainly that they seek a country.

THE Apostle is here exhibiting the excellency of faith, by its glorious effects, and happy issue in the saints of the Old Testament. Having enumerated examples of Abel, Enoch and Noah, of Abraham and Sarah, of Isaac and Jacob, he relates that all "these died in faith, not having received the promises, but having seen them afar off, were persuaded of them and embraced them, and confessed that they were strangers and pilgrims on earth." In these words the apostle seems more immediately to refer to Abraham and Sarah, and their kindred who came with them from Haran, and from

Ur of the Chaldees, as appears by the 15th verse, where he says, "and truly if they had been mindful of that country whence they came out, they might have had opportunity to have returned."

Two things may be here observed.

1. The confession which they made concerning themselves to it, that they were strangers and pilgrims on the earth; of this we have a particular account concerning Abraham, "I am a stranger and a sojourner with you." And it seems to have been a general sense of the patriarchs, by what Jacob says to Pharaoh. "And Jacob said to Pharaoh, the days of the years of my pilgrimage are an hundred and thirty years: few and evil have the days of the years of my life been, and have not attained to the days of the years of the life of my fathers in the days of their pilgrimage. I am a stranger and a sojourner with thee, as all my fathers were."

2. The inference that the apostle draws from hence, viz. *that they sought another country as their home.* "For they that say such things declare plainly that they seek a country." In confessing that they were strangers, they plainly declared that this is not their country, that this is not the place where they are at home. And in confessing themselves to be pilgrims, they declared plainly that this is not their settled abode; but that they have respect to some other country, which they seek and to which they are travelling.

SECTION I.

That this life ought to be so spent by us, as to be only a journey, or pilgrimage, towards heaven.

HERE I would observe,

1. That we ought not to rest in the world and its enjoyments, but should desire heaven. We should *seek first the kingdom of God.* We ought above all things to desire a heavenly happiness; to be with God; and dwell with Jesus Christ. Though surrounded with outward enjoyments, and

settled in families with desirable friends and relations; though we have companions whose society is delightful, and children in whom we see many promising qualifications; though we live by good neighbours, and are generally beloved where known; yet we ought not to take our rest in these things as our portion. We should be so far from resting in them, that we should desire to leave them all, in God's due time. We ought to possess, enjoy, and use them, with no other view but readily to quit them, whenever we are called to it, and to change them willingly and cheerfully for heaven.

A traveller is not wont to rest in what he meets with, however comfortable and pleasing on the road. If he passes through pleasant places, flowery meadows, or shady groves; he does not take up his content in these things, but only takes a transient view of them as he goes along. He is not enticed by fine appearances to put off the thought of proceeding. No, but his journey's end is in his mind. If he meets with comfortable accommodations at an inn; he entertains no thoughts of settling there. He considers that these things are not his own, that he is but a stranger, and when he has refreshed himself, or tarried for a night, he is for going forward. And it is pleasant to him to think that so much of the way is gone.

So should we desire heaven more than the comforts and enjoyments of this life. The apostle mentions it as an encouraging, comfortable consideration to Christians, that they draw nearer their happiness. "Now is our salvation nearer than when we believed."—Our hearts ought to be loose to these things, as that of a man on a journey; that we may as cheerfully part with them whenever God calls. "But this I say, brethren, the time is short: it remaineth, that both they that have wives, be as though they had none; and they that weep, as though they wept not; and they that rejoice, as though they rejoiced not; and they that buy, as though they possessed not; and they that use this world, as not abusing it; for the fashion of this world passeth away."—These things, as only lent to us for a little while, to serve a present turn; but we should set our *hearts* on heaven, as our inheritance for ever.

2. We ought to seek heaven, by travelling in the way that leads thither. This is a way of holiness. We should choose and desire to travel thither in this way and in no other; and part

with all those carnal appetites, which as weights will tend to hinder us. "Let us lay aside every weight, and the sin which doth so easily beset us, and let us run with patience the race that is set before us." However pleasant the gratification of any appetite may be, we must lay it aside, if it be any hindrance, or a stumbling-block in the way to heaven.

We should travel on in the way of obedience to all God's commands, even the difficult as well as the easy; denying all our sinful inclinations and interests. The way to heaven is ascending; we must be content to travel up hill, though it be hard and tiresome, and contrary to the natural bias of our flesh. We should follow Christ; the path he travelled was the right way to heaven. We should take up our cross and follow him, in meekness and lowliness of heart, obedience and charity, diligence to do good, and patience under afflictions. The way to heaven is a heavenly life; an imitation of those who are in heaven, in their holy enjoyments, loving, adoring, serving, and praising God and the Lamb. Even if we *could* go to heaven with the gratification of our lusts, we should prefer a way of holiness and conformity to the spiritual self-denying rules of the gospel.

3. We should travel on in this way in a laborious manner. Long journeys are attended with toil and fatigue; especially if through a wilderness. Persons, in such a case, expect no other than to suffer hardships and weariness. So we should travel in this way of holiness, improving our time and strength, to surmount the difficulties and obstacles that are in the way. The land we have to travel through, is a wilderness; there are many mountains, rocks, and rough places that we must go over, and, therefore, there is a necessity that we should lay out our strength.

4. Our whole lives ought to be spent in travelling this road. We ought to begin *early*. This should be the *first* concern, when persons become capable of acting. When they first set out in the *world*, they should set out on *this* journey. And we ought to travel on with *assiduity*. It ought to be the work of every day. We should often think of our journey's end; and make it our daily work to travel on in the way that leads to it. He who is on a journey, is often thinking of the destined place; and it is his daily care and business to get along; and to improve his time to get towards his journey's end. Thus should heaven be continually in our

thoughts; and the immediate entrance or passage to it, *viz.*
death, should be present with us. We ought to *persevere*
in this way as long as we live.

"Let us run with patience the race that is set before us."
Though the road be difficult, and toilsome, we must hold
out with patience, and be content to endure hardships.
Though the journey be long, yet we must not stop short;
but hold on till we arrive at the place we seek. Nor should
we be discouraged with the length and difficulties of the way,
as the children of Israel were, and be for turning back
again. All our thought, and design, should be to press forward till we arrive.

5. We ought to be continually growing in holiness; and,
in that respect, coming nearer and nearer to heaven. We
should be endeavouring to come nearer to heaven, in being
more heavenly; becoming more and more like the inhabitants of heaven, in respect of holiness, and conformity to
God; the knowledge of God and Christ; in clear views of
the glory of God, the beauty of Christ, and the excellency
of divine things, as we come nearer to the beatific vision.
We should labour to be continually growing in divine love—
that this may be an increasing flame in our hearts, till they
ascend wholly in this flame—in obedience and an heavenly
conversation; that we may do the will of God on earth, as
the angels do in heaven: in comfort and spiritual joy; in sensible communion with God and Jesus Christ. Our path should
be as "the shining light, that shines more and more to the
perfect day." We ought to be hungering and thirsting after
righteousness; after an increase in righteousness. "As new-
born babes desire the sincere milk of the word, that ye
may grow thereby." The perfection of heaven should be our
mark. "This one thing I do, forgetting those things which
are behind, and reaching forth unto those things that are
before, I press toward the mark, for the prize of the high
calling of God in Christ Jesus."

6. All other concerns of life, ought to be entirely subordinate to this. When a man is on a journey, all the steps he
takes are subordinated to the aim of getting to his journey's
end. And, if he carries money or provisions with him, it is to
supply him in his journey. So we ought wholly to subordinate
all our other business, and all our temporal enjoyments, to
this affair of travelling to heaven. When any thing we have,

becomes a clog and hindrance to us, we should quit it immediately. The use of our worldly enjoyments and possessions,
should be with such a view, and in such a manner, as to
further us in our way heaven-ward. Thus we should eat, and
drink, and clothe ourselves, and improve the conversation
and enjoyment of friends. And, whatever business we are
setting about, whatever design we are engaging in, we should
inquire with ourselves, whether this business, or undertaking,
will forward us in our way to heaven? And, if not, we should
quit our design.

SECTION II.

Why the Christian's life is a journey or pilgrimage?

1. THIS world is not our abiding place. Our continuance
here is but very short. Man's days on the earth, are as a
shadow. It was never designed by God that this world should
be our home. Neither did God give us these temporal accommodations for that end. If God has given us ample estates,
and children, or other pleasant friends, it is with no such
design, that we should be furnished here, as for a settled
abode; but with a design that we should use them for the present, and then leave them in a very little time. When we are
called to any secular business, or charged with the care of a
family, if we improve our lives to any other purpose, than as
a journey toward heaven, all our labour will be lost. If we
spend our lives in the pursuit of a temporal happiness; as
riches, or sensual pleasures; credit and esteem from men;
delight in our children, and the prospect of seeing them well
brought up, and well settled, &c.—All these things will be
of little significancy to us. Death will blow up all our hopes,
and will put an end to these enjoyments. "The places that
have known us, will know us no more:" and "the eye that
has seen us, shall see us no more." We must be taken away
for ever from all these things; and it is uncertain when: it
may be soon after we are put into the possession of them.

And then, where will be all our worldly employments and enjoyments, when we are laid in the silent grave! "So man lieth down, and riseth not again, till the heavens be no more."

2. The future world was designed to be our settled and everlasting abode. There it was intended that we should be fixed; and there alone is a lasting habitation, and a lasting inheritance. The present state is short and transitory; but our state in the other world, is everlasting. And as we are there at first, so we must be without change. Our state in the future world, therefore, being eternal, is of so much greater importance than our state here, that all our concerns in this world should be wholly subordinated to it.

3. Heaven is that place alone where our highest end, and highest good is to be obtained. God hath made us for himself. "Of him, and through him, and to him are all things." Therefore, then do we attain to our highest end, when we are brought to God: but that is by being brought to heaven; for that is God's throne, the place of his special presence. There is but a very imperfect union with God to be had in this world, a very imperfect knowledge of him in the midst of much darkness: a very imperfect conformity to God, mingled with abundance of estrangement. Here we can serve and glorify God, but in a very imperfect manner; our service being mingled with sin, which dishonours God.—But when we get to heaven, (if ever that be,) we shall be brought to a perfect union with God, and have more clear views of him. There we shall be fully conformed to God, without any remaining sin: for "we shall see him as he is." There we shall serve God perfectly; and glorify him in an exalted manner, even to the utmost of the powers and capacity of our nature. Then we shall perfectly give up ourselves to God: our hearts will be pure and holy offerings, presented in a flame of divine love.

God is the highest good of the reasonable creature; and the enjoyment of him is the only happiness with which our souls can be satisfied.—To go to heaven fully to enjoy God, is *infinitely* better than the most pleasant accommodations here. Fathers and mothers, husbands, wives, or children, or the company of earthly friends, are but shadows; but the enjoyment of God is the substance. These are but scattered beams; but God is the sun. These are but streams; but God is the fountain. These are but drops; but God is the ocean. —Therefore it becomes us to spend this life only as a journey towards heaven, as it becomes us to make the seeking of our highest end and proper good, the whole work of our lives; to which we should subordinate all other concerns of life. Why should we labour for, or set our hearts on any thing else, but that which is our proper end, and true happiness?

4. Our present state, and all that belongs to it, is designed by him that made all things, to be wholly in order to another world.—This world was made for a place of preparation for another. Man's mortal life was given him, that he might be prepared for his fixed state. And all that God has here given us, is given to this purpose. The sun shines, and the rain falls upon us; and the earth yields her increase to us for this end. Civil, ecclesiastical, and family affairs, and all our personal concerns, are designed and ordered in subordination to a future world, by the maker and disposer of all things. To this therefore they ought to be subordinated by us.

SECTION III.

Instruction afforded by the consideration, that life is a journey, or pilgrimage, towards heaven.

1. THIS doctrine may teach us moderation in our mourning for the loss of such dear friends, who, while they lived, improved their lives to right purposes. If they lived a holy life, then their lives were a journey towards heaven. And why should we be immoderate in mourning, when they are got to their journey's end? Death, though it appears to us with a frightful aspect, is to them a great blessing. Their end is happy, and better than their beginning. *"The day of their death, is better then the day of their birth."* While they lived, they desired heaven, and chose it above this world, or any of its enjoyments. For this they earnestly longed, and why should we grieve that they have obtained it?—Now

they have got to their Father's house. They find more comfort a thousand times, now they are got home, than they did in their journey. In this world they underwent much labour and toil; it was a wilderness they passed through. There were many difficulties in the way; mountains and rough places. It was laborious and fatiguing to travel the road; and they had many wearisome days and nights: but now they have got to their everlasting rest. "And I heard a voice from heaven, saying unto me, Write, blessed are the dead which die in the Lord from henceforth: yea, saith the Spirit, that they may rest from their labours; and their works do follow them." They look back upon the difficulties, and sorrows, and dangers of life, rejoicing that they have surmounted them all.

We are ready to look upon death as their calamity, and to mourn, that those who were so dear to us, should be in the dark grave; that they are there transformed to corruption and worms; taken away from their dear children and enjoyments, &c. as though they were in awful circumstances. But this is owing to our infirmity; they are in a happy condition, inconceivably blessed. They do not mourn, but rejoice with exceeding joy: their mouths are filled with joyful songs, and they drink at rivers of pleasure. They find no mixture of grief that they have changed their earthly enjoyments, and the company of mortals, for heaven. Their life here, though in the best circumstances, was attended with much that was adverse and afflictive: but now there is an end to all adversity. "They shall hunger no more, nor thirst any more; neither shall the sun light on them, nor any heat. For the Lamb which is in the midst of the throne, shall feed them and shall lead them unto living fountains of waters: and God shall wipe away all tears from their eyes."

It is true, we shall see them no more in this world, yet we ought to consider that we are travelling towards the same place; and why should we break our hearts that they have got there before us? We are following after them, and hope, as soon as we get to our journey's end, to be with them again, in better circumstances. A degree of mourning for near relations when departed is not inconsistent with Christianity, but very agreeable to it; for as long as we are flesh and blood, we have animal propensities and affections. But we have just reason that our mourning should be mingled with joy. "But I would not have you to be ignorant, brethren, concerning them that are asleep, that ye sorrow not, even as others that have no hope:" (*i. e.*) that they should not sorrow as the Heathen, who had no knowledge of a future happiness. This appears by the following verse; "*for if we believe that Jesus died and rose again, even so them also which sleep in Jesus, will God bring with him.*"

2. If our lives ought to be only a journey towards heaven; how ill do they improve their lives, that spend them in travelling towards hell?—Some men spend their whole lives, from their infancy to their dying day, in going down the broad way to destruction. They not only draw nearer to hell as to time, but they every day grow more ripe for destruction; they are more assimilated to the inhabitants of the infernal world. While others press forward in the straight and narrow way to life, and laboriously travel up the hill toward Zion, against the inclinations and tendency of the flesh; these run with a swift career down to eternal death. This is the employment of every day, with all wicked men; and the whole day is spent in it. As soon as ever they awake in the morning, they set out anew in the way to hell, and spend every waking moment in it. They begin in early days. "The wicked are estranged from the womb, they go astray as soon as they are born, speaking lies." They hold on it with perseverance. Many of them who live to be old, are never weary in it; though they live to be an hundred years old, they will not cease travelling in the way to hell, till they arrive there. And all the concerns of life are subordinated to this employment. A wicked man is a servant of sin; his powers and faculties are employed in the service of sin; and in fitness for hell. And all his possessions are so used by him as to be subservient to the same purpose. Men spend their time in treasuring up wrath against the day of wrath. Thus do all unclean persons, who live in lascivious practices in secret; all malicious persons; all profane persons, that neglect the duties of religion. Thus do all unjust persons; and those who are fraudulent and oppressive in their dealings. Thus do all backbiters and revilers; all covetous persons, that set their hearts chiefly on the riches of this world. Thus do tavern-haunters, and frequenters of evil company; and many other kinds that might be mentioned. Thus the bulk of mankind are hastening onward in the broad way to destruction; which

is, as it were, filled up with the multitude that are going in it with one accord. And they are every day going to hell out of this broad way by thousands. Multitudes are continually flowing down into the great lake of fire and brimstone, as some mighty river constantly disembogues its water into the ocean.

3. Hence when persons are converted they do but begin their work, and set out in the way they have to go.—They never till then do any thing at that work in which their whole lives ought to be spent. Persons before conversion never take a step that way. Then does a man first set out on his journey, when he is brought home to Christ; and so far is he from having done his work, that his care and labour in his Christian work and business, is then but begun, in which he must spend the remaining part of his life.

Those persons do ill, who when they are converted, and have obtained a hope of their being in a good condition, do not strive as earnestly as they did before, while they were under awakenings. They ought, henceforward, as long as they live, to be as earnest and laborious, as watchful and careful as ever; yea, they should increase more and more. It is no just excuse, that now they have obtained conversion. Should not we be as diligent that we may serve and glorify God, as that we ourselves may be happy? And if we have obtained grace, yet we ought to strive as much that we may obtain the other degrees that are before, as we did to obtain that small degree that is behind. The apostle tells us, that he forgot what was behind, and reached forth towards what was before.

Yea, those who are converted, have now a further reason to strive for grace; for they have seen something of its excellency. A man who has once tasted the blessings of Canaan, has more reason to press towards it than he had before. And they who are converted, should strive to "make their calling and election sure." All those who are converted are not sure of it; and those who are sure, do not know that they shall be always so; and still seeking and serving God with the utmost diligence, is the way to have assurance, and to have it maintained.

SECTION IV.

An exhortation, so to spend the present life, that it may only be a journey towards heaven.

LABOUR to obtain such a disposition of mind that you may choose heaven for your inheritance and home; and may earnestly long for it, and be willing to change this world, and all its enjoyments, for heaven. Labour to have your heart taken up so much about heaven, and heavenly enjoyments, as that you may rejoice when God calls you to leave your best earthly friends and comforts for heaven, there to enjoy God and Christ.

Be persuaded to travel in the way that leads to heaven; *viz.* in holiness, self-denial, mortification, obedience to all the commands of God, following Christ's example; in a way of a heavenly life, or imitation of the saints and angels in heaven. Let it be your daily work, from morning till night, and hold out in it to the end; let nothing stop or discourage you, or turn you aside from this road. And let all other concerns be subordinated to this. Consider the reasons that have been mentioned why you should thus spend your life; that this world is not your abiding place, that the future world is to be your everlasting abode; and that the enjoyments and concerns of this world, are given entirely in order to another. And consider further for motive,

1. How worthy is heaven that your life should be wholly spent as a journey towards it.—To what better purpose can you spend your life, whether you respect your duty or your interest? What better end can you propose to your journey, than to obtain heaven? You are placed in this world, with a choice given you, that you may travel which way you please; and one way leads to heaven. Now can you direct your course better than this way? All men have some aim or other in living. Some mainly seek worldly things; they spend their days in such pursuits. But is not heaven, where is fullness of

joy for ever, much more worthy to be sought by you? How can you better employ your strength, use your means, and spend your days, than in travelling the road that leads to the everlasting enjoyment of God; to his glorious presence; to the new Jerusalem; to the heavenly mount Zion; where all your desires will be filled, and no danger of ever losing your happiness?—No man is at home in this world, whether he choose heaven or not; here he is but a transient person. Where can you choose your home better than in heaven?

2. This is the way to have death comfortable to us.—To spend our lives so as to be only a journeying towards heaven, is the way to be free from bondage, and to have the prospect and forethought of death comfortable. Does the traveller think of his journey's end with fear and terror? Is it terrible to him to think that he has almost got to his journey's end? Were the children of Israel sorry, after forty years' travel in the wilderness, when they had almost got to Canaan? This is the way to be able to part with the world without grief. Does it grieve the traveller, when he has got home, to quit his staff and load of provisions that he had to sustain him by the way?

3. No more of your life will be pleasant to think of when you come to die, than has been spent after this manner.—If you have spent none of your life this way, your whole life will be terrible to you to think of, unless you die under some great delusion. You will see then, that all of your life that has been spent otherwise, is lost. You will then see the vanity of all other aims that you may have proposed to yourself. The thought of what you here possessed and enjoyed, will not be pleasant to you, unless you can think also that you have subordinated them to this purpose.

4. Consider that those who are willing thus to spend their lives as a journey towards heaven, may have heaven.—Heaven, however high and glorious, is attainable for such poor worthless creatures as we are. We may attain that glorious region which is the habitation of angels; yea, the dwelling-place of the Son of God; and where is the glorious presence of the great Jehovah. And we may have it freely; without money and without price; if we are but willing to travel the road that leads to it, and bend our course that way as long as we live; we may and shall have heaven for our eternal resting place.

5. Let it be considered, that if our lives be not a journey towards heaven, they will be a journey to hell. All mankind, after they have been here a short while, go to either of the two great receptacles of all that depart out of this world; the one is *heaven*, whither a small number, in comparison, travel; and the other is *hell,* whither the bulk of mankind throng. And one or the other of these must be the issue of our course in this world.

I shall conclude by giving a few *directions:*

1. Labour to get a sense of the vanity of this world; on account of the little satisfaction that is to be enjoyed here: its short continuance, and unserviceableness when we most stand in need of help, *viz.* on a death-bed.—All men, that live any considerable time in the world, might see enough to convince them of its vanity, if they would but consider.—Be persuaded therefore to exercise consideration, when you see and hear, from time to time, of the death of others. Labour to turn your thoughts this way. See the vanity of the world in such a glass.

2. Labour to be much acquainted with heaven.—If you are not acquainted with it, you will not be likely to spend your life as a journey thither. You will not be sensible of its worth, nor will you long for it. Unless you are much conversant in your mind with a better good, it will be exceeding difficult to you to have your hearts loose from these things, and to use them only in subordination to something else, and be ready to part with them for the sake of that better good.—Labour therefore to obtain a realizing sense of a heavenly world, to get a firm belief of its reality, and to be very much conversant with it in your thoughts.

3. Seek heaven only by Jesus Christ.—Christ tells us that he is the way, and the truth, and the life. He tells that he is the door of the sheep. "I am the door, by me if any man enter in, he shall be saved; and go in and out and find pasture." If we therefore would improve our lives as a journey towards heaven, we must seek it by him, and not by our own righteousness; as expecting to obtain it only for his sake, looking to him, having our dependence on him, who has procured it for us by his merit. And expect strength to walk in holiness, the way that leads to heaven, only from him.

4. Let Christians help one another in going this journey. —There are many ways whereby Christians might greatly

forward one another in their way to heaven, as by religious conference, &c. Therefore let them be exhorted to go this journey as it were in company, conversing together, and assisting one another. Company is very desirable in a journey, but in none so much as this.—Let them go united, and not fall out by the way, which would be to hinder one another; but use all means they can to help each other up the hill.— This would ensure a more successful travelling, and a more joyful meeting at their Father's house in glory.

SINNERS IN THE HANDS OF AN ANGRY GOD

Preached on July 8, 1741, at Enfield, Connecticut, at the height of revival excitement. Its effectiveness owed much to the frenzied moment. Jonathan Edwards was a stranger to this congregation, a fact that added to the effectiveness of his sermon. The power of the familiar doctrine he chose to preach upon lay in part in his ruthless concentration on a single metaphor, *fire*, and on the sense of immediacy he gave to the judgment itself, pressing this past the point of endurance for some in the congregation. "A most Terrible sermon, wch should have had a word of Gospell at ye end of it, tho I think tis all true," Isaac Watts wrote in his own copy of it. Jonathan Edwards often added such a word, but not on this day. The sermon was published immediately, and since then has been printed innumerable times. The text is from *The Works of President Edwards,* edited by S. B. Dwight, Vol. VII, pp. 163–77.

DEUT. xxxii. 35.

—Their foot shall slide in due time.—

IN this verse is threatened the vengeance of God on the wicked unbelieving Israelites, who were God's visible people, and who lived under the means of grace; but who, notwithstanding all God's wonderful works towards them, remained (as ver. 28.) void of counsel, having no understanding in them. Under all the cultivations of heaven, they brought forth bitter and poisonous fruit; as in the two verses next preceding the text.—The expression I have chosen for my text, *Their foot shall slide in due time,* seems to imply the following things, relating to the punishment and destruction to which these wicked Israelites were exposed.

1. That they were always exposed to *destruction;* as one that stands or walks in slippery places is always exposed to fall. This is implied in the manner of their destruction coming upon them, being represented by their foot sliding. The same is expressed, Psalm lxxiii. 18. "Surely thou didst set them in slippery places; thou castedst them down into destruction."

2. It implies, that they were always exposed to sudden unexpected destruction. As he that walks in slippery places is every moment liable to fall, he cannot foresee one moment whether he shall stand or fall the next; and when he does fall, he falls at once without warning: Which is also expressed in Psalm lxxiii. 18, 19. "Surely thou didst set them in slippery places; thou castedst them down into destruction: How are they brought into desolation as in a moment!"

3. Another thing implied is, that they are liable to fall *of themselves,* without being thrown down by the hand of another; as he that stands or walks on slippery ground needs nothing but his own weight to throw him down.

4. That the reason why they are not fallen already, and do not fall now, is only that God's appointed time is not come. For it is said, that when that due time, or appointed time comes, *their foot shall slide.* Then they shall be left to fall, as they are inclined by their own weight. God will not hold them up in these slippery places any longer, but will let them go; and then, at that very instant, they shall fall into destruction; as he that stands on such slippery declining ground, on the edge of a pit, he cannot stand alone, when he is let go he immediately falls and is lost.

The observation from the words that I would now insist upon is this.—"There is nothing that keeps wicked men at any one moment out of hell, but the mere pleasure of God" —By the *mere* pleasure of God, I mean his *sovereign* pleasure, his arbitrary will, restrained by no obligation, hindered by no manner of difficulty, any more than if nothing else but God's mere will had in the least degree, or in any respect whatsoever, any hand in the preservation of wicked men one moment.—The truth of this observation may appear by the following considerations.

1. There is no want of *power* in God to cast wicked men into hell at any moment. Men's hands cannot be strong when God rises up. The strongest have no power to resist him, nor can any deliver out of his hands.—He is not only able to cast wicked men into hell, but he can most easily do it. Sometimes an earthly prince meets with a great deal of difficulty to subdue a rebel, who has found means to fortify himself, and has made himself strong by the numbers of his followers. But it is not so with God. There is no fortress that is any defence from the power of God. Though hand join in hand, and vast multitudes of God's enemies combine and associate themselves, they are easily broken in pieces. They are as great heaps of light chaff before the whirlwind; or large quantities of dry stubble before devouring flames. We find it easy to tread on and crush a worm that we see crawling on the earth; so it is easy for us to cut or singe a slender thread that any thing hangs by: thus easy is it for God, when he pleases, to cast his enemies down to hell. What are we, that we should think to stand before him, at whose rebuke the earth trembles, and before whom the rocks are thrown down?

2. They *deserve* to be cast into hell; so that divine justice never stands in the way, it makes no objection against God's using his power at any moment to destroy them. Yea, on the contrary, justice calls aloud for an infinite punishment of their sins. Divine justice says of the tree that brings forth such grapes of Sodom, "Cut it down, why cumbereth it the ground?" Luke xiii. 7. The sword of divine justice is every moment brandished over their heads, and it is nothing but the hand of arbitrary mercy, and God's mere will, that holds it back.

3. They are already under a sentence of *condemnation* to hell. They do not only justly deserve to be cast down thither, but the sentence of the law of God, that eternal and immutable rule of righteousness that God has fixed between him and mankind, is gone out against them, and stands against them; so that they are bound over already to hell. John iii. 18. "He that believeth not is condemned already." So that every unconverted man properly belongs to hell; that is his place; from thence he is, John viii. 23. "Ye are from beneath:"

And thither he is bound; it is the place that justice, and God's word, and the sentence of his unchangeable law assign to him.

4. They are now the objects of that very same *anger* and wrath of God, that is expressed in the torments of hell. And the reason why they do not go down to hell at each moment, is not because God, in whose power they are, is not then very angry with them; as he is with many miserable creatures now tormented in hell, who there feel and bear the fierceness of his wrath. Yea, God is a great deal more angry with great numbers that are now on earth: yea, doubtless, with many that are now in this congregation, who it may be are at ease, than he is with many of those who are now in the flames of hell.

So that it is not because God is unmindful of their wickedness, and does not resent it, that he does not let loose his hand and cut them off. God is not altogether such an one as themselves, though they may imagine him to be so. The wrath of God burns against them, their damnation does not slumber; the pit is prepared, the fire is made ready, the furnace is now hot, ready to receive them; the flames do now rage and glow. The glittering sword is whet, and held over them, and the pit hath opened its mouth under them.

5. The *devil* stands ready to fall upon them, and seize them as his own, at what moment God shall permit him. They belong to him; he has their souls in his possession, and under his dominion. The scripture represents them as his goods, Luke xi. 12. The devils watch them; they are ever by them at their right hand; they stand waiting for them, like greedy hungry lions that see their prey, and expect to have it, but are for the present kept back. If God should withdraw his hand, by which they are restrained, they would in one moment fly upon their poor souls. The old serpent is gaping for them; hell opens its mouth wide to receive them; and if God should permit it, they would be hastily swallowed up and lost.

6. There are in the souls of wicked men those hellish *principles* reigning, that would presently kindle and flame out into hell fire, if it were not for God's restraints. There is laid in the very nature of carnal men, a foundation for the torments of hell. There are those corrupt principles, in reigning power in them, and in full possession of them, that are

seeds of hell fire. These principles are active and powerful, exceeding violent in their nature, and if it were not for the restraining hand of God upon them, they would soon break out, they would flame out after the same manner as the same corruptions, the same enmity does in the hearts of damned souls, and would beget the same torments as they do in them. The souls of the wicked are in scripture compared to the troubled sea, Isa. lvii. 20. For the present, God restrains their wickedness by his mighty power, as he does the raging waves of the troubled sea, saying, "Hitherto shalt thou come, but no further;" but if God should withdraw that restraining power, it would soon carry all before it. Sin is the ruin and misery of the soul; it is destructive in its nature; and if God should leave it without restraint, there would need nothing else to make the soul perfectly miserable. The corruption of the heart of man is immoderate and boundless in its fury; and while wicked men live here, it is like fire pent up by God's restraints, whereas if it were let loose, it would set on fire the course of nature; and as the heart is now a sink of sin, so if sin was not restrained, it would immediately turn the soul into a fiery oven, or a furnace of fire and brimstone.

7. It is no security to wicked men for one moment, that there are no visible means of death at hand. It is no security to a natural man, that he is now in health, and that he does not see which way he should now immediately go out of the world by any accident, and that there is no visible danger in any respect in his circumstances. The manifold and continual experience of the world in all ages, shows this is no evidence, that a man is not on the very brink of eternity, and that the next step will not be into another world. The unseen, unthought-of ways and means of persons going suddenly out of the world are innumerable and inconceivable. Unconverted men walk over the pit of hell on a rotten covering, and there are innumerable places in this covering so weak that they will not bear their weight, and these places are not seen. The arrows of death fly unseen at noonday; the sharpest sight cannot discern them. God has so many different unsearchable ways of taking wicked men out of the world and sending them to hell, that there is nothing to make it appear, that God had need to be at the expence of a miracle, or go out of the ordinary course of his providence,

to destroy any wicked man, at any moment. All the means that there are of sinners going out of the world, are so in God's hands, and so universally and absolutely subject to his power and determination, that it does not depend at all the less on the mere will of God, whether sinners shall at any moment go to hell, than if means were never made use of, or at all concerned in the case.

8. Natural men's prudence and care to preserve their own lives, or the care of others to preserve them, do not secure them a moment. To this, divine providence and universal experience do also bear testimony. There is this clear evidence that men's own wisdom is no security to them from death; that if it were otherwise we should see some difference between the wise and politic men of the world, and others, with regard to their liableness to early and unexpected death: but how is it in fact? Eccles. ii. 16. "How dieth the wise man? even as the fool."

9. All wicked men's pains and *contrivance* which they use to escape hell, while they continue to reject Christ, and so remain wicked men, do not secure them from hell one moment. Almost every natural man that hears of hell, flatters himself that he shall escape it; he depends upon himself for his own security; he flatters himself in what he has done, in what he is now doing, or what he intends to do. Every one lays out matters in his own mind how he shall avoid damnation, and flatters himself that he contrives well for himself, and that his schemes will not fail. They hear indeed that there are but few saved, and that the greater part of men that have died heretofore are gone to hell; but each one imagines that he lays out matters better for his own escape than others have done. He does not intend to come to that place of torment; he says within himself, that he intends to take effectual care, and to order matters so for himself as not to fail.

But the foolish children of men miserably delude themselves in their own schemes, and in confidence in their own strength and wisdom; they trust to nothing but a shadow. The greater part of those who heretofore have lived under the same means of grace, and are now dead, are undoubtedly gone to hell; and it was not because they were not as wise as those who are now alive: it is not because they did not lay out matters as well for themselves to secure their own escape. If we could speak with them, and inquire of them, one by one, whether they expected, when alive, and when they used to hear about hell, ever to be the subjects of that misery: we doubtless, should hear one and another reply, "No, I never intended to come here: I had laid out matters otherwise in my mind; I thought I should contrive well for myself: I thought my scheme good. I intended to take effectual care; but it came upon me unexpected; I did not look for it at that time, and in that manner; it came as a thief: Death outwitted me: God's wrath was too quick for me. Oh, my cursed foolishness! I was flattering myself, and pleasing myself with vain dreams of what I would do hereafter; and when I was saying, Peace and safety, then suddenly destruction came upon me."

10. God has laid himself under *no obligation,* by any promise to keep any natural man out of hell one moment. God certainly has made no promises either of eternal life, or of any deliverance or preservation from eternal death, but what are contained in the convenant of grace, the promises that are given in Christ, in whom all the promises are yea and amen. But surely they have no interest in the promises of the covenant of grace who are not the children of the convenant, who do not believe in any of the promises, and have no interest in the Mediator of the covenant.

So that, whatever some have imagined and pretended about promises made to natural men's earnest seeking and knocking, it is plain and manifest, that whatever pains a natural man takes in religion, whatever prayers he makes, till he believes in Christ, God is under no manner of obligation to keep him a moment from eternal destruction.

So that, thus it is that natural men are held in the hand of God, over the pit of hell; they have deserved the fiery pit, and are already sentenced to it; and God is dreadfully provoked, his anger is as great towards them as to those that are actually suffering the executions of the fierceness of his wrath in hell, and they have done nothing in the least to appease or abate that anger, neither is God in the least bound by any promise to hold them up one moment; the devil is waiting for them, hell is gaping for them, the flames gather and flash about them, and would fain lay hold on them, and swallow them up; the fire bent up in their own hearts is struggling to break out: and they have no interest in any Mediator, there are no means within reach that can be any security to them. In short, they have no refuge, nothing to take hold of; all that preserves them every moment is the mere arbitrary will, and uncovenanted, unobliged forbearance of an incensed God.

APPLICATION.

The use of this awful subject may be for awakening unconverted persons in this congregation. This that you have heard is the case of every one of you that are out of Christ.—That world of misery, that lake of burning brimstone, is extended abroad under you. There is the dreadful pit of the glowing flames of the wrath of God; there is hell's wide gaping mouth open; and you have nothing to stand upon, nor any thing to take hold of; there is nothing between you and hell but the air; it is only the power and mere pleasure of God that holds you up.

You probably are not sensible of this; you find you are kept out of hell, but do not see the hand of God in it; but look at other things, as the good state of your bodily constitution, your care of your own life, and the means you use for your own preservation. But indeed these things are nothing; if God should withdraw his hand, they would avail no more to keep you from falling, than the thin air to hold up a person that is suspended in it.

Your wickedness makes you as it were heavy as lead, and to tend downwards with great weight and pressure towards hell; and if God should let you go, you would immediately sink and swiftly descend and plunge into the bottomless gulf, and your healthy constitution, and your own care and prudence, and best contrivance, and all your righteousness, would have no more influence to uphold you and keep you out of hell, than a spider's web would have to stop a fallen rock. Were it not for the sovereign pleasure of God, the earth would not bear you one moment; for you are a burden to it; the creation groans with you; the creature is made subject to the bondage of your corruption, not willingly; the sun does not willingly shine upon you to give you light to serve sin and Satan; the earth does not willingly yield her increase to satisfy your lusts; nor is it willingly a stage for your wickedness to be acted upon; the air does not willingly serve you for breath to maintain the flame of life in your vitals, while you spend your life in the service of God's enemies. God's creatures are good, and were made for men to serve God with, and do not willingly subserve to any other purpose, and groan when they are abused to purposes so directly contrary to their nature and end. And the world would spew you out, were it not for the sovereign hand of him who hath subjected it in hope. There are black clouds of God's wrath now hanging directly over your heads, full of the dreadful storm, and big with thunder; and were it not for the restraining hand of God, it would immediately burst forth upon you. The sovereign pleasure of God, for the present, stays his rough wind; otherwise it would come with fury, and your destruction would come like a whirlwind, and you would be like the chaff of the summer threshing floor.

The wrath of God is like great waters that are damned for the present; they increase more and more, and rise higher and higher, till an outlet is given; and the longer the stream is stopped, the more rapid and mighty is its course, when once it is let loose. It is true, that judgment against your evil works has not been executed hitherto; the floods of God's vengeance have been withheld; but your guilt in the mean time is constantly increasing, and you are every day treasuring up more wrath; the waters are constantly rising, and waxing more and more mighty; and there is nothing but the mere pleasure of God, that holds the waters back, that are unwilling to be stopped, and press hard to go forward. If God should only withdraw his hand from the flood-gate, it would immediately fly open, and the fiery floods of the fierceness and wrath of God, would rush forth with inconceivable fury, and would come upon you with omnipotent power; and if your strength were ten thousand times greater than it is, yea, ten thousand times greater than the strength of the stoutest, sturdiest devil in hell, it would be nothing to withstand or endure it.

The bow of God's wrath is bent, and the arrow made

ready on the string, and justice bends the arrow at your heart, and strains the bow, and it is nothing but the mere pleasure of God, and that of an angry God, without any promise or obligation at all, that keeps the arrow one moment from being made drunk with your blood. Thus all you that never passed under a great change of heart, by the mighty power of the Spirit of God upon your souls; all you that were never born again, and made new creatures, and raised from being dead in sin, to a state of new, and before altogether unexperienced light and life, are in the hands of an angry God. However you may have reformed your life in many things, and may have had religious affections, and may keep up a form of religion in your families and closets, and in the house of God, it is nothing but his mere pleasure that keeps you from being this moment swallowed up in everlasting destruction. However unconvinced you may now be of the truth of what you hear, by and by you will be fully convinced of it. Those that are gone from being in the like circumstances with you, see that it was so with them; for destruction came suddenly upon most of them; when they expected nothing of it, and while they were saying, Peace and safety: now they see, that those things on which they depended for peace and safety, were nothing but thin air and empty shadows.

The God that holds you over the pit of hell, much as one holds a spider, or some loathsome insect over the fire, abhors you, and is dreadfully provoked: his wrath towards you burns like fire; he looks upon you as worthy of nothing else, but to be cast into the fire; he is of purer eyes than to bear to have you in his sight; you are ten thousand times more abominable in his eyes, than the most hateful venomous serpent is in ours. You have offended him infinitely more than ever a stubborn rebel did his prince; and yet it is nothing but his hand that holds you from falling into the fire every moment. It is to be ascribed to nothing else, that you did not go to hell the last night; that you was suffered to awake again in this world, after you closed your eyes to sleep. And there is no other reason to be given, why you have not dropped into hell since you arose in the morning, but that God's hand has held you up. There is no other reason to be given why you have not gone to hell, since you have sat here in the house of God, provoking his pure eyes by your sinful wicked manner of attending his solemn worship. Yea, there is nothing else that is to be given as a reason why you do not this very moment drop down into hell.

O sinner! Consider the fearful danger you are in: it is a great furnace of wrath, a wide and bottomless pit, full of the fire of wrath, that you are held over in the hand of that God, whose wrath is provoked and incensed as much against you, as against many of the damned in hell. You hang by a slender thread, with the flames of divine wrath flashing about it, and ready every moment to singe it, and burn it asunder; and you have no interest in any Mediator, and nothing to lay hold of to save yourself, nothing to keep off the flames of wrath, nothing of your own, nothing that you ever have done, nothing that you can do, to induce God to spare you one moment.—And consider here more particularly,

1. *Whose* wrath it is: it is the wrath of the infinite God. If it were only the wrath of man, though it were of the most potent prince, it would be comparatively little to be regarded. The wrath of kings is very much dreaded, especially of absolute monarchs, who have the possessions and lives of their subjects wholly in their power, to be disposed of at their mere will. Prov. xx. 2. "The fear of a king is as the roaring of a lion: Whoso provoketh him to anger, sinneth against his own soul." The subject that very much enrages an arbitrary prince, is liable to suffer the most extreme torments that human art can invent, or human power can inflict. But the greatest earthly potentates in their greatest majesty and strength, and when clothed in their greatest terrors, are but feeble, despicable worms of the dust, in comparison of the great and almighty Creator and King of heaven and earth. It is but little that they can do, when most enraged, and when they have exerted the utmost of their fury. All the kings of the earth, before God, are as grasshoppers; they are nothing, and less than nothing: both their love and their hatred is to be despised. The wrath of the great King of kings, is as much more terrible than theirs, as his majesty is greater. Luke xii. 4, 5. "And I say unto you, my friends, Be not afraid of them that kill the body, and after that, have no more that they can do. But I will forewarn you whom you shall fear: fear him, which after he hath killed,

hath power to cast into hell; yea, I say unto you, Fear him."

2. It is the *fierceness* of his wrath that you are exposed to. We often read of the fury of God; as in Isaiah lix. 18. "According to their deeds, accordingly he will repay fury to his adversaries." So Isaiah lxvi. 15. "For behold, the Lord will come with fire, and with his chariots like a whirlwind, to render his anger with fury, and his rebuke with flames of fire." And in many other places. So, Rev. xix. 15. we read of "the wine press of the fierceness and wrath of Almighty God." The words are exceeding terrible. If it had only been said, "the wrath of God," the words would have implied that which is infinitely dreadful: but it is "the fierceness and wrath of God." The fury of God! the fierceness of Jehovah! Oh, how dreadful must that be! Who can utter or conceive what such expressions carry in them! But it is also "the fierceness and wrath of *Almighty* God." As though there would be a very great manifestation of his almighty power in what the fierceness of his wrath should inflict, as though omnipotence should be as it were enraged, and exerted, as men are wont to exert their strength in the fierceness of their wrath. Oh! then, what will be the consequence! What will become of the poor worms that shall suffer it! Whose hands can be strong? And whose heart can endure? To what a dreadful, inexpressible, inconceivable depth of misery must the poor creature be sunk who shall be the subject of this!

Consider this, you that are here present, that yet remain in an unregenerate state. That God will execute the fierceness of his anger, implies, that he will inflict wrath without any pity. When God beholds the ineffable extremity of your case, and sees your torment to be so vastly disproportioned to your strength, and sees how your poor soul is crushed, and sinks down, as it were, into an infinite gloom; he will have no compassion upon you, he will not forbear the executions of his wrath, or in the least lighten his hand; there shall be no moderation or mercy, nor will God then at all stay his rough wind; he will have no regard to your welfare, nor be at all careful lest you should suffer too much in any other sense, than only that you shall *not suffer beyond what strict justice requires*. Nothing shall be withheld, because it is so hard for you to bear. Ezek. viii. 18. "Therefore will I also deal in fury: mine eye shall not spare, neither will

I have pity; and though they cry in mine ears with a loud voice, yet I will not hear them." Now God stands ready to pity you; this is a day of mercy; you may cry now with some encouragement of obtaining mercy. But when once the day of mercy is past, your most lamentable and dolorous cries and shrieks will be in vain; you will be wholly lost and thrown away of God, as to any regard to your welfare. God will have no other use to put you to, but to suffer misery; you shall be continued in being to no other end; for you will be a vessel of wrath fitted to destruction; and there will be no other use of this vessel, but to be filled full of wrath. God will be so far from pitying you when you cry to him, that it is said he will only "laugh and mock," Prov. i. 25, 26, &c.

How awful are those words, Isa. lxiii. 3, which are the words of the great God. "I will tread them in mine anger, and will trample them in my fury, and their blood shall be sprinkled upon my garments, and I will stain all my raiment." It is perhaps impossible to conceive of words that carry in them greater manifestations of these three things, *viz.* contempt, and hatred, and fierceness of indignation. If you cry to God to pity you, he will be so far from pitying you in your doleful case, or showing you the least regard or favour, that instead of that, he will only tread you under foot. And though he will know that you cannot bear the weight of omnipotence treading upon you, yet he will not regard that, but he will crush you under his feet without mercy; he will crush out your blood, and make it fly, and it shall be sprinkled on his garments, so as to stain all his raiment. He will not only hate you, but he will have you, in the utmost contempt: no place shall be thought fit for you, but under his feet to be trodden down as the mire of the streets.

3. The *misery* you are exposed to is that which God will inflict to that end, that he might show what that wrath of Jehovah is. God hath had it on his heart to show to angels and men, both how excellent his love is, and also how terrible his wrath is. Sometimes earthly kings have a mind to show how terrible their wrath is, by the extreme punishments they would execute on those that would provoke them. Nebuchadnezzar, that mighty and haughty monarch of the Chaldean empire, was willing to show his wrath when enraged with Shadrach, Meshech, and Abednego; and

accordingly gave orders that the burning fiery furnace should be heated seven times hotter than it was before; doubtless, it was raised to the utmost degree of fierceness that human art could raise it. But the great God is also willing to show his wrath, and magnify his awful majesty and mighty power in the extreme sufferings of his enemies. Rom. ix. 22. "What if God, willing to show his wrath, and to make his power known, endure with much long-suffering the vessels of wrath fitted to destruction?" And seeing this is his design, and what he has determined, even to show how terrible the unrestrained wrath, the fury and fierceness of Jehovah is, he will do it to effect. There will be something accomplished and brought to pass that will be dreadful with a witness. Then the great and angry God hath risen up and executed his awful vengeance on the poor sinner, and the wretch is actually suffering the infinite weight and power of his indignation, then will God call upon the whole universe to behold that awful majesty and mighty power that is to be seen in it. Isa. xxxiii. 12–14 "And the people shall be as the burnings of lime, as thorns cut up shall they be burnt in the fire. Hear ye that are far off, what I have done; and ye that are near, acknowledge my might. The sinners in Zion are afraid; fearfulness hath surprised the hypocrites," &c.

Thus it will be with you that are in an unconverted state, if you continue in it; the infinite might, and majesty, and terribleness of the omnipotent God shall be magnified upon you, in the ineffable strength of your torments. You shall be tormented in the presence of the holy angels, and in the presence of the Lamb; and when you shall be in this state of suffering, the glorious inhabitants of heaven shall go forth and look on the awful spectacle, that they may see what the wrath and fierceness of the Almighty is; and when they have seen it, they will fall down and adore that great power and majesty. Isa. lxvi. 23, 24. "And it shall come to pass, that from one new moon to another, and from one sabbath to another, shall all flesh come to worship before me, saith the Lord. And they shall go forth and look upon the carcasses of the men that have transgressed against me; for their worm shall not die, neither shall their fire be quenched, and they shall be an abhorring unto all flesh."

4. It is *everlasting* wrath. It would be dreadful to suffer

this fierceness and wrath of Almighty God one moment; but you must suffer it to all eternity. There will be no end to this exquisite horrible misery. When you look forward, you shall see a long for ever, a boundless duration before you, which will swallow up your thoughts, and amaze your soul; and you will absolutely despair of ever having any deliverance, any end, any mitigation, any rest at all. You will know certainly that you must wear out long ages, millions of millions of ages, in wrestling and conflicting with this almighty merciless vengeance; and then when you have so done, when so many ages have actually been spent by you in this manner, you will know that all is but a point to what remains. So that your punishment will indeed be infinite. Oh, who can express what the state of a soul in such circumstances is! All that we can possibly say about it, gives but a very feeble, faint representation of it; it is inexpressible and inconceivable: For "who knows the power of God's anger?"

How dreadful is the state of those that are daily and hourly in the danger of this great wrath and infinite misery! But this is the dismal case of every soul in this congregation that has not been born again, however moral and strict, sober and religious, they may otherwise be. Oh that you would consider it, whether you be young or old! There is reason to think, that there are many in this congregation now hearing this discourse, that will actually be the subjects of this very misery to all eternity. We know not who they are, or in what seats they sit, or what thoughts they now have. It may be they are now at ease, and hear all these things without much disturbance, and are now flattering themselves that they are not the persons, promising themselves that they shall escape. If we knew that there was one person, and but one, in the whole congregation, that was to be the subject of this misery, what an awful thing would it be to think of! If we knew who it was, what an awful sight would it be to see such a person! How might all the rest of the congregation lift up a lamentable and bitter cry over him! But, alas! instead of one, how many is it likely will remember this discourse in hell? And it would be a wonder, if some that are now present should not be in hell in a very short time, even before this year is out. And it would be no wonder if some persons, that now sit here, in some seats of this meeting-house, in health, quiet and secure, should be there before to-morrow morning. Those of you that finally continue in a natural condition, that shall keep out of hell longest will be there in a little time! your damnation does not slumber; it will come swiftly, and, in all probability, very suddenly upon many of you. You have reason to wonder that you are not already in hell. It is doubtless the case of some whom you have seen and known, that never deserved hell more than you, and that heretofore appeared as likely to have been now alive as you. Their case is past all hope; they are crying in extreme misery and perfect despair; but here you are in the land of the living and in the house of God, and have an opportunity to obtain salvation. What would not those poor damned hopeless souls give for one day's opportunity such as you now enjoy!

And now you have an extraordinary opportunity, a day wherein Christ has thrown the door of mercy wide open, and stands in calling and crying with a loud voice to poor sinners; a day wherein many are flocking to him, and pressing into the kingdom of God. Many are daily coming from the east, west, north and south; many that were very lately in the same miserable condition that you are in, are now in a happy state, with their hearts filled with love to him who has loved them, and washed them from their sins in his own blood, and rejoicing in hope of the glory of God. How awful is it to be left behind at such a day! To see so many others feasting, while you are pining and perishing! To see so many rejoicing and singing for joy of heart, while you have cause to mourn for sorrow of heart, and howl for vexation of spirit! How can you rest one moment in such a condition? Are not your souls as precious as the souls of the people at Suffield, where they are flocking from day to day to Christ?

Are there not many here who have lived long in the world, and are not to this day born again? and so are aliens from the commonwealth of Israel, and have done nothing ever since they have lived, but treasure up wrath against the day of wrath? Oh, sirs, your case, in an especial manner, is extremely dangerous. Your guilt and hardness of heart is extremely great. Do you not see how generally persons of your years are passed over and left, in the present remarkable and wonderful dispensation of God's mercy?

You had need to consider yourselves, and awake thoroughly out of sleep. You cannot bear the fierceness and wrath of the infinite God.—And you, young men, and young women, will you neglect this precious season which you now enjoy, when so many others of your age are renouncing all youthful vanities, and flocking to Christ? You especially have now an extraordinary opportunity; but if you neglect it, it will soon be with you as with those persons who spent all the precious days of youth in sin, and are now come to such a dreadful pass in blindness and hardness.—And you, children, who are unconverted, do not you know that you are going down to hell, to bear the dreadful wrath of that God, who is now angry with you every day and every night? Will you be content to be the children of the devil, when so many other children in the land are converted, and are become the holy and happy children of the King of kings?

And let every one that is yet of Christ, and hanging over the pit of hell, whether they be old men and women, or middle aged, or young people, or little children, now hearken to the loud calls of God's word and providence. This acceptable year of the Lord, a day of such great favours to some, will doubtless be a day of as remarkable vengeance to others. Men's hearts harden, and their guilt increases apace at such a day as this, if they neglect their souls; and never was there so great danger of such persons being given up to hardness of heart and blindness of mind. God seems now to be hastily gathering in his elect in all parts of the land; and probably the greater part of adult persons that ever shall be saved, will be brought in now in a little time, and that it will be as it was on the great out-pouring of the Spirit upon the Jews in the apostles' days; the election will obtain, and the rest will be blinded. If this should be the case with you, you will eternally curse this day, and will curse the day that ever you was born, to see such a season of the pouring out of God's Spirit, and will wish that you had died and gone to hell before you had seen it. Now undoubtedly it is, as it was in the days of John the Baptist, the axe is in an extraordinary manner laid at the root of the trees, that every tree which brings not forth good fruit, may be hewn down and cast into the fire.

Therefore, let every one that is out of Christ, now awake

and fly from the wrath to come. The wrath of Almighty God is now undoubtedly hanging over a great part of this congregation: Let every one fly out of Sodom: "Haste and escape for your lives, look not behind you, escape to the mountain, lest you be consumed."

FAREWELL SERMON

Preached on July 1, 1750, the second Sunday after Jonathan Edwards had been dismissed from his parish on the advice of a church council met in Northampton. Dismissals had been frequent for a decade in New England, and the farewell sermon was invariably a part of the painful experience for both pastor and people. Jonathan Edwards' farewell is a most revealing preachment, for his lack of any spirit of recrimination, for his courage in conviction, and his unqualified sense of right on his side. It is also one of the best statements in print of the colonial preacher's conception of the office he held as one of God's chosen messengers on earth. For the man in the pew and for many in the pulpit, this idea was changing, but not for Jonathan Edwards. The text is from *The Works of President Edwards,* edited by S. B. Dwight, Vol. I, pp. 630–51, with omissions.

2 CORINTHIANS, i. 14.

As also ye have acknowledged us in part, that we are your rejoicing, even as ye also are ours, in the day of the Lord Jesus.

THE Apostle, in the preceding part of the chapter, declares what great troubles he met with, in the course of his ministry. In the text, and two foregoing verses, he declares what were his comforts and supports, under the troubles he met with. There are four things in particular.

1. That he had approved himself to his own conscience. v. 12. *For our rejoicing is this, the testimony of our con-*

science, that in simplicity and godly sincerity, not with flesh-
ly wisdom, but by the grace of God, we have had our conversation in the world, and more abundantly to you wards.

2. Another thing he speaks of as matter of comfort, is,
that as he had approved himself to his own conscience, so he
had also to the consciences of his hearers, the Corinthians to
whom he now wrote, and that they should approve of him at
the day of judgment.

3. The hope he had of seeing the blessed fruit of his
labours and sufferings in the ministry, in their happiness and
glory in that great day of accounts.

4. That in his ministry among the Corinthians, he had approved himself to his Judge, who would approve and reward
his faithfulness in that day.

These three last particulars are signified in my text and the
preceding verse; and indeed all the four are implied in the
text: It is implied, that the Corinthians had acknowledged
him as their spiritual father, and as one that had been faithful among them, and as the means of their future joy and
glory at the day of Judgment, and one whom they should
then see, and have a joyful meeting with as such. It is implied, that the apostle expected, at that time, to have a joyful
meeting with *them*, before the Judge, and, with joy, to behold
their glory, as the fruit of his labours; and so they would be
his rejoicing. It is implied also, that he then expected to be
approved of the great Judge, when he and they should meet
together before him; and that he would then acknowledge his
fidelity, and that this had been the means of their glory; and
that thus he would, as it were, give them to him as his
crown of rejoicing. But this the Apostle could not hope for,
unless he had the testimony of his own conscience in his
favour. And therefore the words do imply, in the strongest
manner, that he had approved himself to his own conscience.

There is one thing implied in each of these particulars, and
in every part of the text, which is that point I shall make
the subject of my present discourse, viz:

DOCTRINE. Ministers, and the people that have been under
their care, must meet one another, before Christ's tribunal, at
the day of judgment.

Ministers, and the people that have been under their care,
must be parted in this world, how well soever they have been
united: If they are not separated before, they must be parted

by death: And they may be separated while life is continued. We live in a world of change, where nothing is certain or stable; and where a little time, a few revolutions of the sun, brings to pass strange things, surprising alterations, in particular persons, in families, in towns and churches, in countries and nations. It often happens, that those, who seem most united, in a little time are most disunited, and at the greatest distance. Thus ministers and people, between whom there has been the greatest mutual regard and strictest union, may not only differ in their judgments, and be alienated in affection; But one may rend from the other, and all relation between them be dissolved; the minister may be removed to a distant place, and they may never have any more to do, one with another, in this world. But if it be so, there is one meeting more that they must have, and that is in the last great day of accounts.

Here I would shew,

I. In what manner, ministers and the people which have been under their care, shall meet one another at the day of judgment.

II. For what purposes.

III. For what reasons God has so ordered it, that ministers and their people shall then meet together in such a manner, and for such purposes.

I. I would shew, in some particulars, in what manner ministers and the people which have been under their care, shall meet one another at the day of judgment. Concerning this, I would observe two things in general.

1. That they shall not then meet merely as all mankind must then meet, but there will be something peculiar in the manner of their meeting.

2. That their meeting together, at that time, shall be very different from what used to be in the house of God in this world.

1. They shall not meet, at that day, merely as all the world must then meet together. I would observe a difference in two things.

(1.) As to a clear actual view, and distinct knowledge and notice of each other.

Although the whole world will be then present, all mankind of all generations gathered in one vast assembly, with all of the angelic nature, both elect and fallen angels; yet we need not suppose, that every one will have a distinct and particular knowledge of each individual of the whole assembled multitude, which will undoubtedly consist of many millions of millions. Though it is probable that men's capacities will be much greater than in their present state, yet they will not be infinite: Though their understanding and comprehension will be vastly extended, yet men will not be deified. There will probably be a very enlarged view, that particular persons will have of the various parts and members of that vast assembly, and so of the proceedings of that great day: but yet it must needs be, that according to the nature of finite minds, some persons and some things, at that day, shall fall more under the notice of particular persons than others; and this, (as we may well suppose,) according as they shall have a nearer concern with some than others, in the transactions of the day. There will be special reason, why those who have had special concerns together, in this world, in their state of probation, and whose mutual affairs will be then to be tried and judged, should especially be set in one another's view. Thus we may suppose, that rulers and subjects, earthly judges and those whom they have judged, neighbours who have had mutual converse, dealings and contests, heads of families and their children and servants, shall then meet, and in a peculiar distinction be set together. And especially will it be thus with ministers and their people. It is evident, by the text, that these shall be in each others' view, shall distinctly know each other, and shall have particular notice one of another at that time.

(2.) They shall meet together, as having special concern, one with another, in the great transactions of that day.

Although they shall meet the whole world at that time, yet they will not have any immediate and particular concern with all. Yea, the far greater part of those who shall then be gathered together, will be such as they have had no intercourse with in their state of probation, and so will have no mutual concerns to be judged of. But as to ministers, and the people that have been under their care, they will be such as have had much immediate concern one with another, in matters of the greatest moment, that ever mankind have to do one with another in. Therefore they especially must meet, and be brought together before the Judge, as having special concern one with another in the design and business of that great day of accounts.

Thus their meeting, as to the manner of it, will be diverse from the meeting of mankind in general.

2. Their meeting, at the day of Judgment, will be very diverse from their meetings one with another in this world.

Ministers and their people, while their relation continues, often meet together in this world: They are wont to meet from sabbath to sabbath, and at other times, for the public worship of God, and administration of ordinances, and the solemn services of God's house: And beside these meetings they have also occasion to meet for the determining and managing their ecclesiastical affairs, for the exercise of church discipline, and the settling and adjusting those things which concern the purity and good order of public administrations. But their meeting at the day of Judgment will be exceeding diverse, in its manner and circumstances, from any such meetings and interviews as they have, one with another, in the present state. I would observe how, in a few particulars.

(1.) Now they meet together in a preparatory mutable state, but then in an unchangeable state.

Now, sinners in the congregation meet their minister in a state wherein they are capable of a saving change, capable of being turned, through God's blessing on the ministrations and labours of their pastor, from the power of Satan unto God, and being brought out of a state of guilt, condemnation and wrath, to a state of peace and favour with God, to the enjoyment of the privileges of his children, and a title to their eternal inheritance. And saints now meet their ministers with great remains of corruption, and sometimes under great spiritual difficulties and affliction: And therefore are yet the proper subjects of means of a happy alteration of their state, consisting in a greater freedom from these things; which they have reason to hope for in the way of an attendance on ordinances; and of which God is pleased commonly to make his ministers the instruments. And ministers and their people now meet in order to the bringing to pass such happy changes; they are the great benefits sought in their solemn meetings in this world.

But when they shall meet together at the day of judgment, it will be far otherwise. They will not then meet in order to the use of means for the bringing to effect any such changes;

for they will all meet in an unchangeable state. Sinners will be in an unchangable state: They who then shall be under the guilt and power of sin, and have the wrath of God abiding on them, shall be beyond all remedy; or possibility of change, and shall meet their ministers without any hopes of relief or remedy, or getting any good by their means. And as for the saints, they will be already perfectly delivered from all their before remaining corruption, temptation and calamities, of every kind, and set forever out of their reach; and no deliverance, no happy alteration will remain to be accomplished in the way of the use of means of grace, under the administration of ministers. It will then be pronounced, *He that is unjust, let him be unjust still; and he that is filthy, let him be filthy still; and he that is righteous, let him be righteous still; and he that is holy, let him be holy still.*

(2.) Then they shall meet together in a state of clear, certain and infallible light.

Ministers are set as guides and teachers, and are represented in Scripture as lights set up in the churches; and in the present state meet their people, from time to time, in order to instruct and enlighten them, to correct their mistakes, and to be a voice behind them, when they turn aside to the right hand or the left, saying, *This is the way, walk ye in it;* to evince and confirm the truth by exhibiting the proper evidences of it, and to refute errors and corrupt opinions, to convince the erroneous and establish the doubting. But when Christ shall come to Judgment, every error and false opinion shall be detected: all deceit and delusion shall vanish away before the light of that day, as the darkness of the night vanishes at the appearance of the rising sun; and every doctrine of the word of God shall then appear in full evidence, and none shall remain unconvinced; all shall know the truth with the greatest certainty, and there shall be no mistakes to rectify.

Now ministers and their people may disagree in their judgments concerning some matters of religion, and may sometimes meet to confer together concerning those things wherein they differ, and to hear the reasons that may be offered on one side and the other; and all may be ineffectual, as to any conviction of the truth; they may meet and part again, no more agreed than before; and that side which was in the wrong, may remain so still: Sometimes the meetings of ministers with their people, in such a case of disagreeing sentiments, are attended with unhappy debate and controversy, managed with much prejudice, and want of candour; not tending to light and conviction, but rather to confirm and increase darkness, and establish opposition to the truth, and alienation of affection one from another. But when they shall hereafter meet together, at the day of Judgment, before the tribunal of the great Judge, the mind and will of Christ will be made known; and there shall no longer be any debate, or difference of opinions; the evidence of the truth shall appear beyond all dispute, and all controversies shall be finally and forever decided.

Now ministers meet their people, in order to enlighten and awaken the consciences of sinners; setting before them the great evil and danger of sin, the strictness of God's law, their own wickedness of heart, and practice, the great guilt they are under, the wrath that abides upon them, and their impotence, blindness, poverty and helpless and undone condition: But all is often in vain; they remain still, notwithstanding all their ministers can say, stupid and unawakened, and their consciences unconvinced. But it will not be so at their last meeting at the day of Judgment; sinners, when they shall meet their Judge, will not meet him with a stupid conscience: they will then be fully convinced of the truth of those things, which they formerly heard from him, concerning the greatness and terrible majesty of God, his holiness and hatred of sin, and his awful justice in punishing it, the strictness of his law, and the dreadfulness and truth of his threatenings, and their own unspeakable guilt and misery; and they shall never more be insensible of these things: the eyes of conscience will now be fully enlightened, and never shall be blinded again: the mouth of conscience shall now be opened, and never shall be shut any more.

Now ministers meet with their people, in public and private, in order to enlighten them concerning the state of their souls; to open and apply the rules of God's word to them, in order to their searching their own hearts, and discerning the state that they are in. But now, ministers have no infallible discerning the state of the souls of their people; and the most skilful of them are liable to mistakes, and often are mistaken in things of this nature; nor are the people able certainly to know the state of their minister, or one another's state; very often, those pass among them for saints, and it may be eminent saints, that are grand hypocrites; and on the other hand, those are sometimes censured, or hardly received into their charity, that are indeed some of God's jewels. And nothing is more common, than for men to be mistaken concerning their own state: Many that are abominable to God, and the children of his wrath, think highly of themselves, as his precious saints and dear children. Yea, there is reason to think, that often some, that are most bold in their confidence of their safe and happy state, and think themselves not only true saints, but the most eminent saints in the congregation, are, in a peculiar manner, a smoke in God's nose. And thus it undoubtedly often is, in those congregations where the word of God is most faithfully dispensed; notwithstanding all that ministers can say in their clearest explications, and most searching applications of the doctrines and rules of God's word to the souls of their hearers, in their meetings one with another. But, in the day of Judgment, they shall have another sort of meeting; then the secrets of every heart shall be made manifest, and every man's state shall be perfectly known. I Cor. iv. 5. *Therefore judge nothing before the time, until the Lord come; who both will bring to light the hidden things of darkness, and will make manifest the counsels of the heart: And then shall every man have praise of God.* Then none shall be deceived concerning his own state, nor shall be any more in doubt about it. There shall be an eternal end to all the self-conceit and vain hopes of deluded hypocrites, and all the doubts and fears of sincere christians. And then shall all know the state of one another's souls: the people shall know whether their minister has been sincere and faithful, and the minister shall know the state of every one of their people, and to whom the word and ordinances of God have been a savour of life unto life, and to whom a savour of death unto death.

Now in this present state, it often happens that, when ministers and people meet together, to debate and manage their ecclesiastical affairs, especially in a state of controversy, they are ready to judge and censure one another, with regard to each other's views and designs, and the principles and ends that each is influenced by; and are greatly mistaken in their judgment, and wrong one another in their censures: but at that future meeting, things will be set in a true and perfect light, and the principles and aims, that every one has acted from, shall be certainly known; and there will be an end to all errors of this kind, and all unrighteous censures.

(3.) In this world, ministers and their people often meet together, to hear of, and wait upon, an unseen Lord; but at the day of Judgment, they shall meet in his most immediate and visible presence.

Ministers, who now often meet their people, to preach to them the King eternal, immortal and invisible, to convince them that there is a God, and declare to them what manner of being he is, and to convince them that he governs, and will judge, the world, and that there is a future state of rewards and punishments, and to preach to them a Christ in heaven, at the right hand of God, in an unseen world, shall then meet their people in the most immediate sensible presence of this great God, Saviour and Judge, appearing in the most plain, visible and open manner, with great glory, with all his holy angels, before them and the whole world. They shall not meet them to hear about an absent Christ, an unseen Lord, and future Judge; but to appear before that Judge, and as being set together in the presence of that supreme Lord, in his immense glory and awful majesty, whom they have heard of so often, in their meetings together on earth.

(4.) The meeting, at the last day, of ministers and the people that have been under their care, will not be attended, by any one, with a careless heedless heart.

With such a heart are their meetings often attended in this world, by many persons, having little regard to him whom they pretend unitedly to adore, in the solemn duties of his public worship, taking little heed to their own thoughts or the frame of their minds, not attending to the business they are engaged in, nor considering the end for which they are come together: but the meeting, at that great day, will be very different; there will not be one careless heart, no sleeping, no wandering of mind, from the great concern of the meeting, no inattentiveness to the business of the day, no regardlessness of the presence they are in, or of those great things which they shall hear from Christ at that meeting, or that they formerly heard from him, and of him, by their ministers, in their meetings in a state of trial, or which they shall now hear their ministers declaring concerning them, before their Judge.

Having observed these things, concerning the manner and circumstances of this future meeting of ministers and the people that have been under their care, before the tribunal of Christ, at the day of Judgment, I now proceed,

II. To observe, to what purposes they shall then meet.

1. To give an account before the great Judge, of their behaviour one to another, in the relation they stood to each other in this world. . . .

2. At that time ministers and the people who have been under their care, shall meet before Christ, that he may judge between them in this world. . . .

3. Ministers and the people that have been under their care, must meet together at that time, to receive an eternal sentence and retribution from the Judge, in the presence of each other, according to their behaviour in the relations they stood in to one another in the present state.

The Judge will not only declare justice, but he will do justice between ministers and their people. He will declare what is right between them, approving him that has been just and faithful, and condemning the unjust; and perfect truth and equity shall take place in the sentence which He passes, in the rewards He bestows, and the punishments which He inflicts. There shall be a glorious reward to faithful ministers. . . .

Thus justice shall be administered, at the great day, to ministers and their people: and to that end they shall meet together, that they may not only receive justice to themselves, but see justice done to the other party: for this is the end of that great day, to *reveal,* or declare *the righteous judgment of God;* Rom, ii 5. Ministers shall have justice done them, and they shall see justice done to their people: and the people shall receive justice themselves from their Judge, and shall see justice done to their minister. And so all things will be adjusted and settled forever between them; every one being sentenced and recompensed according to his works; either in receiving and wearing a crown of eternal joy and glory, or in suffering everlasting shame and pain.

* * *

APPLICATION.

The improvement I would make of the things which have been observed, is to lead the people here present, who have been under my pastoral care, to some reflections, and to give them some advice, suitable to our present circumstances; relating to what has been lately done, in order to our being separated, as to the relation we have heretofore stood in one to another; but expecting to meet each other before the great tribunal at the day of Judgment.

The deep and serious consideration of that our future most solemn meeting, is certainly most suitable at such a time as this; there having so lately been that done, which, in all probability, will (as to the relation we have heretofore stood in) be followed with an everlasting separation.

How often have we met together in the house of God, in this relation? How often have I spoken to you, instructed, counselled, warned, directed and fed you, and administered ordinances among you, as the people which were committed to my care, and whose precious souls I had the charge of? But in all probability, this never will be again.

The prophet Jeremiah, (chap. xxv. 3.) puts the people in mind how long he had laboured among them in the work of the ministry; *From the thirteenth year of Josiah, the son of Amon, king of Judah, even unto this day, (that is, the three and twentieth year,) the word of the Lord came unto me, and I have spoken unto you, rising early and speaking.* I am not about to compare myself with the prophet Jeremiah; but in this respect I can say as he did, that *I have spoken the word of God to you, unto the three and twentieth year, rising early and speaking.* It was three and twenty years, the 15th day of last February, since I have laboured in the work of the ministry, in the relation of a pastor to this church and congregation. And though my strength has been weakness, having always laboured under great infirmity of body, beside my insufficiency for so great a charge, in other respects, yet I have not spared my feeble strength, but have exerted it for the good of your souls. I can appeal to you, as the apostle does to his hearers, Gal. iv. 13. *Ye know how through infirmity of the flesh, I preached the Gospel unto you.* I have spent the prime of my life and strength, in labours for your eternal welfare. You are my witnesses, that what strength I have had I have not neglected in idleness, nor laid out in prosecuting worldly schemes, and managing temporal affairs, for the advancement of my outward estate, and aggrandizing myself and family; but have given myself to the work of the ministry, labouring in it night and day, rising early and applying myself to this great business to which Christ appointed me. I have found the work of the ministry among you to be a great work indeed, a work of exceeding care, labour and difficulty: many have been the heavy burdens that I have borne in it, which my strength has been very unequal to. GOD called me to bear these burdens, and I bless his name, that he has so supported me as to keep me from sinking under them, and that his power herein has been manifested in my weakness; so that although I have often been troubled on every side, yet I have not been distressed; perplexed, but not in despair; cast down, but not destroyed.

But now I have reason to think, my work is finished which I had to do as your minister: you have publicly rejected me, and my opportunities cease.

How highly therefore does it now become us, to consider of that time when we must meet one another before the chief Shepherd? When I must give an account for my stewardship, of the service I have done *for*, and the reception and treatment I have had *among*, the people he sent me to: and you must give an account of your own conduct towards me, and the improvement you have made of those *three and twenty years* of my ministry. For then both you and I must appear together, and we both must give an account, in order to an infallible, righteous and eternal, sentence to be passed upon us, by him who will judge us, with respect to all that we have said or done in our meetings here, all our conduct one towards another, in the house of God and elsewhere, on sabbath-days and on other days; who will try our hearts, and manifest our thoughts, and the principles and frames of our minds, will judge us with respect to all the controversies which have subsisted between us, with the strictest impartiality, and will examine our treatment of each other in those controversies: there is nothing covered, that shall not be revealed, nor hid, which shall not be known; all will be examined in the searching, penetrating light of God's omniscience and glory, and by him whose eyes are as a flame of fire; and truth and right shall be made plainly to appear, being stripped of every veil; and all error, falsehood, unrighteousness and injury, shall be laid open, stripped of every disguise; every specious pretence, every cavil, and all false reasoning, shall vanish in a moment, as not being able to bear the light of that day. And then our hearts will be turned inside out, and the secrets of them will be made more plainly to appear than our outward actions do now. Then it shall appear what the ends are, which we have aimed at, what have been the governing principles which we have acted from, and what have been the dispositions, we have exercised in our ecclesiastical disputes and contests. Then it will appear, whether I acted uprightly, and from a truly conscientious careful, regard to my duty to my great Lord and master, in some former ecclesiastical controversies, which have been attended with exceeding unhappy circumstances, and consequences: it will appear, whether there was any just cause for the resentment which was manifested on those occasions. And then our late grand controversy, concerning the Qualifications necessary for admission to the privileges of members, in complete standing, in the Visible Church of Christ, will be examined and judged, in all its parts and circumstances, and the whole set forth in a clear, certain and perfect light. Then it will appear, whether the doctrine, which I have preached and published, concerning this matter, be Christ's own doctrine, whether he will not own it as one of the precious truths which have proceeded from his own mouth, and vindicate and honour, as such, before the whole universe. Then it will appear, what was meant by *the man that comes without the wedding garment;* for that is the day spoken of, Matt. xxii. 13. wherein such an one *shall be bound hand and foot, and cast into outer darkness, where shall be weeping and gnashing of teeth.* And then it will appear, whether, in declaring this doctrine, and acting agreeably to it, and in my general conduct in this affair, I have been influenced from any regard to my own temporal interest, or honour, or any desire to appear wiser than others; or have acted from any sinister, secular views whatsoever; and whether what I have done has not been from a careful, strict and tender regard to the will of my Lord and Master, and because I dare not offend him, being satisfied what his will was, after a long, diligent, impartial and prayerful, enquiry; having this constantly in view and prospect, to engage me to great solicitude, not rashly to determine truth to be on this side of the question, where I am now persuaded it is, that such a determination would not be for my temporal interest, but every way against it, bringing a long series of extreme difficulties, and plunging me into an abyss of trouble and sorrow. And then it will appear, whether my people have done their duty to their pastor, with respect to this matter; whether they have shown a right temper and spirit on this occasion; whether they have done me justice in hearing, attending to, and considering, what I had to say in evidence of what I believed and taught, as part of the counsel of God; whether I have been treated with that impartiality, candour and regard, which the just Judge esteemed due; and whether, in the many steps which have been taken, and the many things that have been said and done, in the course of this controversy, righteousness and charity and christian decorum have been maintained: or, if otherwise, to how great a degree these things have been violated. Then every step of the conduct of each of us, in this affair, from first to last, and the spirit we have exercised in all, shall be examined and manifested, and our own consciences will speak plain and loud, and each of us shall be convinced, and the world shall know; and never shall there be any more mistake, misrepresentation or misapprehension of the affair, to eternity.

This controversy is now probably brought to an issue, between you and me, as to this world; it has issued in the event of the week before last; but it must have another decision at that great day, which certainly will come, when you and I shall meet together before the great judgment seat: and therefore I leave it to that time, and shall say no more about it at present.

But I would now proceed to address myself particularly to several sorts of persons.

I. To those who are professors of godliness among us. . . .

II. Now I am taking my leave of this people, I would apply myself to such among them as I leave in a christless, graceless condition; and would call on such, seriously to consider of that solemn day, when they and I must meet before the Judge of the world. . . .

III. I would address myself to those who are under some awakenings. . . .

IV. I would apply myself to the young people of the congregation. . . .

V. I would apply myself to the children of the congregation, the lambs of this flock, who have been so long under my care. . . .

*   *   *

I conclude with a few words of advice to all in general, in some particulars, which are of great importance in order to the future welfare and prosperity of this church and congregation.

1. One thing that greatly concerns you, as you would be an happy people, is the maintaining of *family order*. . . .

2. As you would seek the future prosperity of this society, it is of vast importance that you should avoid *contention*. . . .

3. Another thing, that vastly concerns the future prosperity of the town, is, that you should watch against the encroachments of Error; and particularly *Arminianism,* and doctrines of like tendency. . . .

4. Another thing which I would advise to, that you may hereafter be a prosperous people, is, that you would give yourselves much to prayer. . . .

5. The last article of advice, I would give, (which doubtless does greatly concern your prosperity,) is, that you would take great care with regard to the settlement of a minister, to see to it who or what manner of person he is, whom you settle: and particularly in these two respects.

(1.) That he be a man of thoroughly sound principles, in the scheme of doctrine which he maintains. . . .

(2.) Labour to obtain a man, who has an established character, as a person of serious religion and fervent piety. . . .

*   *   *

And let me be remembered, in the prayers of all God's people, that are of a calm spirit, and are peaceable and faithful in Israel, of whatever opinion they may be, with respect to terms of Church Communion.

And let us all remember, and never forget, our future, solemn meeting, on that Great day of the Lord; the day of infallible and of the unalterable sentence. AMEN.

A TREATISE CONCERNING
RELIGIOUS AFFECTIONS

This is Jonathan Edwards' most original work on religious psychology and his mature answer to his lifelong question "What is the nature of true religious experience?" It was rooted in his own personal experience and tested through earnest study and observation during the revivals in his own parish and later under Whitefield's preaching. It was first preached as a series of sermons in his own parish in 1741–42 and first published in 1746. For its theological importance, see Alexander Allen, *Jonathan Edwards*, pp. 218–52. The text is from *The Works of President Edwards*, edited by S. B. Dwight, Vol. V, pp. 7–16, Part I, Sections 1 and 2.

CONCERNING THE NATURE OF THE AFFECTIONS
AND THEIR IMPORTANCE IN RELIGION.

1 PETER i. 8.

Whom having not seen, ye love; in whom though now ye see him not, yet believing, ye rejoice with joy unspeakable and full of glory.

Sect. I.

Introductory Remarks respecting the Affections

IN these words, the apostle represents the state of the Christians to whom he wrote, under persecutions. To these persecutions he has respect, in the two preceding verses, when he speaks of *the trial of their faith,* and of *their being in heaviness through manifold temptations.*

Such *trials* are of threefold benefit to true religion. Hereby the *truth* of it is manifested, it appears to be indeed *true religion.* Trials, above all other things, have a tendency to distinguish true religion and false, and to cause the difference between them evidently to appear. Hence they are called by the name of *trials,* in the verse preceding the text, and innumerable other places.—They try the faith and religion of professors, of what sort it is, as apparent gold is tried in the fire, and manifested, whether it be true gold or not. And the faith of true Christians, being thus tried and proved to be true, is *found to praise, and honour, and glory.*

And then, these trials not only manifest the *truth* of true religion, but they make its genuine *beauty* and *amiableness* remarkably to appear. True virtue never appears so lovely, as when it is most oppressed: and the divine excellency of real Christianity, is never exhibited with such advantage, as when under the greatest trials. Then it is that true faith appears much more precious than gold; and upon this account, is *found to praise, and honour, and glory.*

Again, another benefit of such trials to true religion, is that they *purify* and *increase* it. They not only manifest it to be *true,* but also tend to *refine* it, and deliver it from those mixtures of what is false, which encumber and impede it; that nothing may be left but that which is true. They not only shew the amiableness of true religion to the best advantage, but they tend to increase its beauty by establishing and confirming it; making it more lively and vigorous, and purifying it from those things that obscured its lustre and glory. As gold that is tried in the fire is purged from its alloy, and all remainders of dross, and comes forth more beautiful; so true faith being tried as gold is tried in the fire, becomes more precious; and thus also is *found unto praise, and honour, and glory.* The apostle seems to have respect to each of these benefits in the verse preceding the text.

And, in the text, the apostle observes how true religion *operated* in these Christians under their persecutions, whereby these benefits appeared in them; or what manner of operation it was, whereby their religion, under persecution, was manifested to be *true* religion in its genuine *beauty* and *amiableness,* and also appeared to be *increased* and *purified,* and so was like to be *found unto praise, and honour, and glory, at the appearing of Jesus Christ.* And there were two kinds of operation, or exercise of true religion, in them, under their sufferings, that the apostle takes notice of in the text, wherein these benefits appeared.

1. *Love to Christ. Whom having not seen, ye love.* The world was ready to wonder, what strange principle it was, that influenced them to expose themselves to so great sufferings, to forsake the things that were seen, and renounce all that was dear and pleasant, which was the object of sense. They seemed to the men of the world as if they were beside themselves, and to act as though they hated themselves; there was nothing in *their* view, that could induce them thus to suffer, or to support them under, and carry them through such trials. But although there was nothing that the world saw, or that the Christians themselves ever saw with their bodily eyes, that thus influenced and supported them, yet they had a supernatural principle of love to something *unseen;* they loved Jesus Christ, for they saw him spiritually, whom the world saw not, and whom they themselves had never seen with bodily eyes.

2. *Joy in Christ.* Though their outward sufferings were very grievous, yet their inward spiritual joys were greater than their sufferings; and these supported them, and enabled them to suffer with cheerfulness

There are two things which the apostle takes notice of in the text concerning this joy. 1. The manner in which it rises, the way in which Christ, though unseen, is the foundation of it, *viz.* by *faith;* which is the evidence of things not seen; *In whom, though now ye see him not, yet* BELIEVING, *ye rejoice.* 2. The *nature* of this joy; *unspeakable, and full of glory. Unspeakable* in the *kind* of it; very different from worldly joys, and carnal delights; of a vastly more pure, sublime, and heavenly nature, being something supernatural, and truly divine, and so ineffably excellent! the sublimity and exquisite sweetness of which, there were no words to set forth. Unspeakable also in *degree*; it having pleased God to give them this holy joy with a liberal hand, in their state of persecution.

Their joy was *full of glory.* Although the joy was unspeakable, and no words were sufficient to describe it; yet something might be said of it, and no words more fit to represent its excellency than these, that it was *full of glory;* or, as it is in the original, *glorified joy.* In rejoicing with this joy, their minds were filled, as it were, with a glorious brightness, and their natures exalted and perfected. It was a most worthy, noble rejoicing, that did not corrupt and debase the mind, as many carnal joys do; but did greatly beautify and dignify it. It was a prelibation of the joy of heaven, that raised their minds to a degree of heavenly blessedness; it filled their minds with the light of God's glory, and made themselves to shine with some communication of that glory.

Hence the proposition or doctrine, that I would raise from these words is this, TRUE RELIGION, IN GREAT PART, CONSISTS IN HOLY AFFECTIONS.

We see that the apostle, in remarking the operations and exercises of religion in these Christians, when it had its greatest trial by persecution, as gold is tried in the fire— and when it not only proved true, but was most pure from dross and mixtures—and when it appeared in them most in its genuine excellency and native beauty, and was found to praise, and honour, and glory—he singles out the religious affections of *love* and *joy*, as those exercises, wherein their religion did thus appear *true, pure* and *glorious.*

Here it may be inquired, what the *affections* of the mind are?—I answer, The affections are no other than the more vigorous and *sensible exercises of the inclination and will* of the soul.

God has endued the soul with two principal faculties: The one, that by which it is capable of *perception* and speculation, or by which it discerns, and judges of things; which is called the *understanding.* The other, that by which the soul is some way *inclined* with respect to the things it views or considers: or it is the faculty by which the soul beholds things—not as an indifferent unaffected spectator, but— either as liking or disliking, pleased or displeased, approving or rejecting. This faculty is called by various names: it is sometimes called the *inclination;* and, as it respects the actions determined and governed by it, the *will:* and the *mind,* with regard to the exercises of this faculty, is often called the *heart.*

The *exercises* of this last faculty are of two sorts; either those by which the soul is carried out towards the things in view in *approving* them, being pleased with, and inclined to them; or, those in which the soul opposes the things in view, in *disapproving* them; and in being displeased with, averse from, and rejecting them. And as the exercises of the inclination are various in their *kinds,* so they are much more various in their *degrees.* There are some exercises of pleasedness or displeasedness, inclination or disinclination, wherein the soul is carried but a little beyond a state of perfect indifference. And there are other degrees, wherein the approbation or dislike, pleasedness or aversion, are stronger; wherein we may rise higher and higher, till the soul comes to act vigorously and sensibly, and its actings are with that strength, that (through the laws of union which the Creator has fixed between soul and body) the motion of the blood and animal spirits begins to be sensibly altered: whence oftentimes arises some bodily sensation, especially about the *heart* and vitals, which are the fountain of the fluids of the body. Whence it comes to pass, that the *mind*, with regard to the exercises of this faculty, perhaps in all nations and ages, is called *the heart.* And it is to be noted, that they are these more vigorous and sensible exercises of this faculty, which are called the *affections*.

The *will*, and the *affections* of the soul, are not two faculties; the affections are not essentially distinct from the will, nor do they differ from the mere *actings* of the will and inclination, but only in the liveliness and sensibility of exercise.—It must be confessed, that language is here somewhat imperfect, the meaning of words in a considerable measure loose and unfixed, and not precisely limited by custom which governs the use of language. In some sense, the affection of the soul differs nothing at all from the will and inclination, and the will never is in any exercise further than it is *affected;* it is not moved out of a state of perfect indifference, any otherwise than as it is *affected* one way or other. But yet there are many actings of the will and inclination, that are not so commonly called *affections.* In every thing we do, wherein we act voluntarily, there is an exercise of the will and inclination. It is our inclination that governs us in our actions; but *all the actings* of the inclination and will, are not ordinarily called affections. Yet, what are commonly called affections are not essentially different from them, but only in the *degree* and *manner* of exercise. In every act of the will whatsoever, the soul either likes or dislikes, is either inclined or disinclined to what is in view. These are not *essentially* different from the affections of *love* and *hatred*. A liking or inclination of the soul to a thing, if it be in a high degree vigorous and lively, is the very same thing with the affection of *love:* and a disliking and disinclining, if in a great degree, is the very same with *hatred*. In every act of the will *for,* or *towards* something not present, the soul is in some degree *inclined* to that thing; and that inclination, if in a considerable degree, is the very same with the affection of *desire*. And in every degree of an act of the will, wherein the soul approves of something present, there is a degree of pleasedness; and that pleasedness, if it be in a considerable degree, is the very same with the affection of *joy* or *delight*. And if the will disapproves of what is present, the soul is in some degree displeased, and if that displeasedness be great, it is the very same with the affection of *grief* or *sorrow*.

Such seems to be our nature, and such the laws of the union of soul and body, that there never is in any case whatsoever, any lively and vigorous exercise of the inclination, without some effect upon the body, in some alteration of the motion of its fluids, and especially of the animal spirits. And, on the other hand, from the same laws of union, over the constitution of the body, and the motion of its fluids, may promote the exercise of the affections. But yet, it is not the body, but the mind only, that is the proper seat of the affections. The body of man is no more capable of being really the subject of love or hatred, joy or sorrow, fear or hope, than the body of a tree, or than the same body of man is capable of thinking and understanding. As it is the soul only that has ideas, so it is the soul only that is pleased or displeased with its ideas. As it is the soul only that thinks, so it is the soul only that loves or hates, rejoices or is grieved at what it thinks of. Nor are these motions of the animal spirits, and fluids of the body, any thing properly belonging to the *nature* of the affections; though they always *accompany* them in the present state; but are only effects or concomitants of the affections, which are entirely distinct from the affections themselves, and no way essential to them; so that an unbodied spirit may be

as capable of love and hatred, joy or sorrow, hope or fear, or other affections, as one that is united to a body.

The *affections* and *passions* are frequently spoken of as the same; and yet, in the more common use of speech, there is in some respect a difference. *Affection* is a word, that in its ordinary signification, seems to be something more extensive than *passion*, being used for all vigorous lively actings of the will or inclination; but *passion* is used for those that are more sudden, and whose effects on the animal spirits are more violent, the mind being more overpowered, and less in its own command.

As all the exercises of inclination and will are concerned either in approving and liking, or disapproving and rejecting; so the affections are of two sorts; they are those by which the soul is carried out to what is in view, cleaving *to* it, or *seeking* it; or those by which it is averse *from* it, and *opposes* it. Of the former sort are *love, desire, hope, joy, gratitude, complacence.* Of the latter kind, are *hatred, fear, anger, grief,* and such like; which it is needless now to stand particularly to define.

And there are some affections wherein there is a *composition* of each of the aforementioned kinds of actings of the will; as in the affection of *pity,* there is something of the *former kind,* towards the person suffering, and something of the *latter,* towards what he suffers. And so in *zeal,* there is in it high *approbation* of some person or thing, together with vigorous *opposition* to what is conceived to be contrary to it.

SECT. II.

True Religion, in great part, consists in the Affections.

1. WHAT has been said of the *nature* of the affections makes this evident; and may be sufficient, without adding any thing further, to put this matter out of doubt; for who will deny that true religion consists, in a great measure, in vigorous

and lively actings of the *inclination* and *will* of the soul, or the fervent exercises of the *heart?* That religion which God requires, and will accept, does not consist in weak, dull, and lifeless wishes, raising us but a little above a state of indifference. God, in his word, greatly insists upon it, that we be in good earnest, *fervent in spirit,* and our hearts vigorously engaged in religion: Rom. xii. 11. *Be ye fervent in spirit, serving the Lord.* Deut. x. 12. *And now Israel, what doth the Lord thy God require of thee, but to fear the Lord thy God, to walk in all his ways, and to love him, and to serve the Lord thy God with all thy heart, and with all thy soul?* And chap. vi. 4, 5. *Hear, O Israel, the Lord our God is one Lord; and thou shalt love the Lord thy God with all thy heart, and with all thy soul, and with all thy might.* It is such a fervent, vigorous engagedness of the heart in religion, that is the fruit of a real circumcision of the heart, or true regeneration, and that has the promises of life; Deut. xxx. 6. *And the Lord thy God will circumcise thine heart, and the heart of thy seed, to love the Lord thy God with all thy heart, and with all thy soul, that thou mayest live.*

If we be not in good earnest in religion, and our wills and inclinations be not strongly exercised, we are nothing. The things of religion are so great, that there can be no suitableness in the exercises of our hearts, to their nature and importance, unless they be lively and powerful. In nothing is vigour in the actings of our inclinations so requisite, as in religion; and in nothing is lukewarmness so odious. True religion is evermore a powerful thing; and the power of it appears, in the first place, in its exercises in the heart, its principal and original seat. Hence true religion is called the *power of godliness,* in distinction from external appearances, which are *the form* of it, 2 Tim. iii. 5. *Having a form of godliness, but denying the power of it.* The Spirit of God, in those who have sound and solid religion, is a spirit of powerful holy affection; and, therefore, God is said *to have given them the Spirit of power, and of love, and of a sound mind,* (2 Tim. i. 7.) And such, when they receive the Spirit of God in his sanctifying and saving influences, are said to be *baptized with the Holy Ghost, and with fire;* by reason of the power and fervour of those exercises which the Spirit of God excites in them, and whereby *their hearts,* when grace is in exercise, may be said to *burn within them.* (Luke xxiv. 32.)

The business of *religion* is, from time to time, compared to those *exercises,* wherein men are wont to have their hearts and strength greatly exercised and engaged; such as running, wrestling or agonizing for a great prize or crown, and fighting with strong enemies that seek our lives, and warring as those that by violence take a city or kingdom. Though true grace has various degrees, and there are some who are but babes in Christ, in whom the exercise of the inclination and will towards divine and heavenly things, is comparatively weak; yet every one that has the power of godliness, has his inclinations and heart exercised towards God and divine things with such strength and vigour, that these holy exercises prevail in him above all carnal or natural affections, and are effectual to overcome them; for every true disciple of Christ, *loves him above father or mother, wife and children, brethren and sisters, houses and lands, yea more than his own life.* Hence it follows, that wherever true religion is, there are vigorous exercises of the inclination and will towards divine objects: but by what was said before, the vigorous, lively, and sensible exercises of the will, are no other than the *affections* of the soul,

2. The Author of our nature has not only given us affections, but has made them very much the spring of actions. As the *affections* not only necessarily belong to the *human nature,* but are a very *great part* of it; so (inasmuch as by regeneration persons are renewed in the whole man) *holy affections* not only necessarily belong to *true religion,* but are a very great part of such religion. And as true religion is practical, and God hath so constituted the human nature, that the affections are very much the spring of men's actions, this also shews, that true religion must consist very much in the affections.

Such is man's nature, that he is very inactive, any otherwise than he is influenced by either *love* or *hatred, desire, hope, fear,* or some other affection. These affections we see to be the moving springs in all the affairs of life, which engage men in all their pursuits; and especially in all affairs wherein they are earnestly engaged, and which they pursue with vigour. We see the world of mankind exceedingly busy and active; and their affections are the springs of motion; take away all *love* and *hatred,* all *hope* and *fear,* all *anger, zeal,* and affectionate *desire,* and the world would be, in a great measure, motionless and dead: there would be no such thing as activity amongst mankind, or any earnest pursuit whatsoever. It is affection that engages the covetous man, and him that is greedy of worldly profits; it is by the affections that the ambitious man is put forward in his pursuit of worldly glory; and the affections also actuate the voluptuous man, in his pleasure and sensual delights. The world continues, from age to age, in a continual commotion and agitation, in pursuit of these things; but take away affection, and the *spring* of all this motion would be gone; the motion itself would cease. And as in worldly things, worldly affections are very much the spring of men's motion and action; so in religious matters, the spring of their actions are very much religious affections: he that has doctrinal knowledge and speculation only, without affection, never is *engaged* in the business of religion.

3. Nothing is more manifest *in fact,* than that the things of religion take hold of men's souls no further than they *affect* them. There are multitudes who often hear the word of God, things infinitely great and important, and which most nearly concern them, yet all seems to be wholly ineffectual upon them, and to make no alteration in their disposition or behaviour; the reason is, they are not *affected* with what they hear. There are many who often hear of the glorious perfections of God, his almighty power, boundless wisdom, infinite majesty, and that holiness by which he is of purer eyes than to behold evil, and cannot look on iniquity; together with his infinite goodness and mercy. They hear of the great works of God's wisdom, power, and goodness, wherein there appear the admirable manifestations of these perfections. They hear particularly of the unspeakable love of God and Christ, and what Christ has done and suffered. They hear of the great things of another world, of eternal misery, in bearing the fierceness and wrath of almighty God; and of endless blessedness and glory in the presence of God, and the enjoyment of his love. They also hear the peremptory commands of God, his gracious counsels and warnings, and the sweet invitations of the gospel. Yet they remain as before, with no sensible alteration, either in heart or practice, because they are not *affected* with what they hear. I am bold to assert, that there never was any considerable change wrought in the mind or conversation of any person, by any thing of a religious na-

ture that ever he read, heard or saw, who had not his affections moved. Never was a natural man engaged earnestly to seek his salvation; never were any such brought to cry after wisdom, and lift up their voice for understanding, and to wrestle with God in prayer for mercy; and never was one humbled, and brought to the foot of God, from any thing that ever he heard or imagined of his own unworthiness and deservings of God's displeasure: nor was ever one induced to fly for refuge unto Christ, while his heart remained *unaffected.* Nor was there ever a saint awakened out of a cold, lifeless frame, or recovered from a declining state in religion, and brought back from a lamentable departure from God, without having his heart *affected.* And, in a word, there never was any thing *considerable* brought to pass in the heart or life of any man living, by the things of religion, that had not his heart *deeply affected* by those things.

4. The holy scriptures every where place religion very much in the affections; such as fear, hope, love, hatred, desire, joy, sorrow, gratitude, compassion, and zeal.

The scriptures place much of religion in godly *fear;* insomuch that an experience of it is often spoken of as the character of those who are truly religious persons. *They tremble at God's word,* they *fear before him, their flesh trembles for fear of him, they are afraid of his judgments, his excellency makes them afraid, and his dread falls upon them,* &c. An appellation commonly given the saints in scripture, is, *fearers of God,* or *they that fear the Lord.* And because this is a great part of true godliness, hence true godliness in general is very commonly called *the fear of God.*

So *hope* in God, and in the promises of his word, is often spoken of in the scripture, as a very considerable *part of true religion.* It is mentioned as one of the three great things of which religion consists, 1 Cor. xiii. 13. Hope in the Lord is also frequently mentioned as the *character of the saints:* Psal. cxlvi. 5. *Happy is he that hath the God of Jacob for his help, whose* HOPE *is in the Lord his God.* Jer. xvii. 7. *Blessed is the man that trusteth in the Lord, and whose* HOPE *the Lord is.* Psal. xxxi 24. *Be of good courage, and he shall strengthen your heart, all ye that* HOPE *in the Lord.* And the like in many other places. Religious fear and hope are, once and again, joined together, as jointly constituting the character of the true saints; Psal. xxxiii. 18. *Behold, the eye of the Lord is upon them that* FEAR *him, upon them that* HOPE *in his mercy.* Psal. cxlvii. 11. *The Lord taketh pleasure in them that* FEAR *him, in those that* HOPE *in his mercy.* Hope is so great a part of true religion, that the apostle says *we are saved by* HOPE, Rom. viii. 24. And this is spoken of as *the helmet* of the Christian soldier, 1 Thess. v. 8. *And for an helmet the* HOPE *of salvation;* and the sure and stedfast *anchor* of the soul, which preserves it from being cast away by the storms of this evil world, Heb. vi. 19. *Which* HOPE *we have as an anchor of the soul, both sure and stedfast, and which entereth into that within the veil.* It is spoken of as a great benefit which true saints receive by Christ's resurrection, 1 Pet. i. 3. *Blessed be the God and Father of our Lord Jesus Christ, which, according to his abundant mercy, hath begotten us again unto a lively* HOPE, *by the resurrection of Jesus Christ from the dead.*

The scriptures place religion very much in the affection of *love;* love to God, and the Lord Jesus Christ; love to the people of God, and to mankind. The texts in which this is manifest, both in the Old Testament and New, are innumerable. But of this more afterwards. . . .

FREEDOM OF THE WILL

Written in Stockbridge and published in 1754. Easily his most famous book and his most successful polemic. Modern students should keep in mind his title, which imposes limitations on a complete study. He was writing *A Careful and Strict Enquiry into the Modern Prevailing Notions of that Freedom of Will which is supposed to be Essential to Moral Agency, Vertue and Vice, Reward and Punishment, Praise and Blame.* He set out to demolish the arguments of his Arminian opponents against the Calvinistic position. This limitation is largely responsible for the lukewarmness of later scholars for whom the battle of the will has greatly changed with the centuries. In fairness to Edwards the treatise should be judged in the light of its main purpose and against the background of 1754. This was a late day in the long battle. For discussions of theological importance, see Alexander Allen, *Jonathan Edwards*, pp. 281–301; Perry Miller, *Jonathan Edwards*, pp. 235–63; Conrad Wright, "Edwards and the Arminians on the Freedom of the Will," *Harvard Theological Review*, October, 1942, pp. 241–61. The text is from *The Works of President Edwards*, edited by S. B. Dwight, Vol. II, pp. 15–41, Part I, with omissions.

WHEREIN ARE EXPLAINED AND STATED VARIOUS TERMS AND THINGS BELONGING TO THE SUBJECT OF THE ENSUING DISCOURSE.

Sect. I.

Concerning the Nature of the Will.

196

It may possibly be thought, that there is no great need of going about to define or describe the *Will*; this word being generally as well understood as any other words we can use to explain it: and so perhaps it would be, had not philosophers, metaphysicians and polemic divines brought the matter into obscurity by the things they have said of it. But since it is so, I think it may be of some use, and will tend to greater clearness in the following discourse, to say a few things concerning it.

And therefore I observe, that the *Will* (without any metaphysical refining) is *That by which the mind chooses any thing.* The faculty of the *Will,* is that power, or principle of mind, by which it is capable of *choosing:* an act of the *Will* is the same as an act of *choosing* or *choice.*

If any think it is a more perfect definition of the Will, to say, that it is that by which the soul either *chooses* or *refuses;* I am content with it: though I think it enough to say, It is that by which the soul chooses: for in every act of Will whatsoever, the mind chooses one thing rather than another; it chooses something rather than the contrary, or rather than the want or non-existence of that thing. So in every act of refusal, the mind chooses the absence of the thing refused; the positive and the negative are set before the mind for its choice, and it chooses the negative; and the mind's making its choice in that case is properly the act of the Will: the Will's determining between the two, is a voluntary determination; but that is the same thing as making a choice. So that by whatever names we call the act of the Will, choosing, refusing, approving, disapproving, liking, disliking, embracing, rejecting, determining, directing, commanding, forbidding, inclining or *being* averse, *being* pleased or displeased *with;* all may be reduced to this of *choosing.* For the soul to act *voluntarily,* is evermore to act *electively.*

Mr. LOCKE says, "The Will signifies nothing but a power or ability to *prefer* or *choose.*" And, in the foregoing page, he says, "The word *preferring* seems best to express the act of volition;" but adds, that "it does it not precisely; for, though a man would *prefer* flying to walking, yet who can say he ever *wills* it?" But the instance he mentions, does not prove that there is any thing else in *willing,* but merely *preferring:* for it should be considered what is the immediate object of the Will, with respect to a man's walking, or any other external action; which is not being removed from one place to another; on the earth, or through the air; these are remoter objects of preference; but such or such an immediate *exertion* of himself. The thing next chosen, or preferred, when a man wills to walk, is not his being removed to such a place where he would be, but such an exertion and motion of his legs and feet, &c. in order to it. And his willing such an alteration in his body in the present moment, is nothing else but his choosing or preferring such an alteration in his body at such a moment, or his liking it better than the forbearance of it. And God has so made and established the human nature, the soul being united to a body in proper state, that the soul preferring or choosing such an immediate exertion or alteration of the body, such an alteration instantaneously follows. There is nothing else in the actions of my mind, that I am conscious of while I walk, but only my preferring or choosing, through successive moments, that there should be such alterations of my external sensations and motions; together with a concurring habitual expectation that it will be so; having ever found by experience, that on such an immediate preference, such sensations and motions do actually, instantaneously, and constantly arise. But it is not so in the case of flying: though a man may be said *remotely* to choose or prefer flying: yet he does not prefer, or desire, under circumstances in view, any *immediate exertion* of the members of his body in order to it; because he has no expectation that he should obtain the desired end by any such exertion; and he does not prefer, or incline to, any bodily exertion, under this apprehended circumstance, of its being wholly in vain. So that if we carefully distinguish the *proper objects* of the several acts of the Will, it will not appear by this, and such like instances, that there is any difference between *volition* and *preference;* or that a man's choosing, liking best, or being best pleased with a thing, are not the same with his *willing* that thing. Thus an act of the Will is commonly expressed by *its pleasing a man* to do thus or thus; and a man doing as he *wills,* and doing as he *pleases,* are in common speech the same thing.

Mr. Locke says, "The Will is perfectly distinguished from Desire; which in the very same action may have a quite contrary tendency from that which our Wills set us upon. A man, says he, whom I cannot deny, may oblige me to use persuasions to another, which, at the same time I am speaking, I may wish may not prevail on him. In this case, it is plain the Will and Desire run counter." I do not suppose, that *Will* and *Desire* are words of precisely the same signification: *Will* seems to be a word of a more general signification, extending to things present and absent. *Desire* respects something absent. I may prefer my present situation and posture, suppose sitting still, or having my eyes open, and so may *will* it. But yet I cannot think they are so entirely distinct, that they can ever be properly said to run counter. A man never, in any instance, wills any thing contrary to his desires, or desires any thing contrary to his Will. The forementioned instance, which MR. LOCKE produces, is no proof that he ever does. He may, on some consideration or other *will* to utter speeches which have a tendency to persuade another, and still may *desire* that they may not persuade him; but yet his Will and Desire do not run counter at all: the thing which he wills, the very same he desires; and he does not will a thing, and desire the *contrary*, in any particular. In this instance, it is not carefully observed, what is the thing willed, and what is the thing desired: if it were, it would be found, that Will and Desire do not clash in the least. The thing willed on some consideration, is to utter such words; and certainly, the same consideration so influences him, that he does not desire the contrary; all things considered, he chooses to utter such words, and does not desire not to utter them. And so as to the thing which Mr. LOCKE speaks of as *desired*, viz. That the words, though they tend to persuade, should not be effectual to that end, his Will is not contrary to this; he does not will that they should be effectual, but rather wills that they should not, as he desires. In order to prove that the Will and Desire may run counter, it should be shown that they may be contrary one to the other in the same thing, or with respect to the *very same object* of Will or desire: but here the objects are two; and in each, taken by themselves, the Will and Desire agree. And it is no wonder that they should not agree in *different* things, though but little distinguished in their nature. The Will may not agree with the Will, nor Desire agree with Desire, in different things. As in this very instance which MR. LOCKE mentions, a person may, on *some* consideration, desire to use persuasions, and at the same time may desire they may not prevail; but yet no body will say, that *Desire* runs counter to *Desire;* or that this proves that *Desire* is perfectly a distinct thing from *Desire.*—The like might be observed of the other instance MR. LOCKE produces, of a man's desiring to be eased of pain, &c.

But, not to dwell any longer on this, whether *Desire* and *Will,* and whether *Preference* and *Volition* be precisely the same things, I trust it will be allowed by all, that in every act of *will* there is an act of *choice;* that in every *volition* there is a *preference,* or a prevailing inclination of the soul, whereby, at that instant, it is out of a state of perfect indifference, with respect to the direct object of the volition. So that in every act, or going forth of the Will, there is some preponderation of the mind, one way rather than another; and the soul had rather *have* or *do* one thing, than another, or than *not* to have or do that thing; and that where there is absolutely no preferring or choosing, but a perfect, continuing equilibrium, there is no volition.

Sect. II.

Concerning the Determination of the Will.

By *determining* the Will, if the phrase be used with any meaning, must be intended, *causing* that the act of the Will or Choice should be thus, and not otherwise: and the Will is said to be determined, when, in consequence of some action, or influence, its choice is directed to, and fixed upon a particular object. As when we speak of the determination of motion, we mean causing the motion of the body to be in such a direction, rather than another.

The Determination of the Will, supposes an effect, which must have a cause. If the Will be determined, there is a Determiner. This must be supposed to be intended even by them that say the Will determines itself. If it be so, the Will is both Determiner and determined; it is a cause that acts and produces effects upon itself, and is the object of its own influence and action.

With respect to that grand enquiry, "What determines the

Will?" it would be very tedious and unnecessary, at present, to examine all the various opinions, which have been advanced concerning this matter; nor is it needful that I should enter into a particular discussion of all points debated in disputes on that other question, "Whether the Will always follows the last dictate of the understanding?" It is sufficient to my present purpose to say, *It is that motive, which, as it stands in the view of the mind, is the strongest, that determines the Will.* But it may be necessary that I should a little explain my meaning.

By *motive,* I mean the whole of that which moves, excites, or invites the mind to volition, whether that be one thing singly, or many things conjunctly. Many particular things may concur, and unite their strength, to induce the mind; and when it is so, all together are as one complex motive. And when I speak of the *strongest* motive, I have respect to the strength of the whole that operates to induce a particular act of volition, whether that be the strength of one thing alone, or of many together.

Whatever is objectively a motive, in this sense, must be something that is *extant in the view or apprehension of the understanding,* or perceiving faculty. Nothing can induce or invite the mind to will or act any thing, any further than it is perceived, or is some way or other in the mind's view; for what is wholly unperceived and perfectly out of the mind's view, cannot affect the mind at all. It is most evident, that nothing is in the mind, or reaches it, or takes any hold of it, any otherwise than as it is perceived or thought of.

And I think it must also be allowed by all, that every thing that is properly called a motive, excitement, or inducement to a perceiving, willing agent, has some sort and degree of *tendency,* or *advantage* to move or excite the Will, previous to the effect, or to the act of the Will excited. This previous tendency of the motive is what I call the *strength* of the motive. That motive which has a less degree of previous advantage, or tendency to move the will, or which appears less inviting, as it stands in the view of the mind, is what I call a *weaker* motive. On the contrary, that which appears most inviting, and has, by what appears concerning it to the understanding or apprehension, the greatest degree of previous tendency to excite and induce the choice, is what I call the *strongest* motive. And in this sense, I suppose the Will is always determined by the strongest motive.

Things that exist in the view of the mind have their strength, tendency, or advantage to move, or excite its Will, from many things appertaining to the nature and circumstances of the *thing viewed*, the nature and circumstances of the *mind that views*, and the degree and manner of its *view;* of which it would perhaps be hard to make a perfect enumeration. But so much I think may be determined in general, without room for controversy, that whatever is perceived or apprehended by an intelligent and voluntary agent, which has the nature and influence of a motive to volition or choice, is considered or viewed *as good;* nor has it any tendency to engage the election of the soul in any further degree than it appears such. For to say otherwise, would be to say, that things that appear, have a tendency, by the appearance they make, to engage the mind to elect them, some other way than by their appearing eligible to it; which is absurd. And therefore it must be true, in some sense, that *the Will always is, as the greatest apparent good is*. But only, for the right understanding of this, two things must be well and distinctly observed.

1. It must be observed in what sense I use the term "good;" namely, as of the same import with "agreeable." To appear *good* to the mind, as I use the phrase, is the same as to *appear agreeable,* or *seem pleasing* to the mind. Certainly, nothing appears inviting and eligible to the mind, or tending to engage its inclination and choice, considered as *evil* or *disagreeable;* nor indeed, as *indifferent,* and neither agreeable nor disagreeable. But if it tends to draw the inclination, and move the Will, it must be under the notion of that which *suits* the mind. And therefore that must have the greatest tendency to attract and engage it, which, as it stands in the mind's view, suits it best, and pleases it most; and in that sense, is the greatest apparent good: to say otherwise, is little, if any thing, short of a direct and plain contradiction.

The word "good," in this sense, includes in its signification, the removal or avoiding of evil, or of that which is disagreeable and uneasy. It is agreeable and pleasing, to avoid what is disagreeable and displeasing, and to have uneasiness removed. So that here is included what MR. LOCKE supposes

determines Will. For when he speaks of "uneasiness," as
determining the Will, he must be understood as supposing
that the end or aim which governs in the volition or act of
preference, is the avoiding or the removal of that uneasiness;
and that is the same thing as choosing and seeking what is
more easy and agreeable.

2. When I say, that the Will is as the greatest apparent
good, or, (as I have explained it) that volition has always for
its object the thing which appears most agreeable; it must be
carefully observed, to avoid confusion and needless objection,
that I speak of the *direct* and *immediate* object of the act of
volition; and not some object to which the act of Will has
only an indirect and remote respect. Many acts of volition
have some remote relation to an object, that is different from
the thing most immediately willed and chosen. Thus, when a
drunkard has his liquor before him, and he has to choose
whether to drink it, or no; the immediate objects, about which
his present volition is conversant, and between which his
choice now decides, are his own *acts,* in drinking the liquor,
or letting it alone; and this will certainly be done according
to what, in the present view of his mind, taken in the whole
of it, is most agreeable to him. If he chooses to drink it,
and not to let it alone; then this action, as it stands in the
view of his mind, with all that belongs to its appearance
there, is more agreeable and pleasing than letting it alone.

But the objects to which this act of volition may relate
more remotely, and between which his choice may determine
more indirectly, are the present pleasure the man expects by
drinking, and the future misery which he judges will be the
consequence of it; he may judge that this future misery,
when it comes, will be more disagreeable and unpleasant, than
refraining from drinking now would be. But these two things
are not the proper objects that the act of volition spoken of
is next conversant about. For the act of Will spoken of, is
concerning present drinking or forbearing to drink. If he
wills to drink, then *drinking* is the proper object of the act of
his Will; and drinking, on some account or other, now appears most agreeable to him, and suits him best. If he chooses
to refrain, then *refraining* is the immediate object of his Will,
and is most pleasing to him. If in the choice he makes in the
case, he prefers a present pleasure to a future advantage,
which he judges will be greater when it comes; then a lesser

present pleasure appears more agreeable to him than a greater advantage at a distance. If on the contrary a future advantage is preferred, then that appears most agreeable, and suits him best. And so still, the present volition is, as the greatest apparent good at present is.

I have rather chosen to express myself thus, "that the Will always is as the greatest apparent good," or "as what appears most agreeable," than to say that the Will "*is determined by* the greatest apparent good," or "by what seems most agreeable;" because an appearing most agreeable to the mind, and the mind's preferring, seem scarcely distinct. If strict propriety of speech be insisted on, it may more properly be said, that the *voluntary action,* which is the immediate *consequence* of the mind's choice, is *determined* by that which appears most agreeable, than the choice itself; but that *volition* itself is always determined by that in or about the mind's view of the object, which *causes it to appear* most agreeable. I say, "in or about the mind's view of the object;" because what has influence to render an object in view agreeable, is not only what appears *in* the object viewed, but also *the manner* of the view, and *the state and circumstances* of the mind that views. Particularly to enumerate all things pertaining to the mind's view of the objects of volition, which have influence in their appearing agreeable to the mind, would be a matter of no small difficulty, and might require a treatise by itself, and is not necessary to my present purpose. I shall therefore only mention some things in general.

I. One thing that makes an object proposed to choice agreeable, is the *apparent nature* and *circumstances of the object.* And there are various things of this sort, that have influence in rendering the object more or less agreeable; as

1. That which appears *in* the object, rendering it *beautiful* and pleasant, or *deformed* and irksome to the mind; viewing it as it is *in itself.*

2. The apparent degree of pleasure or trouble *attending* the object, or the *consequence* of it. Such concomitants and consequences being viewed as circumstances of the object, are to be considered as belonging to it; and as it were parts of it, as it stands in the mind's view a proposed object of choice.

3. The *apparent state* of the pleasure or trouble that appears, with respect to *distance of time;* being either nearer or

farther off. It is a thing in itself agreeable to the mind, to have pleasure speedily; and disagreeable to have it delayed: so that if there be two equal degrees of pleasure set in the mind's view, and all other things are equal, but one is beheld as near, and the other afar off; the nearer will appear most agreeable, and so will be chosen. Because, though the agreeableness of the objects be exactly equal, as viewed in themselves, yet not as viewed in their circumstances; one of them having the additional agreeableness of the circumstance of nearness.

II. Another thing that contributes to the agreeableness of an object of choice, as it stands in the mind's view, is the *manner of the view*. If the object be something which appears connected with future pleasure, not only will the degree of apparent pleasure have influence, but also the manner of the view, especially in two respects.

1. With respect to the degree of *assent,* with which the mind judges the pleasure to be future. Because it is more agreeable to have a *certain* happiness, than an *uncertain* one; and a pleasure viewed as more probable, all other things being equal, is more agreeable to the mind, than that which is viewed as less probable.

2. With respect to the degree of the *idea* or apprehension of the future pleasure. With regard to things which are the subject of our thoughts, either past, present or future, we have much more of an idea or apprehension of some things than others; that is, our idea is much more clear, lively and strong. Thus the ideas we have of sensible things by immediate sensation, are usually much more lively than those we have by mere imagination, or by contemplation of them when absent. My idea of the sun, when I look upon it, is more vivid, than when I only think of it. Our idea of the sweet relish of a delicious fruit is usually stronger when we taste it, than when we only imagine it. And sometimes, the idea we have of things by contemplation, are much stronger and clearer, than at other times. Thus, a man at one time has a much stronger idea of the pleasure which is to be enjoyed in eating some sort of food that he loves, than at another. Now the strength of the idea or the sense that men have of future good or evil, is one thing that has great influence on their minds to excite volition. When two kinds of future pleasure are presented for choice, though both are supposed exactly equal by the judgment, and both equally certain, yet of one

the mind has a far more lively sense, than of the other; this last has the greatest advantage by far to affect and attract the mind, and move the Will. It is now more agreeable to the mind, to take the pleasure of which it has a strong and lively sense, than that of which it has only a faint idea. The view of the former is attended with the strongest appetite, and the greatest uneasiness attends the want of it; and it is agreeable to the mind to have uneasiness removed, and its appetite gratified. And if several future enjoyments are presented together, as competitors for the choice of the mind, some of them judged to be greater, and others less; the mind also having a more lively idea of the good of some, and of others a less; and some are viewed as of greater certainty or probability than others; and those enjoyments that appear most agreeable in one of these respects, appear least so in others: in this case, all other things being equal, the agreeableness of a proposed object of choice will be in a degree some way compounded of the degree of good supposed by the judgment, the degree of apparent probability or certainty of that good, and the degree of liveliness of the idea the mind has of that good; because all together concur to constitute the degree in which the object appears at present agreeable; and accordingly will volition be determined.

I might further observe, that the *state of the mind* which views a proposed object of choice, is another thing that contributes to the agreeableness or disagreeableness of that object; the particular temper which the mind has by nature, or that has been introduced and established by education, example, custom, or some other means; or the frame or state that the mind is in on a particular occasion. That object which appears agreeable to one, does not so to another. And the same object does not always appear alike agreeable to the same person, at different times. It is most agreeable to some men, to follow their reason; and to others, to follow their appetites: to some men, it is more agreeable to deny a vicious inclination, than to gratify it: others it suits best to gratify the vilest appetites. It is more disagreeable to some men than others, to counter-act a former resolution. In these respects, and many others which might be mentioned, different things will be most agreeable to different persons; and not only so, but to the same persons at different times.

But possibly it is needless to mention the "state of the

mind," as a ground of the agreeableness of objects distinct from the other two mentioned before; *viz.* The apparent *nature and circumstances* of the objects viewed, and the *manner* of the view. Perhaps, if we strictly consider the matter, the different temper and state of the mind makes no alteration as to the agreeableness of objects, any other way, than as it makes the objects themselves appear differently *beautiful or deformed,* having apparent pleasure or pain attending them; and, as it occasions the *manner* of the view to be different, causes the idea of beauty or deformity, pleasure or uneasiness to be more or less lively.

However, I think so much is certain, that volition, in no one instance that can be mentioned, is otherwise than the greatest apparent good is, in the manner which has been explained. The choice of the mind never departs from that which, at the time, and with respect to the direct and immediate objects of decision, appears most agreeable and pleasing, all things considered. If the immediate objects of the will are a man's own actions, then those actions which appear most agreeable to him he wills. If it be now most agreeable to him, all things considered, to walk, then he now wills to walk. If it be now, upon the whole of what at present appears to him, most agreeable to speak, then he chooses to speak: if it suits him best to keep silence, then he chooses to keep silence. There is scarcely a plainer and more universal dictate of the sense and experience of mankind, than that, when men act voluntarily, and do what they please, then they do what suits them best, or what is most *agreeable to them.* To say, that they do what *pleases* them, but yet not what is *agreeable* to them, is the same thing as to say, they do what they please, but do not act their pleasure; and that is to say, that they do what they please, and yet do not what they please.

It appears from these things, that in some sense, *the Will always follows the last dictate of the understanding.* But then the *understanding* must be taken in a large sense, as including the whole faculty of perception or apprehension, and not merely what is called *reason* or *judgment.* If by the dictate of the understanding is meant what reason declares to be best, or most for the person's happiness, taking in the whole of its duration, it is not true, that the Will always follows the last dictate of the understanding. Such a dictate of reason is quite a different matter from things appearing now most *agreeable,* all things being put together which pertain to the mind's present preceptions in any respect: although that dictate of reason, when it takes place, has concern in the compound influence which moves the Will; and should be considered in estimating the degree of that appearance of good which the Will always follows; either as having its influence added to other things, or subducted from them. When such dictate of reason concurs with other things, then its weight is added to them, as put into the same scale; but when it is against them, it is as a weight in the opposite scale, resisting the influence of other things: yet its resistance is often overcome by their greater weight, and so the act of the Will is determined in opposition to it.

These things may serve, I hope, in some measure, to illustrate and confirm the position laid down in the beginning of this section, viz. "That the Will is always determined by the strongest motive," or by that view of the mind which has the greatest degree of *previous* tendency to excite volition. But whether I have been so happy as rightly to explain the thing wherein consists the strength of motives, or not, yet my failing in this will not overthrow the position itself; which carries much of its own evidence with it, and is a point of chief importance to the purpose of the ensuing discourse: And the truth of it, I hope, will appear with great clearness before I have finished what I have to say on the subject of human liberty.

Sect. III.

Concerning the Meaning of the Terms Necessity, Impossibility, Inability, &c. and of Contingence.

The words *necessary, impossible,* &c. are abundantly used in controversies about Free-Will and Moral Agency; and therefore the sense in which they are used, should be clearly understood.

Here I might say, that a thing is then said to be *necessary,* when it *must* be, and cannot be otherwise. But this would not properly be a definition of Necessity, any more than if I explained the word *must* by the phrase, there being a Necessity. The words *must, can,* and *cannot,* need explication as much as the words *necessary* and *impossible;* excepting that the former are words that in earliest life we more commonly use.

The word *necessary,* as used in common speech, is a relative term; and relates to some supposed opposition made to the existence of a thing, which opposition is overcome, or proves insufficient to hinder or alter it. That is necessary, in the original and proper sense of the word, which is, or will be, notwithstanding all supposable opposition. To say, that a thing is necessary, is the same thing as to say, that it is impossible, it should not be. But the word *impossible* is manifestly a relative term, and has reference to supposed power exerted to bring a thing to pass, which is insufficient for the effect; as the word *unable* is relative, and has relation to ability, or endeavour, which is insufficient. Also the word *irresistible* is relative, and has always reference to resistance which is made, or may be made, to some force or power tending to an effect, and is insufficient to withstand the power, or hinder the effect. The common notion of Necessity and Impossibility implies something that frustrates endeavour or desire.

Here several things are to be noted.

1. Things are said to be necessary in *general,* which are or will be notwithstanding any supposable opposition from whatever quarter. But things are said to be necessary *to us,* which are or will be notwithstanding all opposition supposable in the case *from us.* The same may be observed of the word *impossible,* and other such like terms.

2. These terms *necessary, impossible, irresistible,* &c. more especially belong to controversies about liberty and moral agency, as used in the latter of the two senses now mentioned, *viz.* as necessary or impossible *to us,* and with relation to any supposable opposition or endeavour *of ours.*

3. As the word *Necessity,* in its vulgar and common use, is relative, and has always reference to some supposable insufficient opposition; so when we speak of any thing as necessary *to us,* it is with relation to some supposable opposition of *our Wills,* or some voluntary exertion or effect of ours to the contrary. For we do not properly make opposition to an event, any otherwise than as we *voluntarily* oppose it. Things are said to be what must be, or *necessarily* are, *as to us,*

when they are, or will be, though we desire or endeavour the contrary, or try to prevent or remove their existence: but such opposition of ours always either consists in, or implies opposition of our wills.

It is manifest that all such like words and phrases, as vulgarly used, are understood in this manner. Anything is said to be *necessary,* when we cannot help it, let us do what we will. So any thing is said to be *impossible* to us, when we would do it, or would have it brought to pass, and endeavour it; or at least may be supposed to desire and seek it; but all our desires and endeavours are, or would be vain. And that is said to be *irresistible,* which overcomes all our opposition, resistance, and endeavour to the contrary. And we are said to be *unable* to do a thing, when our supposable desires and endeavours are insufficient.

We are accustomed, in the common use of language, thus to apply and understand these phrases: we grow up with such a habit; which, by the daily use of these terms from our childhood, becomes fixed and settled; so that the idea of a relation to a supposed will, desire, and endeavour of ours, is strongly connected with these terms, whenever we hear the words used. Such ideas, and these words, are so associated, that they unavoidably go together; one suggests the other, and never can be easily separated as long as we live. And though we use the words, as terms of art, in another sense, yet, unless we are exceedingly circumspect, we shall insensibly slide into the vulgar use of them, and so apply the words in a very inconsistent manner, which will deceive and confound us in our reasonings and discourses, even when we pretend to use them as terms of art.

4. It follows from what has been observed, that when these terms *necessary, irresistible, unable,* &c are used in cases wherein no insufficient will is supposed, or can be supposed, but the very nature of the supposed case itself excludes any opposition, will or endeavour, they are then not used in their proper signification. The reason is manifest; in such cases we cannot use the words with reference to a supposable opposition, will or endeavour. And therefore if any man uses these terms in such cases, he either uses them nonsensically, or in some new sense, diverse from their original and proper meaning. As for instance; if any one should affirm after this manner, That it is *necessary* for a

man, or what *must* be, that he should choose virtue rather
than vice, during the time that he prefers virtue to vice; and
that it is a thing impossible and irresistible, that it should be
otherwise than that he should have this choice, so long as
this choice continues; such a one would use the terms *must,
irresistible,* &c. with either perfect insignificance, or in some
new sense, diverse from their common use; which is with
reference, as has been observed, to supposable opposition,
unwillingness and resistance; whereas, here, the very supposition excludes and denies any such thing: for the case
supposed is that of being willing, and choosing.

5. It appears from what has been said, that these terms
necessary, impossible, &c. are often used by philosophers and
metaphysicians in a sense quite diverse from their common
and original signification; for they apply them to many cases
in which no opposition is supposable. Thus they use them
with respect to God's existence before the creation of the
world, when there was no other being; with regard to many
of the dispositions and acts of the divine Being, such as his
loving himself, his loving righteousness, hating sin, &c. So
they apply them to many cases of the inclinations and
actions of created intelligent beings, wherein all opposition of
the Will is excluded in the very supposition of the case.

Metaphysical or *Philosophical* Necessity is nothing different from their certainty. I speak not now of the certainty
of knowledge, but the certainty that is in things themselves,
which is the foundation of the certainty of the knowledge,
or that wherein lies the ground of the infallibility of the
proposition which affirms them.

What is sometimes given as the definition of philosophical
Necessity, namely, *"That by which a thing cannot but be,"*
or *"whereby it cannot be otherwise,"* fails of being a proper
explanation of it, on two accounts: *First,* the words *can,* or
cannot, need explanation as much as the word *Necessity;*
and the former may as well be explained by the latter, as
the latter by the former. Thus, if any one asked us what we
mean, when we say, a thing *cannot but be,* we might explain
ourselves by saying, it must necessarily be so; as well as explain Necessity, by saying, it is that by which a thing cannot but be. And *Secondly,* this definition is liable to the
forementioned great inconvenience; the words *cannot,* or *unable,* are properly relative, and have relation to power ex-

erted, or that may be exerted, in order to the thing spoken of; to which as I have now observed, the word *Necessity,* as used by philosophers, has no reference.

Philosophical Necessity is really nothing else than the FULL AND FIXED CONNECTION BETWEEN THE THINGS SIGNIFIED BY THE SUBJECT AND PREDICATE OF A PROPOSITION, which affirms something to be true. When there is such a connection, then the thing affirmed in the proposition is necessary, in a philosophical sense; whether any opposition, or contrary effort be supposed, or no. When the subject and predicate of the proposition, which affirms the existence of any thing, either substance, quality, act, or circumstance, have a full and CERTAIN CONNECTION, then the existence or being of that thing is said to be *necessary* in a metaphysical sense. And in this sense I use the word *Necessity,* in the following discourse, when I endeavour to prove *that Necessity is not inconsistent with Liberty.* . . .

Sect. IV.

Of the Distinction of natural and moral Necessity, and Inability.

That Necessity which has been explained, consisting in an infallible connection of the things signified by the subject and predicate of a proposition, as intelligent beings are the subjects of it, is distinguished into *moral* and *natural* Necessity.

I shall not now stand to enquire whether this distinction be a proper and perfect distinction; but shall only explain how these two sorts of Necessity are understood, as the terms are sometimes used, and as they are used in the following discourse.

The phrase, *moral Necessity,* is used variously; sometimes it is used for a necessity of moral obligation. So we say, a man is under Necessity, when he is under bonds of *duty* and conscience, from which he cannot be discharged. Again, the word *Necessity* is often used for great obligation in point of *interest.* Sometimes by moral Necessity is meant that apparent connection of things, which is the ground of *moral evidence;* and so is distinguished from *absolute Necessity,* or that sure connection of things, that is a foundation for *infallible certainty.* In this sense, moral Necessity signifies much the same as that high degree of *probability,* which is ordinarily sufficient to satisfy mankind, in their conduct and behaviour in the world, as they would consult their own safety and interest, and treat others properly as members of society. And sometimes by moral Necessity is meant that Necessity of connection and *consequence,* which arises from such *moral causes,* as the strength of inclination, or motives, and the connection which there is in many cases between these, and such certain volitions and actions. And it is in *this* sense, that I use the phrase, *moral Necessity,* in the following discourse.

By *natural Necessity,* as applied to men, I mean such Necessity as men are under through the force of natural causes; as distinguished from what are called moral causes, such as habits and dispositions of the heart, and moral motives and inducements. Thus men placed in certain circumstances, are the subjects of particular sensations by Necessity: they feel pain when their bodies are wounded; they see the objects presented before them in a clear light, when their eyes are opened: so they assent to the truth of certain propositions, as soon as the terms are understood; as that two and two make four, that black is not white, that two parallel lines can never cross one another; so by a natural Necessity men's bodies move downwards, when there is nothing to support them.

But here several things may be noted concerning these two kinds of Necessity.

1. Moral Necessity may be as *absolute,* as natural Necessity. That is, the effect may be as perfectly connected with its moral cause, as a natural necessary effect is with its natural cause. Whether the Will in every case is necessarily determined by the strongest motive, or whether the Will ever makes any resistance to such a motive, or can ever oppose the strongest present inclination, or not; if that matter should be controverted, yet I suppose none will deny, but that, in some cases, a previous bias and inclination, or the motive presented, may be so powerful, that the act of the Will may be certainly and indissolubly connected

therewith. When motives or previous bias are very strong, all will allow that there is some *difficulty* in going against them. And if they were yet stronger, the difficulty would be still greater. And therefore, if more were still added to their strength, to a certain degree, it would make the difficulty so great, that it would be wholly *impossible* to surmount it; for this plain reason, because whatever power men may be supposed to have to surmount difficulties, yet that power is not infinite; and so goes not beyond certain limits. If a man can surmount ten degrees of difficulty of this kind with twenty degrees of strength, because the degrees of strength are beyond the degrees of difficulty; yet if the difficulty be increased to thirty, or an hundred, or a thousand degrees, and his strength not also increased, his strength will be wholly insufficient to surmount the difficulty. As therefore it must be allowed, that there may be such a thing as a *sure* and *perfect* connection between moral causes and effects; so this only is what I call by the name of *moral Necessity.*

2. When I use this distinction of *moral* and *natural Necessity,* I would not be understood to suppose, that if any thing come to pass by the former kind of Necessity, the *nature* of things is not concerned in it, as well as in the latter. I do not mean to determine, that when a *moral* habit or motive is so strong, that the act of the Will infallibly follows, this is not owing to the *nature of things.* But *natural* and *moral* are the terms by which these two kinds of Necessity have usually been called; and they must be distinguished by some names, for there is a difference between them, that is very important in its consequences. This difference, however, does not lie so much in the nature of the *connection,* as in the two terms *connected.* The cause with which the effect is connected, is of a particular kind; *viz.* that which is of a moral nature; either some previous habitual disposition, or more motive exhibited to the understanding. And the effect is also of a particular kind; being likewise of a moral nature; consisting in some inclination or volition of the soul, or voluntary action.

I suppose, that Necessity which is called *natural* in distinction from *moral* necessity, is so called, because *mere nature* as the word is vulgarly used, is concerned, without any thing of *choice.* The word *nature* is often used in opposition to *choice;* not because nature has indeed never any hand in our choice; but, probably, because we first get our notion of nature from that obvious course of events, which we observe in many things where our choice has no concern; and especially in the material world; which, in very many parts of it, we easily perceive to be in a settled course; the stated order, and manner of succession, being very apparent. But where we do not readily discern the rule and connection, (though there be a connection, according to an established law, truly taking place) we signify the manner of event by some other name. Even in many things which are seen in the material and inanimate world, which do not obviously come to pass according to any settled course, men do not call the manner of the event by the name of *nature,* but by such names as *accident, chance, contingence,* &c. So men make a distinction between nature and choice; as if they were completely and universally distinct. Whereas, I suppose none will deny but that choice, *in many cases,* arises from nature, as truly as other events. But the connection between acts of choice, and their causes, according to established laws, is not so obvious. And we observe that choice is, as it were, a new principle of motion and action, different from that established order of things which is most obvious, and seen especially in corporeal things. The choice also often interposes, interrupts, and alters the chain of events in these external objects, and causes them to proceed otherwise than they would do, if let alone. Hence it is spoken of as if it were a principle of motion entirely distinct from nature, and properly set in opposition to it. Names being commonly given to things, according to what is most obvious, and is suggested by what appears to the senses without reflection and research.

3. It must be observed, that in what has been explained, as signified by the name of *moral Necessity,* the word *Necessity* is not used according to the original design and meaning of the word: for, as was observed before, such terms, *necessary, impossible, irresistible,* &c. in common speech, and their most proper sense, are always relative; having reference to some supposable voluntary opposition or endeavour, that is insufficient. But no such opposition, or contrary will and endeavour, is supposable in the case of moral Necessity; which is a certainty of the inclination and

will itself; which does not admit of the supposition of a will to oppose and resist it. For it is absurd, to suppose the same individual will to oppose itself, in its present act; or the present choice to be opposite to, and resisting present choice: as absurd as it is to talk of two contrary motions, in the same moving body, at the same time.—And therefore the very case supposed never admits of any trial, whether an opposing or resisting will can overcome this Necessity.

What has been said of natural and moral Necessity, may serve to explain what is intended by natural and moral *Inability*. We are said to be *naturally* unable to do a thing, when we cannot do it if we will, because what is most commonly called *nature* does not allow of it, or because of some impending defect or obstacle that is extrinsic to the will; either in the faculty of understanding, constitution of body, or external objects. *Moral* Inability consists not in any of these things; but either in the want of inclination; or the strength of a contrary inclination; or the want of sufficient motives in view, to induce and excite the act of the will, or the strength of apparent motives to the contrary. Or both these may be resolved into one; and it may be said in one word, that moral Inability consists in the opposition or want of inclination. For when a person is unable to will or choose such a thing, through a defect of motives, or prevalence of contrary motives, it is the same thing as his being unable through the want of an inclination, or the prevalence of a contrary inclination, in such circumstances, and under the influence of such views.

To give some instances of this *moral Inability*.—A woman of great honour and chastity may have a moral Inability to prostitute herself to her slave. A child of great love and duty to his parents, may be thus unable to kill his father. A very lascivious man, in case of certain opportunities and temptations, and in the absence of such and such restraints, may be unable to forbear gratifying his lust. A drunkard, under such and such circumstances, may be unable to forbear taking strong drink. A very malicious man may be unable to exert benevolent acts to an enemy, or to desire his prosperity; yea, some may be so under the power of a vile disposition, that they may be unable to love those who are most worthy of their esteem and affection. A strong habit of virtue, and a great degree of holiness, may cause a moral Inability to love wickedness in general, and may render a man unable to take complacence in wicked persons or things; or to choose a wicked, in preference to a virtuous life. And on the other hand, a great degree of habitual wickedness may lay a man under an Inability to love and choose holiness; and render him utterly unable to love an infinitely holy Being, or to choose and cleave to him as his chief good.

Here it may be of use to observe this distinction of moral Inability, viz. of that which is *general and habitual,* and that which is *particular and occasional.* By a *general and habitual* moral Inability, I mean an Inability in the heart to all exercises or acts of will of that kind, through a fixed and habitual inclination, or an habitual and stated defect, or want of a certain kind of inclination. Thus a very ill-natured man may be unable to exert such acts of benevolence, as another, who is full of good nature, commonly exerts; and a man whose heart is habitually void of gratitude, may be unable to exert grateful acts, through that stated defect of a grateful inclination. By *particular and occasional* moral Inability, I mean an Inability of the will or heart to a particular act, through the strength or defect of present motives, or of inducements presented to the view of the understanding, *on this occasion.*——If it be so, that the will is always determined by the strongest motive, then it must always have an Inability, in this latter sense, to act otherwise than it does; it not being possible, in any case, that the will should, at present, go against the motive which has now, all things considered, the greatest advantage to induce it.——The former of these kinds of moral Inability, is most commonly called by the name of *Inability;* because the word, in its most proper and original signification, has respect to some *stated defect.* And this especially obtains the name of *Inability* also upon another account:—because, as before observed, the word Inability in its original and most common use, is a relative term; and has respect to will and endeavour, as supposable in the case, and as insufficient to bring to pass the thing desired and endeavoured. Now there may be more of an appearance and shadow of this, with respect to the acts which arise from a fixed and strong habit, than others that arise only from transient occasions and causes. Indeed will and endeavour against, or diverse from *present* acts of the will are in no case supposable, whether those acts be occasional or habitual; for that would be to suppose the will, at present, to be otherwise than, at present, it is. But yet there may be will and endeavour against *future* acts of the will, or volitions that are likely to take place, as viewed at a distance. It is no contradiction, to suppose that the acts of the will at one time, may be against the acts of the will at another time; and there may be desires and endeavours to prevent or excite future acts of the will; but such desires and endeavours are, in many cases, rendered insufficient and vain, through fixedness of habit: when the occasion returns, the strength of habit overcomes, and baffles all such opposition. In this respect, a man may be in miserable slavery and bondage to a strong habit. But it may be comparatively easy to make an alteration with respect to such future acts, as are only occasional and transient; because the occasion or transient cause, if foreseen, may often easily be prevented or avoided. On this account, the moral inability that attends fixed habits, especially obtains the name of *Inability*. And then, as the will may remotely and indirectly resist itself, and do it in vain, in the case of strong habits; so reason may resist present acts of the will, and its resistance be insufficient: and this is more commonly the case also, when the acts arise from strong habit.

But it must be observed concerning moral Inability, in each kind of it, that the word *Inability* is used in a sense very diverse from its original import. The word signifies only a natural Inability, in the proper use of it; and is applied to such cases only wherein a present will or inclination to the thing, with respect to which a person is said to be unable, is supposable. It cannot be truly said, according to the ordinary use of language, that a malicious man, let him be never so malicious, cannot hold his hand from striking, or that he is not able to shew his neighbour kindness; or that a drunkard, let his appetite be never so strong, cannot keep the cup from his mouth. In the strictest propriety of speech, a man has a thing in his power, if he has it in his choice, or at his election: and a man cannot be truly said to be unable to do a thing, when he can do it if he will. It is improperly said, that a person cannot perform those external actions, which are dependent on the act of the will, and which would be easily performed, if the act of the will were present. And if it be improperly said, that he cannot perform those external voluntary actions, which depend on the will, it is in some respect more improperly said, that he is unable to exert the acts of the will themselves; because it is more evidently false, with respect to these, that he cannot if he will; for to say so, is a downright contradiction; it is to say, he *cannot* will, if he *does* will. And in this case, not only is it true, that it is easy for a man to do the thing if he will, but the very willing is the doing; when once he has willed, the thing is performed; and nothing else remains to be done. Therefore, in these things, to ascribe a non-performance to the want of power or ability, is not just; because the thing wanting is not a being *able,* but a being *willing.* There are faculties of mind, and a capacity of nature, and every thing else, sufficient, but a disposition: nothing is wanting but a will.

Sect. V.

Concerning the Notion of Liberty, and of Moral Agency.

The plain and obvious meaning of the words *Freedom* and *Liberty,* in common speech, is *The power, opportunity, or advantage that any one has, to do as he pleases.* Or in other words, his being free from hindrance or impediment in the way of doing, or conducting in any respect as he wills. And the contrary to Liberty, whatever name we call that by, is a person's being hindered or unable to conduct as he will, or being necessitated to do otherwise.

If this which I have mentioned be the meaning of the word Liberty, in the ordinary use of language; as I trust that none that has ever learned to talk, and is unprejudiced, will deny; then it will follow, that in propriety of speech, neither Liberty, nor its contrary, can properly be ascribed to any being or thing, but that which has such a faculty, power, or property, as is called will. For that which is possessed of no *will,* cannot have any *power* or *opportunity* of doing *according to its will,* nor be necessitated to act *con-*

trary to its will, nor be restrained from acting agreeably to it. And therefore to talk of Liberty, or the contrary, as belonging to the *very will itself,* is not to speak good sense; if we judge of sense, and nonsense, by the original and proper signification of words.—For the *will itself* is not an Agent that *has a will:* the power of choosing, itself, has not a power of choosing. That which has the power of volition is the man, or the soul, and not the power of volition itself. And he that has the Liberty of doing according to his will, is the Agent who is possessed of the will; and not the will which he is possessed of. We say with propriety, that a bird let loose has power and liberty to fly; but not that the bird's power of flying has a power and Liberty of flying. To be free is the property of an agent, who is possessed of powers and faculties, as much as to be cunning, valiant, bountiful, or zealous. But these qualities are the properties of persons; and not the properties of properties.

There are two things contrary to what is called Liberty in common speech. One is *constraint;* otherwise called *force, compulsion,* and *coaction;* which is a person's being necessitated to do a thing *contrary* to his will. The other is *restraint;* which is, his being hindered, and not having power to do *according* to his will. But that which has no will cannot be the subject of these things.—I need say the less on this head, Mr. LOCKE having set the same thing forth, with so great clearness, in his *Essay on the Human Understanding.*

But one thing more I would observe concerning what is vulgarly called *Liberty*; namely, that power and opportunity for one to do and conduct as he will, or according to his choice, is all that is meant by it, without taking into the meaning of the word, any thing of the *cause* of that choice; or at all considering how the person came to have such a volition; whether it was caused by some external motive, or internal habitual bias; whether it was determined by some internal antecedent volition, or whether it happened without a cause; whether it was necessarily connected with something foregoing, or not connected. Let the person come by his choice any how, yet, if he is able, and there is nothing in the way to hinder his pursuing and executing his will, the man is perfectly free, according to the primary and common notion of freedom.

What has been said may be sufficient to shew what is

meant by *Liberty,* according to the common notions of mankind, and in the usual and primary acceptation of the word: but the word, as used by *Arminians, Pelagians* and others, who oppose the *Calvinists,* has an entirely different signification.—These several things belong to their notion of Liberty. 1. That it consists in a *self-determining power* in the will, or a certain sovereignty the will has over itself, and its own acts, whereby it determines its own volitions; so as not to be dependent in its determinations, on any cause without itself, nor determined by any thing prior to its own acts. 2. *Indifference* belongs to Liberty in their notion of it, or that the mind, previous to the act of volition, be *in equilibrio.* 3. *Contingence* is another thing that belongs and is essential to it; not in the common acceptation of the word, as that has been already explained, but as opposed to all *necessity* or any fixed and certain connection with some previous ground or reason of its existence. They suppose the essence of Liberty so much to consist in these things, that unless the will of man be free in this sense, he has no real freedom, how much soever he may be at Liberty to act according to his will.

A *moral Agent* is a being that is capable of those actions that have a *moral* quality, and which can properly be denominated good or evil in a moral sense, virtuous or vicious, commendable or faulty. To moral Agency belongs a *moral faculty,* or sense of moral good and evil, or of such a thing as desert or worthiness, of praise or blame, reward or punishment; and a capacity which an Agent has of being influenced in his actions by moral inducements or motives, exhibited to the view of understanding and reason, to engage to a conduct agreeable to the moral faculty.

The sun is very excellent and beneficial in its actions and influence on the earth, in warming and causing it to bring forth its fruits; but it is not a moral Agent: its action, though good, is not virtuous or meritorious. Fire that breaks out in a city, and consumes great part of it, is very mischievous in its operation; but is not a moral Agent: what it does is not faulty or sinful, or deserving of any punishment. The brute creatures are not moral Agents: the actions of some of them are very profitable and pleasant; others are very hurtful: yet seeing they have no moral faculty, or sense of desert, and do not act from choice guided by understanding, or with a capacity of reasoning and reflecting, but only from instinct, and are not capable of being influenced by moral inducements, their actions are not properly sinful or virtuous; nor are they properly the subjects of any such moral treatment for what they do, as moral Agents are for their faults or good deeds.

Here it may be noted, that there is a circumstantial difference between the moral Agency of a *ruler* and a *subject*. I call it *circumstantial,* because it lies only in the difference of moral inducements, by which they are capable of being influenced, arising from the difference of *circumstances.* A *ruler* acting in that capacity only, is not capable of being influenced by a moral law, and its sanctions of threatenings and promises, rewards and punishments, as the *subject* is; though both may be influenced by a knowledge of moral good and evil. And therefore the moral Agency of the Supreme Being, who acts only in the capacity of a *ruler* towards his creatures, and never as a *subject,* differs in that respect from the moral Agency of created intelligent beings. God's actions, and particularly those which he exerts as a moral governor, have moral qualifications, and are morally good in the highest degree. They are most perfectly holy and righteous; and we must conceive of Him as influenced in the highest degree, by that which, above all others, is properly a moral inducement; viz. the moral good which He sees in such and such things: and therefore He is, in the most proper sense, a moral Agent, the source of all moral ability and Agency, the fountain and rule of all virtue and moral good; though by reason of his being supreme over all, it is not possible He should be under the influence of law or command, promises or threatenings, rewards or punishments, counsels or warnings. The essential qualities of a moral Agent are in God, in the greatest possible perfection; such as understanding, to perceive the difference between moral good and evil; a capacity of discerning that moral worthiness and demerit, by which some things are praiseworthy, others deserving of blame and punishment; and also a capacity of choice, and choice guided by understanding, and a power of acting according to his choice or pleasure, and being capable of doing those things which are in the highest sense praiseworthy. And herein does very much consist that image of God wherein he made man, (which we read of *Gen.* i.

26, 27, and *chap*. ix. 6.) by which God distinguished man from the beasts, *viz*. in those faculties and principles of nature, whereby He is capable of moral Agency. Herein very much consists the *natural* image of God; whereas the *spiritual* and *moral* image, wherein man was made at first, consisted in that moral excellency with which he was endowed.

CHRISTIAN DOCTRINE OF ORIGINAL SIN DEFENDED

In press at the time of his death and published several months later, 1758. Once again he is fighting as the champion of Calvinism, using some of the arguments basic to the freedom-of-the-will polemic. He is attacking specifically Dr. John Taylor's *The Scripture Doctrine of Original Sin Proposed to a Free and Candid Examination,* which for twenty years had been a target for defenders of the orthodox position. Jonathan Edwards came late to the battle. For modern students one of the main interests of this book theologically is the theory of the unity of the race, which is the Edwards basis for the continuing corruption of man from Adam to all men. See Alexander Allen, *Jonathan Edwards,* pp. 302–13, for theological issues involved. The text is from *The Works of President Edwards,* edited by S. B. Dwight, Vol. II, pp. 309–16, Part I, Section 1.

WHEREIN ARE CONSIDERED SOME EVIDENCES OF ORIGINAL SIN FROM FACTS AND EVENTS, AS FOUNDED BY OBSERVATION AND EXPERIENCE, TOGETHER WITH REPRESENTATIONS AND TESTIMONIES OF HOLY SCRIPTURE, AND THE CONFESSION AND ASSERTION OF OPPOSERS.

The Evidence of Original Sin from what appears in Fact of the Sinfulness of Mankind.

All Mankind constantly, in all Ages, without Fail in any one Instance, run into that moral Evil, which is in effect their

own utter and eternal Perdition in a total privation of
GOD's Favour, and suffering of his Vengeance and Wrath.

By *Original Sin* as the phrase has been most commonly used
by divines, is meant the *innate sinful depravity of the heart.*
But yet when the *doctrine* of original sin is spoken of, it is
vulgarly understood in that latitude, which includes not only
the *depravity of nature,* but the *imputation* of Adam's first
sin; or, in other words, the liableness or exposedness of
Adam's posterity, in the divine judgment, to partake of the
punishment of that sin. So far as I know, most of those
who have held one of these, have maintained the other; and
most of those who have opposed one, have opposed the
other: both are opposed by the Author chiefly attended to in
the following discourse, in his book against original sin: And
it may perhaps appear in our future consideration of the subject, that they are closely connected; that the arguments
which prove the one establish the other, and that there are
no more difficulties attending the allowing of one, than the
other.

I shall in the first place, consider this doctrine more especially with regard to the *corruption of nature;* and as we
treat of this the other will naturally come into consideration, in the prosecution of the discourse, as connected with
it. As all moral qualities, all principles either of virtue or
vice, lie in the disposition of the heart, I shall consider
whether we have any evidence that the heart of man is naturally of a corrupt and evil disposition. This is strenuously
denied by many late writers who are enemies to the doctrine
of original sin; and particularly by Dr. TAYLOR.

The way we come by the idea of any such thing as
disposition or *tendency* is by observing what is constant or
general in *event;* especially under a great variety of circumstances; and above all, when the effect or event continues
the same through great and various opposition, much and
manifold force and means used to the contrary not prevailing
to hinder the effect. I do not know that such a prevalence
of effects is denied to be an evidence of prevailing tendency
in causes and agents; or that it is expressly denied by the
opposers of the doctrine of original sin, that if, in the course
of events, it universally or generally proves that mankind

are actually corrupt, this would be an evidence of a prior corrupt propensity in the world of mankind; whatever may be said by some, which, if taken with its plain consequences, may seem to imply a denial of this; which may be considered afterwards. But by many the fact is denied; that is, it is denied, that corruption and moral evil are commonly prevalent in the world: on the contrary, it is insisted on, that good preponderates, and that virtue has the ascendant.

To this purpose, Dr. TURNBULL says, "With regard to the prevalence of vice in the world, men are apt to let their imagination run out upon all the robberies, piracies, murders, perjuries, frauds, massacres, assassinations they have either heard of, or read in history; thence concluding all mankind to be very wicked. As if a court of justice were a proper place to make an estimate of the morals of mankind, or an hospital of the healthfulness of a climate. But ought they not to consider that the number of honest citizens and farmers far surpasses that of all sorts of criminals in any state, and that the innocent and kind actions of even criminals themselves surpass their crimes in numbers; that it is the rarity of crimes in comparison of innocent or good actions, which engages our attention to them and makes them to be recorded in history, while honest, generous domestic actions are overlooked only because they are so common? as one great danger, or one month's sickness shall become a frequently repeated story during a long life of health and safety.—Let not the vices of mankind be multiplied or magnified. Let us make a fair estimate of human life, and set over against the shocking, the astonishing instances of barbarity and wickedness that have been perpetrated in any age, not only the exceeding generous and brave actions with which history shines, but the prevailing innocency, good-nature, industry, felicity, and cheerfulness of the greater part of mankind at all times; and we shall not find reason to cry out, as objectors against Providence do on this occasion, that all men are vastly corrupt and that there is hardly any such thing as virtue in the world. Upon a fair computation the fact does indeed come out, that very great villanies have been very uncommon in all ages and looked upon as monstrous; so general is the sense and esteem of virtue."—It seems to be with a like view that Dr. TAYLOR says, "We must not take the measure of our health and enjoyments from a lazar-house, nor of our understanding from *Bedlam,* nor of our morals from a jail." (p. 77. S.)

With respect to the propriety and pertinence of such a representation of things, and its force as to the consequence designed, I hope we shall be better able to judge, and in some measure to determine whether the natural disposition of the hearts of mankind be corrupt or not, when the things which follow have been considered. But for the greater clearness, it may be proper here to premise one consideration that is of great importance in this controversy, and is very much overlooked by the opposers of the doctrine of original sin in their disputing against it.

That it is to be looked upon as the *true* tendency of the innate disposition of man's heart, which appears to be its tendency, when we consider things as they are in themselves, or in their own nature, without the *interposition of divine grace.*—Thus, that state of man's nature, that disposition of the mind, is to be looked upon as evil and pernicious, which, as it is in itself, tends to extremely pernicious consequences, and would certainly end therein, were it not that the free mercy and kindness of God interposes to prevent that issue. It would be very strange if any should argue that there is no evil tendency in the case, because the mere favour and compassion of the Most High may step in and oppose the tendency and prevent the sad effect. Particularly, if there be any thing in the nature of man whereby he has an universal unfailing tendency to that moral evil which, according to the real nature and true demerit of things as they are in themselves, implies his utter ruin, that must be looked upon as an evil tendency or propensity; however divine grace may interpose to save him from deserved ruin, and to over-rule things to an issue contrary to that which they tend to of themselves. Grace is sovereign, exercised according to the good pleasure of God, bringing good out of evil. The effect of it belongs not to the nature of things themselves, that otherwise have an ill tendency, any more than the remedy belongs to the disease; but is something altogether independent on it, introduced to oppose the natural tendency, and reverse the course of things. But the event to which things tend, according to their own *demerit,* and according to divine *justice,* is the event to which they tend in their own nature; as Dr. *T.'s* own words fully imply (*Pref*

to. Par. on Rom. p. 131.) "God alone (says he) can declare
whether he will pardon or punish the ungodliness and unrighteousness of mankind, which is in ITS OWN NATURE
punishable." Nothing is more precisely according to the truth
of things than divine justice: it weighs things in an even
balance; it views and estimates things no otherwise than
they are truly in their own nature. Therefore undoubtedly
that which implies a tendency to ruin, according to the
estimate of divine *justice*, does indeed imply such a tendency
in its *own nature*.

And then it must be remembered, that it is a *moral
depravity* we are speaking of; and therefore when we are
considering whether such depravity do not appear by a tendency to a bad effect or issue, it is a *moral tendency* to such
an issue that is the thing to be taken into the account. A
moral tendency or influence is by *desert*. Then may it be
said man's nature or state is attended with a pernicious or
destructive tendency in a *moral* sense, when it tends to
that which *deserves* misery and destruction. And therefore it
equally shews the moral depravity of the nature of mankind in their present state, whether that nature be universally
attended with an effectual tendency to destructive vengeance
actually executed, or to their *deserving* misery and ruin,
or their just *exposedness* to destruction, however that
fatal consequence may be prevented by grace, or whatever
the actual event be.

One thing more is to be observed here, that the topic
mainly insisted on by the opposers of the doctrine of original
sin, is the *justice* of God; both in their objections against
the *imputation* of *Adam's* sin, and also against its being
so ordered, that men should come into the world with a
corrupt and ruined nature, without having merited the displeasure of their Creator by any personal fault. But the latter is not repugnant to God's justice, if men *actually are*
born into the world with a tendency to sin, and to misery
and ruin for their sin, which actually will be the consequence unless *mere grace* steps in and prevents it. If this
be allowed, the argument from *justice* is given up: for it is
to suppose, that their liableness to misery and ruin comes
in a way of justice; otherwise there would be no need of
the interposition of divine grace to save them. Justice alone
would be sufficient security, if exercised, without grace. It is

all one in this dispute about what is just and righteous, whether men are born in a miserable state by a tendency to ruin which *actually follows*, and that *justly;* or whether they are born in such a state as tends to a *desert* of ruin, which *might justly* follow, and *would actually follow* did not grace prevent. For the controversy is not what grace *will* do, but what justice *might* do.

I have been the more particular on this head, because it enervates many of the reasonings and conclusions by which Dr. *T.* makes out his scheme; in which he argues from that state which mankind are in *by divine grace*, yea, which he himself supposes to be by divine grace; and yet not making any allowance for this, he from hence draws conclusions against what others suppose of the deplorable and ruined state mankind are in by the fall. Some of his arguments and conclusions to this effect, in order to be made good, must depend on such a supposition as this:—that God's dispensations of grace are rectifications or amendments of his foregoing constitutions and proceedings, which were merely legal; as though the dispensations of grace, which succeed those of mere law, implied an acknowledgment that the preceding legal constitution would be unjust if left as it was, or at least very hard dealing with mankind; and that the other were of the nature of a satisfaction to his creatures for former injuries, or hard treatment. So that, put together the injury with the satisfaction, the legal and injurious dispensation taken with the following good dispensation, which our author calls grace, and the unfairness or improper severity of the former amended by the goodness of the latter, both together made up one righteous dispensation.

The reader is desired to bear in mind what I have said concerning the interposition of divine grace not altering the nature of things as they are in themselves. Accordingly, when I speak of such and such an evil *tendency* of things belonging to the present nature and state of mankind, understand me to mean their tendency *as they are in themselves,* abstracted from any consideration of that remedy the sovereign and infinite grace of God has provided. Having premised these things, I now assert, that mankind are all naturally in such a state, as is attended, without fail, with this consequence or issue; that THEY UNIVERSALLY RUN THEMSELVES INTO THAT WHICH IS, IN EFFECT, THEIR OWN UTTER

ETERNAL PERDITION, as being finally accursed of God and the subject of his remediless wrath through sin.—From which I infer, that the natural state of the mind of man, is attended with a *propensity of nature,* which is prevalent and effectual, to such an issue; and that therefore their nature is corrupt and depraved with a moral depravity that amounts to and implies their utter undoing.

Here I would first consider the *truth* of the proposition; and then would shew the certainty of the *consequences* which I infer from it. If both can be clearly and certainly proved, then I trust none will deny but that the doctrine of original depravity is evident, and so the falseness of Dr. *T.'s* scheme demonstrated; the greatest part of whose book called *the Scripture Doctrine of Original Sin,* &c. is against the doctrine of *innate depravity.* In p. 107, S. he speaks of the conveyance of a corrupt and sinful nature to *Adam's* posterity as *the grand point* to be proved by the maintainers of the doctrine of original sin.

In order to demonstrate what is asserted in the proposition laid down, there is need only that these two things should be made manifest: *one* is this fact, that all mankind come into the world in such a state as without fail comes to this issue, namely, the universal commission of sin; or that every one who comes to act in the world as a moral agent, is, in a greater or less degree, guilty of sin. The *other* is, that all sin deserves and exposes to utter and eternal destruction under God's wrath and curse; and would end in it, were it not for the interposition of divine grace to prevent the effect. Both which can be abundantly demonstrated to be agreeable to the word of God, and to Dr. *T.'s* own doctrine.

That every one of mankind, at least such as are capable of acting as moral agents, are guilty of sin (not now taking it for granted that they come guilty into the world) is most clearly and abundantly evident from the holy scriptures: 1 Kings viii. 46. *If any man sin against thee; for there is no man that sinneth not.* Eccl. vii. 20. *There is not a just man upon earth that doeth good and sinneth not.* Job. ix. 2, 3. *I know it is so of a truth,* (i. e. as *Bildad* had just before said, that God would not cast away a perfect man, &c.) *but how should man be just with God? If he will contend with him, he cannot answer him one of a thousand.* To the like purpose, Psal. cxliii. 2. *Enter not into judgment with*

thy servant; for in thy sight shall no man living be justified.
So the words of the apostle (in which he has apparent reference to those of the Psalmist.) Rom. iii. 19, 20. "That every mouth may be stopped, and all the world become guilty before God. Therefore by the deeds of the law there shall no flesh be justified in his sight: for by the law is the knowledge of sin." So, Gal. ii. 16. 1, John i. 7–10. "If we walk in the light, the blood of Christ cleanseth us from all sin. If we say that we have no sin, we deceive ourselves, and the truth is not in us. If we confess our sins, he is faithful and just to forgive us our sins, and to cleanse us from all unrighteousness. If we say that we have not sinned, we make him a liar, and his word is not in us." In this, and innumerable other places, confession and repentance of sin are spoken of as duties proper for ALL; as also prayer to God for pardon of sin: also forgiveness of those that injure us, from that motive, that we hope to be *forgiven* of God. Universal guilt of sin might also be demonstrated from the appointment, and the declared use and end of the ancient sacrifices; and also from the ransom which every one that was numbered in *Israel* was directed to pay, to make atonement for his soul. (*Exod.* xxx. 11–16.) All are represented, not only as being sinful, but as having great and manifold iniquity. (*Job.* ix. 2, 3, *Jam.* iii. 1, 2.)

There are many scriptures which both declare the *universal sinfulness* of mankind, and also that all sin *deserves* and justly exposes to *everlasting destruction,* under the wrath and curse of God; and so demonstrate both parts of the proposition I have laid down. To which purpose that passage in Gal. iii. 10. is exceeding full: *For as many as are of the works of the law are under the curse; for it is written, cursed is every one that continueth not in all things which are written in the book of the law, to do them.* How manifestly is it implied in the apostle's meaning here, that there is no man but what fails in some instances of doing all things that are written in the book of the law, and therefore as many as have their dependence on their fulfilling the law, are under that curse which is pronounced on them that fail of it? And hence the apostle infers in the next verse, *that* NO MAN *is justified by the law in the sight of God:* as he had said before in the preceding chapter, ver. 16. *By the works of the law shall no flesh be justified.* The apostle shews us he understands, that by this place which he cites from Deuter-onomy, *the scripture hath concluded, or shut up all under sin.* (Gal. iii. 22.) So that here we are plainly taught, both that every one of mankind is a *sinner,* and that every sinner is under the *curse* of God.

To the like purpose is *Rom.* iv. 14, also 2 *Cor.* iii. 6, 7, 9, where the law is called *the letter that kills, the ministration of death, and the ministration of condemnation.* The wrath, condemnation, and death, which is threatened in the law to all its transgressors, is final perdition, the second death, eternal ruin; as is very plain, and indeed is confessed. And this punishment which the law threatens for every sin is a *just* punishment; being what every sin truly *deserves;* God's law being a righteous law, and the sentence of it a righteous sentence. . . .

CONCERNING THE END FOR WHICH GOD CREATED THE WORLD

One of the most spirited of all Jonathan Edwards' writings. It is speculative and mystical rather than strictly theological. A lifetime of thought and personal religious experience lies between this concept of God and that of the early days in the East Windsor meadows. The text is from *The Works of President Edwards,* edited by S. B. Dwight, Vol. III, pp. 81–87, Chapter II, Section 7.

SHEWING, THAT THE ULTIMATE END OF THE CREATION OF THE WORLD IS BUT ONE, AND WHAT THAT ONE END IS.

From what has been observed in the last section, it appears, if the whole of what is said relating to this affair be duly weighed, and one part compared with another, we shall have reason to think that the design of the Spirit of God is not to represent God's ultimate end as *manifold,* but as ONE. For though it be signified by various names, yet they appear not to be names of *different* things, but various names involving each other in their meaning; either different names of the *same thing,* or names of several parts of *one whole;* or of the same whole viewed in *various lights,* or in its *different respects* and relations. For it appears, that all that is ever spoken of in the scripture as an ultimate end of God's works, is included in that one phrase, *the glory of*

God; which is the name by which the ultimate end of God's works is most commonly called in scripture; and seems most aptly to signify the thing.

The thing signified by that name, *the glory of God,* when spoken of as the supreme and ultimate end of all God's works, is the emanation and true external expression of God's internal glory and fulness; meaning by his *fulness,* what has already been explained; or, in other words, God's internal glory, in a true and just exhibition, or external existence of it. It is confessed, that there is a degree of obscurity in these definitions; but perhaps an obscurity which is unavoidable, through the imperfection of language to express things of so sublime a nature. And therefore the thing may possibly be better understood, by using a variety of expressions, by a particular consideration of it, as it were, by parts, than by any short definition.

It includes the *exercise* of God's perfections to produce a proper *effect,* in opposition to their lying eternally dormant and ineffectual: as his power being eternally without any act or fruit of that power; his wisdom eternally ineffectual in any wise production, or prudent disposal of any thing, &c. The *manifestation* of his internal glory to created understandings. The *communication* of the infinite fulness of God to the creature. The creature's high *esteem* of God, love to him, and complacence and joy in him; and the proper *exercises* and *expressions* of these.

These at first view may appear to be entirely distinct things: but if we more closely consider the matter, they will all appear to be ONE thing, in a variety of views and relations. They are all but the *emanation of God's glory;* or the excellent brightness and fulness of the divinity *diffused, overflowing,* and as it were *enlarged;* or in one word, *existing and extra.* God *exercising* his perfection to produce a proper *effect,* is not distinct from the emanation or *communication* of his *fulness:* for this is the effect, viz. his *fulness communicated,* and the producing of this effect is the communication of his fulness; and there is nothing in this effectual exerting of God's perfection, but the emanation of God's internal glory.

Now God's *internal* glory is either in his understanding or will. The glory or fulness of his *understanding* is his knowledge. The internal glory and fulness of God, having its special seat in his *will*, is his holiness and happiness. The *whole* of God's *internal* good or glory is in these three things, viz. his infinite *knowledge;* his infinite virtue or *holiness,* and his infinite joy and *happiness.* Indeed there are a great many attributes in God, according to our way of conceiving them: but all may be reduced to these; or to their degree, circumstances and relations. We have no conception of God's *power,* different from the degree of these things, with a certain relation of them to effects. God's *infinity* is not properly a distinct *kind* of good, but only expresses the *degree* of good there is in him. So God's *eternity* is not a distinct good; but is the duration of good. His *immutability* is still the same good, with a negation of change. So that, as I said, the *fulness* of the Godhead is the fulness of his *understanding,* consisting in his knowledge; and the fulness of his *will,* consisting in his virtue and happiness.

And therefore, the *external* glory of God consists in the *communication* of these. The communication of his knowledge is chiefly in giving the *knowledge of himself:* for this is the knowledge in which the fulness of God's understanding chiefly consists. And thus we see how the manifestation of God's glory to created understandings, and their seeing and knowing it, is not distinct from an emanation or communication of God's fulness, but clearly implied in it. Again, the communication of God's virtue or holiness is principally in communicating the *love of himself.* And thus we see how, not only the creature's seeing and knowing God's excellence, but also supremely esteeming and loving him, belongs to the communication of *God's fulness.* And the communication of God's joy and happiness consists chiefly in communicating to the creature that happiness and joy which consists in *rejoicing in God,* and in his glorious excellency; for in such joy God's own happiness does principally consist. And in these things, *knowing* God's excellency, *loving* God for it, and *rejoicing* in it; and in the *exercise* and *expression* of these, consists God's honour and praise; so that these are clearly implied in that glory of God, which consists in the *emanation* of his internal glory.

And though all these things, which seem to be so various, are signified by that glory which the scripture speaks of as the ultimate end of all God's works; yet it is manifest there is no greater, and no other variety in it, than in the internal and essential glory of God itself. God's internal glory is partly in his understanding, and partly in his will. And this internal glory, as seated in the will of God, implies both his holiness and his happiness: both are evidently God's glory, according to the use of the phrase. So that as God's external glory is only the emanation of his internal, this variety necessarily follows. And again, it hence appears that here is no other variety or distinction, but what necessarily arises from the distinct faculties of the creature to which the communication is made, as created in the image of God: even as having these two faculties of understanding and will. God communicates himself to the *understanding* of the creature, in giving him the *knowledge* of his glory; and to the *will* of the creature, in giving him *holiness,* consisting primarily in the love of God: and in giving the creature *happiness* chiefly consisting in *joy* in God. These are the sum of that emanation of divine fulness called in scripture, *the glory of God.* The first part of this glory is called *truth,* the latter *grace,* John i. 14. "We beheld his *glory,* the glory of the only begotten of the Father, full of *grace* and *truth.*"

Thus we see that the great end of God's works, which is so variously expressed in scripture, is indeed but ONE; and this *one* end is most properly and comprehensively called, THE GLORY OF GOD; by which name it is most commonly called in scripture; and is fitly compared to an effulgence or emanation of light from a luminary. Light is the external expression, exhibition, and manifestation of the excellency of the luminary, of the sun for instance: It is the abundant, extensive emanation and communication of the fulness of the sun to innumerable beings that partake of it. It is by this that the sun itself is seen, and his glory beheld, and all other things are discovered: it is by a participation of this communication from the sun, that surrounding objects receive all their lustre, beauty, and brightness. It is by this that all nature receives life, comfort, and joy. Light is abundantly used in scripture to represent and signify these three things, knowledge, holiness, and happiness.

What has been said may be sufficient to shew, how those things, which are spoken of in scripture as ultimate ends of God's works, though they may seem at first view to be distinct, are all plainly to be reduced to this *one* thing, viz. *God's internal glory or fulness existing in its emanation.* And though

God in seeking this end, seeks the creature's good; yet therein appears his supreme regard to himself.

The emanation or communication of the divine fulness, consisting in the knowledge of God, love to him, and joy in him, has relation indeed both to *God* and the *creature:* but it has relation to God as its *fountain,* as the thing communicated, is something of his internal fulness. The water in the stream is something of the fountain; and the beams of the sun are something of the sun. And again they have relation to God as their *object:* for the knowledge communicated is the knowledge of God; and the love communicated, is the love of God: and the happiness communicated, is joy in God. In the creature's knowing, esteeming, loving, rejoicing in, and praising God, the glory of God is both *exhibited* and *acknowledged;* his fulness is *received* and *returned.* Here is both an *emanation* and *remanation.* The refulgence shines upon and into the creature, and is reflected back to the luminary. The beams of glory come from God, are something of God, and are refunded back again to their original. So that the whole is *of* God, and *in* God, and *to* God; and he is the beginning, and the middle, and the end.

And though it be true that God has respect to the *creature* in these things; yet his respect to himself, and to the creature, are not properly a double and divided respect. What has been said (chap. I. sect. 3, 4) may be sufficient to shew this. Nevertheless, it may not be amiss here briefly to say a few things; though mostly implied in what has been said already.

When God was about to create the world, he had respect to that *emanation of his glory*, which is *actually* the consequence of the creation, both with regard to himself and the creature. He had regard to it as an *emanation* from himself, a *communication* of himself, and, as the *thing communicated,* in its nature *returned* to himself, as its final term. And he had regard to it also as the *emanation* was *to* the creature, and as the *thing communicated* was *in* the creature, as its subject.

And God had regard to it in this manner, as he had a supreme regard to himself, and value for his own infinite, internal glory. It was this value for himself that caused him to value and seek that his internal glory should *flow forth* from himself. It was from his value for his glorious perfections of wisdom, righteousness, &c. that he valued the proper *exercise* and effect of these perfections, in wise and righteous acts and effects. It was from his infinite value for his internal glory and fulness, that he valued the *thing itself* communicated, which is something of the same, extant in the creature. Thus because he infinitely values his own glory, consisting in the knowledge of himself, love to himself, and complacence and joy in himself; he therefore valued the image, communication, or participation of these in the creature. And it is because he values himself, that he delights in the knowledge, and love, and joy of the creature; as being himself the object of this knowledge, love, and complacence. For it is the necessary consequence of true esteem and love that we value others' esteem of the same object, and dislike the contrary. For the same reason, God approves of others' esteem and love of himself.

Thus it is easy to conceive, how God should seek the good of the creature, consisting in the creature's knowledge and holiness, and even his happiness, for a supreme regard to *himself;* as his happiness arises from that which is an image and participation of God's own beauty: and consists in the creature's exercising a supreme regard to God, and complacence in him; in beholding God's glory, in esteeming and loving it, and rejoicing in it, and in his exercising and testifying love and supreme respect to God: which is the same thing with the creature's exalting God as his chief good, and making him his supreme end.

And though the emanation of God's fulness, intended in the creation, is to the creature as its *object;* and though the creature is the *subject* of the fulness communicated, which is the creature's good; yet it does not necessarily follow, that even in so doing, God did not make *himself* his end. It comes to the same thing. God's respect to the creature's good, and his respect to himself, is not a divided respect; but both are united in one, as the happiness of the creature aimed at is happiness in union with himself. The creature is no further happy with this happiness which God makes his ultimate end, than he becomes one with God. The more happiness the greater union; when the happiness is perfect, the union is perfect. And as the happiness will be increasing to eternity, the union will become more and more strict and perfect; nearer and more like to that between God the Father and the Son; who are so united that their interest is perfectly one.—If the happiness of the creature be considered in the whole of the creature's eternal duration, with all the infinity of its progress, and infinite increase of nearness and union to God; in this view, the creature must be looked upon as united to God in an infinite strictness.

If God has respect to something in the creature, which he views as of everlasting duration, and as rising higher and higher through that infinite duration, and that not with constantly diminishing (but perhaps an increasing) celerity; then he has respect to it, as, in the whole, of infinite height; though there never will be any particular time when it can be said already to have come to such a height.

Let the most perfect union with God be represented by something at an infinite height above us: and the eternally increasing union of the saints with God, by something that is ascending constantly towards that infinite height, moving upwards with a given velocity; and that is to continue thus to move to all eternity. God who views the whole of this eternally increasing height, views it as an infinite height. And if he has respect to it, and makes it his end, as in the whole of it, he has respect to it as an infinite height, though the time will never come when it can be said it has already arrived at this infinite height.

God aims at that which the motion or progression which he causes, aims at, or tends to. If there be many things supposed to be so made and appointed, that by a constant and eternal motion, they all tend to a certain centre; then it appears that he who made them, and is the cause of their motion, aimed at that centre; that term of their motion, to which they eternally tend, and are eternally, as it were, striving after.—And if God be the centre, then God aimed at himself. And herein it appears, that as he is the first author of their being and motion, so he is the last end, the final term to which is their ultimate tendency and aim.

We may judge of the end that the Creator aimed at, in the being, nature, and tendency he gives the creature, by the mark or term which they constantly aim at in their tendency and eternal progress; though the time will never come, when it can be said it is attained to, in the most absolutely perfect manner.

But if strictness of union to God be viewed as thus infinitely exalted; then the creature must be regarded as nearly and closely united to God. And viewed thus, their interest must be viewed as one with God's interest; and so is not regarded properly with a disjunct and separate, but an undivided respect. And as to any difficulty of reconciling God's not making the creature his ultimate end, with a respect properly distinct from a respect to himself; with his benevolence and free grace, and the creature's obligation to gratitude, the reader must be referred to chap. I. sect. 4. obj. 4. where this objection has been considered and answered at large.

If by reason of the strictness of the union of a man and his family, their interest may be looked upon as one, how much more so is the interest of Christ and his church,—whose first union in heaven is unspeakably more perfect and exalted, than that of an earthly father and his family—if they be considered with regard to their eternal and increasing union? Doubtless it may justly be esteemed so much one, that it may be sought, not with a distinct and separate, but an undivided respect. It is certain that what God aimed at in the creation of the world, was the good that would be the consequence of the creation, in the whole continuance of the thing created.

It is no solid objection against God aiming at an infinitely perfect union of the creature with himself, that the particular time will never come when it can be said, the union is now infinitely perfect. God aims at satisfying justice in the eternal damnation of sinners: which will be satisfied by their damnation, considered no otherwise than with regard to its eternal duration. But yet there never will come that particular moment when it can be said, that now justice is satisfied. But if this does not satisfy our modern free-thinkers, who do not like the talk about satisfying justice with an infinite punishment; I suppose it will not be denied by any, that God, in glorifying the saints in heaven with eternal felicity, aims to satisfy his infinite grace or benevolence, by the bestowment of a good infinitely valuable, because eternal: and yet there never will come the moment when it can be said, that *now* this infinitely valuable good has been actually bestowed.

THE NATURE OF TRUE VIRTUE

Written during the Stockbridge years and published posthumously as one of *Two Dissertations,* the other being "Concerning the End for Which God Created the World." The main idea of this piece is that virtue is not of the intellect, but of the emotions. Argument proceeds from the same basic conviction as the "Religious Affections," to which it might be called a sequel. The text is from *The Works of President Edwards,* edited by S. B. Dwight, Vol. III, pp. 93–100, Chapter I.

SHEWING WHEREIN THE ESSENCE OF TRUE VIRTUE CONSISTS.

WHATEVER controversies and variety of opinions there are about the *nature* of virtue, yet all excepting some sceptics, who deny any real difference between virtue and vice, mean by it something *beautiful,* or rather some kind of *beauty* or excellency. It is not *all* beauty that is called virtue; for instance, not the beauty of a building, of a flower, or of the rainbow; but some beauty belonging to beings that have *perception* and *will.* It is not all beauty of *mankind* that is called virtue; for instance, not the external beauty of the countenance or shape, gracefulness of motion, or harmony of voice: but it is a beauty that has its original seat in the mind. But yet perhaps not *every* thing that may be called a beauty of *mind,* is properly called virtue. There is a beauty of understanding and speculation; there is something in the ideas and conceptions of great philosophers and statesmen, that may be called beautiful: which is a different thing from what is most commonly meant by virtue.

But virtue is the beauty of those qualities and acts of the mind that are of a *moral* nature, *i. e.* such as are attended with desert or worthiness of *praise* or *blame*. Things of this sort it is generally agreed, so far as I know, do not belong merely to speculation: but to the *disposition* and *will,* or (to use a general word I suppose commonly well understood) to the *heart*. Therefore I suppose I shall not depart from the common opinion when I say, that virtue is the beauty of the qualities and exercises of the heart, or those actions which proceed from them. So that when it is enquired, what is the nature of true *virtue?* This is the same as to enquire what that is, which renders any habit, disposition, or exercise of the heart truly *beautiful?*

I use the phrase *true* virtue, and speak of things *truly* beautiful, because I suppose it will generally be allowed, that there is a distinction to be made between some things which are *truly* virtuous, and others which only *seem* to be so, through a partial and imperfect view of things: that some actions and dispositions appear beautiful, if considered partially and superficially, or with regard to some things belonging to them, and in some of their circumstances and tendencies, which would appear otherwise in a more extensive and comprehensive view, wherein they are seen clearly in their whole nature, and the extent of their connections in the universality of things.

There is a general and particular beauty. By a *particular* beauty, I mean that by which a thing appears beautiful when considered only with regard to its connection with, and tendency to, some particular things within a limited, and as it were a private sphere. And a *general* beauty is that by which a thing appears beautiful when viewed most perfectly, comprehensively and universally, with regard to all its tendencies, and its connections with every thing to which it stands related. The former may be without and against the latter. As a few notes in a tune, taken only by themselves and in their relation to one another, may be harmonious, which, when considered with respect to all the notes in the tune, or the entire series of sounds they are connected with, may be very discordant, and disagreeable. *That only,* therefore, is what I mean by *true* virtue, which, belonging to the *heart* of an intelligent being, is beautiful by a *general* beauty, or beautiful in a comprehensive view, as it is in itself, and as related to every thing with which it stands connected. And therefore, when we are enquiring concerning the nature of true virtue—wherein this true and general beauty of the heart does most essentially consist—this is my answer to the enquiry:—

True virtue most essentially consists in BENEVOLENCE TO BEING IN GENERAL. Or perhaps, to speak more accurately, it is that consent, propensity and union of heart to being in general, which is immediately exercised in a general good will.

The things before observed respecting the nature of true virtue, naturally lead us to such a notion of it. If it has its seat in the heart, and is the general goodness and beauty of the disposition and its exercise, in the most comprehensive view, considered with regard to its universal tendency, and as related to every thing with which it stands connected; what can it consist in, but a consent and good will to being in general? Beauty does not consist in discord and dissent, but in consent and agreement. And if every intelligent being is some way related to being in general, and is a part of the universal system of existence; and so stands in connection with the whole; what can its general and true beauty be, but its union and consent with the great whole?

If any such thing can be supposed as an union of heart to some particular being, or number of beings, disposing it to benevolence to a private circle or system of beings, which are but a small part of the whole; not implying a tendency to an union with the great system, and not at all inconsistent with enmity towards being in general, this I suppose not to be of the nature of true virtue; although it may in some respects be good, and may appear beautiful in a confined and contracted view of things.—But of this more afterwards.

It is abundantly plain by the holy scriptures, and generally allowed, not only by christian divines, but by the more considerable Deists, that virtue most essentially consists in love. And I suppose it is owned by the most considerable writers, to consist in general love of benevolence, or kind affection: though it seems to me the meaning of some in this affair is not sufficiently explained; which perhaps occasions some error or confusion in discourses on this subject.

When I say true virtue consists in *love to being in general*, I shall not be likely to be understood, that no one act of the mind or exercise of love is of the nature of true virtue, but what has being in general, or the great system of universal existence, for its *direct* and *immediate* object: so that no exercise of love, or kind affection to any one particular being, that is but a small part of this whole, has any thing of the nature of true virtue. But that the nature of true virtue consists in a *disposition* to benevolence towards being in general; though from such a disposition may arise exercises of love to *particular* beings, as objects are presented and occasions arise. No wonder that he who is of a *generally* benevolent disposition, should be more disposed than another to have his heart moved with benevolent affection to *particular* persons, with whom he is acquainted and conversant, and from whom arise the greatest and most frequent *occasions* for exciting his benevolent temper. But my meaning is, that no affections towards particular persons or beings are of the nature of true virtue, but such as arise from a generally benevolent temper, or from that habit or frame of mind, wherein consists a disposition to love being in general.

And perhaps it is needless for me to give notice to my readers, that when I speak of an intelligent being having a heart united and benevolently disposed to being in general, I thereby mean *intelligent* being in general. Not inanimate things, or beings that have no perception or will; which are not properly capable objects of benevolence.

Love is commonly distinguished into love of benevolence, and love of complacence. Love of *benevolence* is that affection or propensity of the heart to any being, which causes it to incline to its well-being, or disposes it to desire and take pleasure in its happiness. And if I mistake not, it is agreeable to the common opinion, that beauty in the object is not always the ground of this propensity; but that there may be a disposition to the welfare of those that are *not* considered as beautiful, unless mere existence be accounted a beauty. And benevolence or goodness in the divine Being is generally supposed, not only to be prior to the beauty of many of its objects, but to their existence; so as to be the ground both of their existence and their beauty, rather than the foundation of God's benevolence; as it is supposed that it is God's goodness which moved him to give them both being and beauty. So that if all virtue primarily consists in that affection of heart to being, which is exercised in benevolence, or an inclination to its good, then God's virtue is so extended as to include a propensity not only to being actually existing, and actually beautiful, but to possible being, so as to incline him to give a being beauty and happiness.

What is commonly called love of *complacence,* presupposes beauty. For it is no other than delight in beauty; or complacence in the person or being beloved for his beauty. If virtue be the beauty of an intelligent being, and virtue consists in love, then it is a plain inconsistence, to suppose that virtue primarily consists in any love to its object for its beauty; either in a love of complacence, which is delight in a being for his beauty, or in a love of benevolence, that has the beauty of its object for its foundation. For that would be to suppose, that the beauty of intelligent beings primarily consists in love to beauty; or that their virtue first of all consists in their love to virtue. Which is an inconsistence, and going in a circle. Because it makes virtue, or beauty of mind, the foundation or first motive of that love wherein virtue originally consists, or wherein the very first virtue consists; or, it supposes the first virtue to be the consequence and effect of virtue. Which makes the first virtue both the ground and the consequence, both cause and effect of itself. Doubtless virtue primarily consists in something else besides any effect or consequence of virtue. If virtue consists primarily in love to virtue, then virtue, the thing loved, is the love of virtue: so that virtue must consist in the love of the love of virtue—and so on *in infinitum.* For there is no end of going back in a circle. We never come to any beginning or foundation; it is without beginning, and hangs on nothing.— Therefore, if the essence of *virtue,* or *beauty* of mind, lies in love, or a disposition to love, it must primarily consist in something *different* both from complacence, which is a delight in beauty, and also from any benevolence that has the beauty of its object for its foundation. Because it is absurd to say, that virtue is primarily and first of all the consequence of itself; which makes virtue primarily prior to itself.

Nor can virtue primarily consist in *gratitude;* or one being's benevolence to another for his benevolence to him. Because this implies the same inconsistence. For it supposes a benevolence prior to gratitude, which is the cause of gratitude. The *first* benevolence cannot be gratitude. Therefore there is room left for no other conclusion, than that the primary object of virtuous love is being, simply considered; or that true virtue primarily consists, not in love to any particular beings, because of their virtue or beauty, nor in gratitude, because they love us; but in a propensity and union of heart to being simply considered; exciting *absolute* benevolence, if I may so call it, to being in general. I say true virtue *primarily* consists in this. For I am far from asserting, that there is no true virtue in any other love than this absolute benevolence. But I would express what appears to me to be the truth on this subject, in the following particulars.

The *first* object of a virtuous benevolence is *being,* simply considered; and if being, *simply* considered, be its object, then being *in general* is its object; and what it has an ultimate propensity to is the *highest good* of being in general. And it will seek the good of every *individual* being unless it be conceived as not consistent with the highest good of being in general. In which case the good of a particular being, or some beings, may be given up for the sake of the highest good of being in general. And particularly, if there be any being statedly and irreclaimably opposite, and an enemy to being in general, then consent and adherence to being in general will induce the truly virtuous heart to forsake that enemy, and to oppose it.

Further, if BEING, simply considered, be the first object of a truly virtuous benevolence, then that object who has *most* of being, or has the greatest share of existence, *other things being equal,* so far as such a being is exhibited to our faculties, will have the *greatest* share of the propensity and benevolent affections of the heart. I say, "other things being equal," especially because there is a *secondary* object of virtuous benevolence, that I shall take notice of presently, which must be considered as the ground or motive to a purely virtuous benevolence. Pure benevolence in its *first* exercise is nothing else but being's uniting consent, or propensity to being; and inclining to the general highest good, and to each being, whose welfare is consistent with the highest general good, in proportion to the degree of *existence,** understand, "other things being equal."

---

* I say, "in proportion to the degree of *existence,*" because one

The *second* object of a virtuous propensity of heart is *benevolent* being. A secondary ground of love of pure benevolence is virtuous benevolence itself in its object. When any one under the influence of general benevolence, sees another being possessed of the like general benevolence, this attaches his heart to him, and draws forth greater love to him, than merely his having existence: because so far as the being beloved has love to being in general, so far his own being is, as it were, enlarged; extends to, and in some sort comprehends being in general: and therefore, he that is governed by love to being in general, must of necessity have complacence in him, and the greater degree of benevolence to him, as it were out of gratitude to him for his love to general existence, that his own heart is extended and united to, and so looks on its interest as its own. It is because his heart is thus united to being in general, that he looks on a benevolent propensity to being in general, wherever he sees it, as the beauty of the being in whom it is; an excellency that renders him worthy of esteem, complacence, and the greater good-will. But several things may be noted more particularly concerning this *secondary* ground of a truly virtuous love.

1. That loving a being on *this* ground necessarily arises from pure benevolence to being *in general,* and comes to the same thing. For he that has a simple and pure good will to general existence, must love that temper in others, that agrees and conspires with itself. A spirit of consent to being must agree with consent to being. That which truly and sincerely seeks the good of others, must approve of, and love that which joins with him in seeking the good of others.

2. This secondary ground of virtuous love is the thing wherein true moral or spiritual *beauty* primarily consists. Yea, spiritual beauty consists wholly in this, and in the

---

being may have more *existence* than another, as he may be greater than another. That which is *great* has more existence, and is further from nothing, than that which is *little.* One being may have every thing positive belonging to it, or every thing which goes to its positive existence (in opposition to defect) in an higher degree than another; or a greater capacity and power, greater understanding, every faculty and every positive quality in an higher degree. An *archangel* must be supposed to have more existence, and to be every way further removed from *nonentity,* than a *worm.*

various qualities and exercises of mind which proceed from it, and the external actions which proceed from these internal qualities and exercises. And in these things consists all true *virtue,* viz. in this love of being, and the qualities and acts which arise from it.

3. As all spiritual beauty lies in these virtuous principles and acts, so it is primarily *on this account* they are beautiful, viz. that they imply *consent* and *union* with being *in general.* This is the primary and most essential beauty of every thing that can justly be called by the name of virtue, or is any moral excellency in the eye of one that has a perfect view of things. I say, "the *primary* and *most essential* beauty," because there is a secondary and inferior sort of beauty; which I shall take notice of afterwards.

4. This spiritual beauty, which is but a *secondary* ground of virtuous benevolence, is the ground not only of benevolence, but *complacence,* and is the *primary* ground of the latter; that is, when the complacence is truly virtuous. Love to us in particular, and kindness received may be a secondary ground: but this is the primary objective foundation of it.

5. It must be noted, that the *degree* of the *amiableness* of true virtue primarily consisting in consent, and a benevolent propensity of heart to being in general, is not in the *simple* proportion of the degree of benevolent affection seen, but in a proportion *compounded* of the greatness of the benevolent being, or the degree of *being* and the degree of *benevolence.* —One that loves being in general, will necessarily value good will to being in general, whenever he sees it. But if he sees the same benevolence in *two* beings, he will value it *more* in two, than in one only. Because it is a greater thing, more favourable to being in general, to have two beings to favour it, than only one of them. For there is more being that favours being: both together having more being than one alone. So if one being be as great as two, has as much existence as both together, and has the same degree of general benevolence, it is more favourable to being in general, than if there were general benevolence in a being that had but half that share of existence. As a large quantity of gold, with the same quality, is more valuable than a small quantity of the same metal.

6. It is impossible that any one should truly *relish* this beauty, consisting in general benevolence, who has *not* that

temper himself. I have observed, that if any being is possessed of such a temper, he will unavoidably be pleased with the same temper in another. And it may in like manner be demonstrated, that it is such a spirit, and nothing else, which will relish such a spirit. For if a being destitute of benevolence, should love benevolence to being in general, it would prize and seek that for which it had no value. For how should one love and value a *disposition* to a thing, or a *tendency* to *promote* it, and for that very reason, when the *thing* itself is what he is regardless of, and has no value for, nor desires to have promoted.

THE IMAGES OR SHADOWS OF DIVINE THINGS

From a homemade notebook entitled "The Images of Divine Things, The Shadows of Divine Things, The Language and Lessons of Nature," as edited by Perry Miller, Yale University Press, New Haven, 1948. Grateful acknowledgment is herewith given for permission to quote these brief excerpts from this book. The whole contains two hundred and twelve entries, each of which is presumed to be the earthly image of a spiritual truth. The essay "The Beauty of the World" ends the volume. Jonathan Edwards had not intended publication in the form of these jottings assembled over the years, but even in this disjointed form the piece has unity. As he looked out on the physical world of sun, moon, stars, birds, grass, trees, and flowers, each part became a shadow of metaphysical reality. He believed that if human intelligence were pure it could read these signs as the language of God Himself.

57. It is very fit and becoming of God who is so infinitely wise, so to order things that there should be a voice of His in His works, instructing those that behold him and painting forth and shewing divine mysteries and things more immediately appertaining to Himself and His spiritual kingdom. The works of God are but a kind of voice or language of God to instruct intelligent beings in things pertaining to Himself. And why should we not think that he would teach and instruct by His works in this way as well as in others, viz., by representing divine things by His works and so painting them forth, especially since we know that God hath so much delighted in this way of instruction.

7. If we look on these shadows of divine things as the

voice of God purposely by them teaching us these and those spiritual and divine things, to show of what excellent advantage it will be, how agreeably and clearly it will tend to convey instruction to our minds, and to impress things on the mind and to affect the mind, by that we may, as it were, have God speaking to us. Wherever we are, and whatever we are about, we may see divine things excellently represented and held forth. And it will abundantly tend to confirm the Scriptures, for there is an excellent agreement between these things and the holy Scripture.

156. The book of Scripture is the interpreter of the book of nature two ways, viz., by declaring to us those spiritual mysteries that are indeed signified and typified in the constitution of the natural world; and secondly, in actually making application of the signs and types in the book of nature as representations of those spiritual mysteries in many instances.

212. The immense magnificence of the visible world in inconceivable vastness, the incomprehensible height of the heavens, etc., is but a type of the infinite magnificence, height and glory of God's work in the spiritual world: the most incomprehensible expression of His power, wisdom, holiness and love in what is wrought and brought to pass in the world, and the exceeding greatness of the moral and natural good, the light, knowledge, holiness and happiness which shall be communicated to it, and therefore to that magnificence of the world, height of heaven. These things are often compared in such expressions: Thy mercy is great above the heavens, thy truth reacheth; thou hast for thy glory above the heavens, etc. (See Image 21.)

THE BEAUTY OF THE WORLD

The beauty of the world consists wholly of sweet mutual consents, either within itself or with the supreme being. As to the corporeal world, though there are many other sorts of consents, yet the sweetest and most charming beauty of it is its resemblance of spiritual beauties. The reason is that spiritual beauties are infinitely the greatest, and bodies being but the shadows of beings, they must be so much the more charming as they shadow forth spiritual beauties. This beauty is peculiar to natural things, it surpassing the art of man.

Thus there is the resemblance of a decent trust, dependence and acknowledgment in the planets continually moving around the sun, receiving his influences by which they are made happy, bright and beautiful: a decent attendance in the secondary planets, an image of majesty, power, and glory, and beneficence in the sun in the midst of all, and so in terrestrial things, as I have shown in another place.

It is very probable that the wonderful suitableness of green for the grass and plants, the blue of the skie, the white of the clouds, the colours of flowers, consists in a complicated proportion that these colours make one with another, either in their magnitude of the rays, the number of vibrations that are caused in the atmosphere, or some other way. So there is a great suitableness between the objects of different senses, as between sounds, colours, and smells; as between colours of the woods and flowers and the smells and the singing of birds, which it is probable consist in a certain proportion of the vibrations that are made in the different organs. So there are innumerable other agreeablenesses of motions, figures, etc. The gentle motions of waves, of the lily, etc., as it is agreeable to other things that represent calmness, gentleness and benevolence, etc., the fields and woods seem to rejoice, and how joyfull do the birds seem to be in it. How much a resemblance is there of every grace in the field covered with plants and flowers when the sun shines serenely and undisturbedly upon them, how a resemblance, I say, of every grace and beautiful disposition of mind, of an inferiour towards a superiour cause, preserver, benevolent benefactor, and a fountain of happiness.

How great a resemblance of a holy and virtuous soul is a calm, serene day. What an infinite number of such like beauties is there in that one thing, the light, and how complicated an harmony and proportion it is probable belongs to it.

There are beauties that are more palpable and explicable, and there are hidden and secret beauties. The former pleases, and we can tell why; we can explain the particular point for the agreement that renders the thing pleasing. Such are all artificial regularities; we can tell wherein the regularity lies that affects us. [The] latter sort are those beauties that delight us and we cannot tell why. Thus, we find ourselves pleased in beholding the colour of the violets, but we know not what secret regularity or harmony it is that creates that pleasure in our minds. These hidden beauties are commonly by far the greatest, because the more complex a beauty is, the more hidden is it. In this latter fact consists principally the beauty of the world, and very much in light and colours. Thus mere light is pleasing to the mind. If it be to the degree of effulgence, it is very sensible, and mankind have agreed in it: they all represent glory and extraordinary beauty by brightness. The reason of it is either that light or our organ of seeing is so contrived that an harmonious motion is excited in the animal spirits and propagated to the brain. That mixture we call white is a proportionate mixture that is harmonious, as Sir Isaac Newton has shown, to each particular simple colour, and contains in some harmony or other that is delightfull. And each sort of rays play a distinct tune to the soul, besides those lovely mixtures that are found in nature. Those beauties, how lovely is the green of the face of the earth in all manner of colours, in flowers, the colour of the skies, and lovely tinctures of the morning and evening.

Corollary: Hence the reason why almost all men, and those that seem to be very miserable, love life, because they cannot bear to lose sight of such a beautiful and lovely world. The ideas, that every moment whilst we live have a beauty that we take not distinct notice of, brings a pleasure that, when we come to the trial, we had rather live in such pain and misery than lose.

SELECTED BIBLIOGRAPHY

Allen, Alexander V. G. *Jonathan Edwards.* Boston: Houghton Mifflin Company, 1890.

Edwards, Jonathan. *Freedom of the Will.* (Ed. by Paul Ramsey.) New Haven: Yale University Press, 1957.

————. *The Images or Shadows of Divine Things.* (Ed. by Perry Miller.) New Haven: Yale University Press, 1948.

————. *A Treatise Concerning Religious Affections.* (Ed. by John E. Smith.) New Haven: Yale University Press, 1959.

————. *The Works of President Edwards.* (Ed. by Sereno B. Dwight.) 10 vols. New York: S. Converse, 1829–30.

Elwood, Douglas J. *The Philosophical Theology of Jonathan Edwards.* New York: Columbia University Press, 1960.

Howard, Leon. *"The Mind" of Jonathan Edwards: A Reconstructed Text.* Berkeley and Los Angeles: University of California Press, 1963.

Johnson, Thomas H. *The Printed Writings of Jonathan Edwards, 1703–1758: A Bibliography.* Princeton, N. J.: Princeton University Press, 1940.

Locke, John. *An Essay Concerning Human Understanding.* (Ed. by Alexander Campbell Fraser.) 2 vols. New York and London: Oxford University Press, 1894.

Miller, Perry. *Jonathan Edwards.* New York: William Sloane Associates, Inc., 1949.

————. "Jonathan Edwards on the Sense of the Heart," *Harvard Theological Review,* XLI, pp. 123–45.

Winslow, Ola Elizabeth. *Jonathan Edwards, 1703–1758: A Biography.* New York: The Macmillan Company, 1940.

JONATHAN EDWARDS was born on October 5, 1703, the only son of Timothy Edwards, pastor in East Windsor, Connecticut. He grew up in that frontier village, and in 1716, shortly before his thirteenth birthday, he entered Yale College. He received his A.B. degree in 1720, his M.A. in 1723; and in May, 1724, he became tutor at the college. For six months, beginning in August, 1722, Jonathan Edwards preached to a Scotch Presbyterian congregation in New York City. He was ordained associate pastor in the parish of his grandfather, Solomon Stoddard, in Northampton, Massachusetts, on February 15, 1727. The following year he wed Sarah Pierrepont of New Haven; they were married thirty years and had twelve children. In the years 1735-1737 Jonathan Edwards' preaching inspired a revival movement in his church that aroused widespread interest. After religious activity had abated, a long and bitter controversy arose in the parish—the chief cause being Edwards' insistence on a stricter basis for full church membership than that instituted by his grandfather. On June 30, 1750, after twenty-three years' service, Jonathan Edwards was dismissed from his pastorate by a church council met in Northampton. He then served for six years as a missionary to the Housatonic Indians in the outpost of Stockbridge, Massachusetts, writing some of his best-known works during this period. On September 29, 1757, he was invited to the presidency of the College of New Jersey (now Princeton). The town of Princeton was, at that time, in the throes of an epidemic; Edwards was inoculated on his arrival there, but he suffered a secondary infection and died on March 22, 1758.